Michel Foucault: Personal Autonomy and Education

Philosophy and Education

VOLUME 7

The titles published in this series are listed at the end of this volume.

Michel Foucault: Personal Autonomy and Education

by

JAMES D. MARSHALL
The University of Auckland, New Zealand

KLUWER ACADEMIC PUBLISHERS
DORDRECHT / BOSTON / LONDON

Library of Congress Cataloging-in-Publication Data

Marshall, James (James D.)
Michel Foucault : personal autonomy and education / by James D. Marshall.
p. cm. -- (Philosophy and education ; v. 7)
Includes bibliographical references (p.) and indexes.
ISBN 0-7923-4016-7 (hb : alk. paper)
1. Foucault, Michel. 2. Foucault, Michel--Contributions in philosophy of education. 3. Postmodernism and education. 4. Autonomy (Philosophy) I. Title. II. Series.
B2430.F724M36 1996
194--dc20 96-11697

ISBN 0-7923-4016-7

Published by Kluwer Academic Publishers,
P.O. Box 17, 3300 AA Dordrecht, The Netherlands.

Kluwer Academic Publishers incorporates
the publishing programmes of
D. Reidel, Martinus Nijhoff, Dr W. Junk and MTP Press.

Sold and distributed in the U.S.A. and Canada
by Kluwer Academic Publishers,
101 Philip Drive, Norwell, MA 02061, U.S.A.

In all other countries, sold and distributed
by Kluwer Academic Publishers Group,
P.O. Box 322, 3300 AH Dordrecht, The Netherlands.

Printed on acid-free paper

Printed in the Netherlands

TABLE OF CONTENTS

ACKNOWLEDGEMENTS

I wish to acknowledge the following sources in which some of my ideas from my reading of Foucault have been presented.

Some earlier ideas on Foucault were presented in: 'Foucault and Education,' *Australian Journal of Education* 33(2), pp. 97-111, 1989; and, 'Foucault and Educational Research,' in Stephen Ball ed., *Foucault and Education: Discipline and Knowledge*, London and New York, Routledge, pp. 11-28, 1990.

Some of my more recent views are to be found also in: 'The Autonomous Chooser and 'Reforms' in Education,' *Studies in Philosophy and Education* 15(1) (forthcoming); 'Wittgenstein and Foucault: Resolving Philosophical Puzzles,' *Studies in Philosophy and Education* 14(2-3), pp. 329-344, 1995; 'Pedagogy and Apedagogy: Lyotard and Foucault at Vincennes,' in Michael Peters ed., *Education and the Post-modern Condition*, New York, Bergin and Garvey, pp. 167-192, 1995; and, 'Michel Foucault: Governmentality and Liberal Education,' *Studies in Philosophy and Education* 14(1), pp. 23-34, 1995.

I also wish to acknowledge my indebtedness to the following scholars, whose accounts I use in the text: Gary Gutting for his account of Bachelard and Canguilhelm; Roy Boyne for his discussion of Foucault on madness; and Huck Gutman for his account of Rousseau and the Romantic self.

PREFACE

This book is designed to serve two purposes. First it provides an introduction to the ideas and works of Michel Foucault. It should be particularly appropriate for education students for whom, in general, Foucault is a shadowy presence. Second, it provides a Foucault based critique of a central plank of Western liberal education, the notion of the autonomous individual or personal autonomy.

There are several introductions to Foucault but they tend to be written from a particular theoretical position, or with a particular interest in Foucault's ideas and works. For example Smart (1986) and Poster (1984) exemplify the former, and Dreyfus and Rabinow (1983) the latter. There is no substantial work in education on Foucault, apart from Ball (1990), which is an edited collection of papers by educationalists. The writer started reading Foucault from a position in education which was in the liberal framework, somewhere between Dewey, Freire and Habermas, but with an interest in punishment, authority and power. The book is the outcome of several years of trying to introduce students in education to his ideas and works in an educationally relevant manner. But an introduction, on its own, cannot show this relevance to education. Unless his ideas are put to work, unless they are *used* as opposed to *mentioned* in some sphere or area of education, then they may be of little relevance.

In order to understand Foucault it is necessary to have some knowledge and understanding of the intellectual climate(s) in France post World War II, and the ideas, works and thinkers against which, and against whom, he defined and elaborated his thought. Also it is necessary to be aware of ideas, positions, and methods, that he adopted, adapted and made to groan. To comprehend the relevance of his work for education these ideas must be put to work. That is the intention of this book - to show that he provides the basis for a powerful critique of the post-Enlightenment ideal of personal autonomy. It is not just that this ideal is difficult to attain in education but that it is fundamentally incoherent; instead of liberating the individual and guaranteeing independence it promotes dependence, subjection and domination.

According to Foucault:

> one writes things in part because one thinks them but also so one won't have to think them any more. Finishing a book is also not wanting to see it any more. As long as one has some love for his book one works on it. Once one no longer loves it, one stops

writing it. (quoted in Eribon, 1991: 277)

This book is now finished, but it has been a long time in the writing, mainly because of constraints upon my energy and time from administrative duties. It has both suffered and prospered from short periods of intensive work whilst in Paris, during four visits in 1990-1992, and as a visiting professor at Simon Fraser University in 1991. It was substantially rewritten whilst I was a visiting fellow at Edith Cowan University in March/April 1994. I am grateful to the space and hospitality afforded me by these two universities, and to my friends Robin Barrow and Bruce Haynes in particular. I am also grateful for the patience of staff at the Biliothèque Nationale and the Bibliothèque Saulchoir, and for the assistance of M.Thierry Holzer of Mission des Archives du Ministère de l'Education Nationale.

It was my former colleague Eric Braithwaite who, several years ago, passed me a copy of Foucault's *Discipline and Punish*. There are many of us who have intellectual debts to Eric.

Finally, I would wish to acknowledge the continuing intellectual support for my work on Foucault of my friend and colleague Michael Peters, and the support over many years of Bridget. Josie Lander, Bridget Holland, Hilary Stewart, Denise Davies and Bev Cooke assisted with the preparation of the manuscript.

James Marshall
The University of Auckland

INTRODUCTION

A THOUSAND MASKS

One of the more interesting and controversial thinkers to have emerged in the Western World in the twentieth century is Michel Foucault. According to *Libération* (30 July,1984); "Sans doute la dernier grande voix d'aujourd'hui". Yet he does not seem to impinge directly and explicitly upon educational thought and practice. Where he has influenced Western thought it might be argued that it was at the periphery, perhaps heralding the end of traditional philosophy in the company of Jacques Derrida, or the end of history in the company of Nietzsche. If he has been seen as a visiting European scholar at North American Universities he may not have been taken as a serious philosopher, historian, whatever, but rather as a *visitor* to established intellectual fortresses, or as a vagabond without the gates demanding entrance. How can any one who says this be taken seriously by University academics?:

> I think I have in fact been situated in most of the squares on the political checkerboard, one after another and sometimes simultaneously: as anarchist, leftist, ostentatious or disguised marxist, nihilist, explicit or secret anti-marxist, technocrat in the service of Guallism, new liberal etc. An American professor complained that a crypto-marxist like me was invited to the U.S.A., and I was denounced by the press in Eastern Europe for being an accomplice of the dissidents. None of these descriptions is important by itself; taken together, on the other hand, they mean something. And I must admit that I rather like what they mean. (Foucault, 1984a, p. 383f)

The distinguished historian of religion, Georges Dumezil, was to say that there were a thousand Foucaults; "he wore masks, and he was always changing them", so that for Dumezil there was no true identity to be discovered beneath these masks and disguises (quoted in Eribon,1991, p. xi). There was Foucault as scholar at a desk in the Bibliothèque Nationale almost daily, there was Foucault the dandy, the academic, the Government advisor, the committed philosopher, engaged homme de gauche, masked philosopher, and so on. If Dumezil rejected some of the alleged masks he never rejected Foucault.

Academics seem exasperated that Foucault does not appear to fit into recognisable categories and does not employ reputable or even recognizable methodologies. Some historians (e.g., Maxcy 1977: Megill,1979) see him as a structuralist - which he vehemently denied, e.g., in the introduction to *Words and Things* - Foucault, 1973a); others object that he plays fast and loose with historical data and time, appealing to concepts like rupture and discontinuity which, they claim, fail to explain (Megill 1979). Philosophers find him to be incoherent (Taylor, 1986: Walzer, 1986), or protest that his methodology wavers between the philosophical, the politically strategic, and a moral onslaught (Fraser 1985). Marxists believe that what appears as a radical position on the Left cuts across the central and basic tenets of Marxism (or perhaps transcends Marxism by critiquing its fundamental assumptions). In some cases, Foucault is seen as providing important insights into individualisation and the operation of forms of power, even if the final account of power is inadequate (e.g., in relation to state power: Walzer,1986; Poulantzas,1978). One former Marxist suggests, more radically, that 'the classic discourse of socialism is rendered problematic' (Smart 1983,1986).

But Foucault, like many other French intellectuals, did not write either for a narrow disciplinary or even for an intellectual audience alone as, for example, *Discipline and Punish; the birth of the prison* (Foucault,1979a) was read by both criminologists and criminals alike. As a member of Le Group d'Information sur les Prisons (G.I.P.) he wrote on prison riots. Independently, as "un homme de gauche" he wrote upon and discussed with workers elements of the class struggle (see, e.g. the discussion with a worker named José, in *Libération*, May 1973b). Yet he denied the title of intellectual: even that he knew any intellectuals (Foucault, 1980b). He was involved in a number of political causes, and both demonstrated (with Sartre!) and lobbied politicians (Eribon, 1991). However a burgeoning array of academic critiques attest to the interest that his work has aroused in both academic and professional circles. But,in general, Foucault has been ignored by educationalists - with the exception of a scattering of journal articles and an edited collection by Stephen Ball (1990).

I would argue that Foucault should be taken for himself and not as some other person neatly classified into recognisable categories.

At the time when he was at the height of his influence upon French intellectual life, when he had begun to occupy a position held formerly by Jean Paul Sartre, Michel Foucault died at the untimely age of 57. Paul Veyne, a distinguished classical historian and former colleague at the College of France, was to declare in an obituary in *Le Monde* that Foucault's work was "the most important event in thought of our century". Although Veyne cannot be considered as impartial towards Foucault (they were normaliens at the École Normale Supérieure, and remained close both academically and personally - Eribon, 1991; et. passim), this is a claim worthy of consideration. What grounds are there for judgements such as those made by Veyne? Why might philosophers of education and educationalists be interested in Foucault?

In what follows answers to these questions will be attempted. Whether these answers are ultimately satisfactory must be determined by the reader. At the outset however certain difficulties in attempting to answer these questions must be identified. As can be seen in the quotation above Foucault makes no claim to any particular disciplinary background. Yet the examiners of his Ph.D. emphasised that his approach was conceptual and philosophical. According to Lemert and Gillen (1982) he appears to come from nowhere, but as will be argued below, that is not correct. Nor did he normally enter into long and protracted arguments with his colleagues and contemporaries, though there were attempts in interviews to draw him into critical debates (especially in relation to Sartre - see Foucault 1966a,1968,1969). Nor did he revel in polemics (though see Foucault (1971b) where, in a vitriolic response to a critic, he sounds like a drill sergeant, telling his critic to "Report himself to page x "!). If he was guilty of intellectual polemics as a member of the left wing intellectual group Fuchs (*Libération*,1984) most of this he avoided in later life. Often when attempts were made to draw him into critical debate he responded by paying tributes to alleged adversaries - for example to Sartre, Merleau-Ponty and the "generation des *Temps Modernes*" (Foucault,1966a), though in private he was more caustic. Seldom did he acknowledge his intellectual forbears. Certainly he did not follow them *explicitly*, as even Nietzsche is made to "groan and protest" (Foucault,1977a). However, in the important article "The Discourse on Language" (Foucault,1971a), he acknowledges academic debts to Georges Dumezil, Georges Canguilhem and Jean Hyppolite, especially the latter: "a large part of my indebtedness is to Jean Hyppolite". And this was more than any required and polite homage to his predecessor. He talks of Hyppolite's conception of philosophy:

Instead of conceiving of philosophy as a totality ultimately

> capable of dispersing and regrouping itself in the movement Jean Hyppolite transformed it into an endless task.....it was a task without end.....of countless recommencement.....it was that which presents and reveals itself as the recurring question in life, death and in memory. (Foucault, 1971a, p. 236)

In 1975, and some seven years after Hyppolite's death (Master Hippal as Foucault referred to him), Foucault sent a copy of *Discipline and Punish* to Madame Hyppolite with this dedication: "For Madame Hyppolite, in memory of the man to whom I owe everything" (Eribon, 1991, p. 18).

And it was Georges Dumezil, whom he had not met but was later to be a close friend, who assisted him into the formal academic position in Sweden after obtaining only an assistant position at Lille (Eribon,1991: Piel,1986). Canguilhelm first interviewed him for the École Normale Supérieure, examined his Ph.D. and supported him always, especially in his election to the Collège de France.

Foucault was to return to this theme of Hyppolite's later, e.g., in another important paper, "What is Enlightenment" (Foucault,1984b). In accepting Kant's earlier title, in discussing both Kant's paper and the slumbers that he alleged Kant's work had unfortunately engendered, Foucault interprets Kant positively as conceiving the message of the Enlightenment as the adoption of an attitude. This was an attitude of constant critique of the present - "a task without end".

The problems for thinking about Foucault in relation to education are accentuated further because he said little explicitly about it. In *Discipline and Punish* (Foucault,1979a) he talks about schools but these are used as illustrations of the development of modern power. He does not address schools and education *directly*. He was however a master of the interview and it is there that some more explicit comments on schools and education can be found. Nevertheless these are very limited and his critique of education and schooling must be constructed, in the main, from what is implicit. However, as we shall see below, there may be no need for him to say anything more directly or more explicitly about schooling, as he tends to see it as but one side of "corriger" - to punish or to teach (Foucault,1972c).

Michel Foucault was born in Poitiers in 1926. His full name was Paul-Michel Foucault and at school was known by either name. Later he was to drop the Paul, probably in opposition to his father and the notion of a family name (Eribon,1991). He was raised in a middleclass bourgeois family - his father was a surgeon - and he attended local schools. Of these he was to say:

> For someone like me, brought up as a provincial petty bourgeois, learning comes with your baby bottle before you even go to primary school. Knowledge was the rule of existence....(it was) the kind of learning that amounted to a prohibition against knowing certain things.... (yet) learning is something erotic.... (but) teachers manage to make learning unpleasant, depressing, grey, unerotic. We need to understand how that serves the needs of society.... you have to make learning rebarbative if you want to restrict the number of people who have access to knowledge. (Foucault, 1974, p. 52)

According to his school friends in Poitiers (*Libération*, 1984) he said little of his family. He had fond memories of growing up and, with the exception of his father, was close to his family. In later years he was to buy a house close to his mother and she was to say: "He always gave me his August" (quoted in Eribon, 1991, p. 14). His emotional memories seem to have been related to the political situation against the constant menace of war (Foucault, 1983a, p. 7). "Our private life was really threatened". He noted particularly the influence of the impending war and the actual war upon himself and his contemporaries; "boys and girls of this generation had their childhood formed by these great historical events" (loc.cit.).

He commenced at the local Lycée Henry IV but was moved to boarding at the college Saint Stanislas, where it was thought by his parents that the local priests would discipline the rather corrosive aspects of Michel's character (*Libération*, 1984). He hated those three years at St. Stanislas and later, was difficult in any form of institutionalised and communal living (Eribon, 1991). However after his baccalauréat he was to return to a local lycée to prepare for the entrance exam to the prestigious ecole, the École Normale Supérieure. He failed at his first attempt but after further study in Paris at the prestigious Lycée Henri IV he was accepted at the second attempt. At Henri IV he was taught by Hyppolite, and Cauguilhelm was on his oral panel for the École Normale Supérieure. He studied there, but did not attend very much at the Sorbonne. His formative years then can be associated with such distinguished thinkers as Jean Hyppolite (the translator and interpreter of Hegel), Georges Canguilhelm (the distinguished philosopher and historian of science), the phenomenologist Maurice Merleau-Ponty, Jacques Lacan the psychotherapist, and the marxist structuralist Louis Althusser, who became both teacher, friend and colleague. Later there was Georges Dumezil (the historian of religion).

He took his licence de philosophie in 1948 but he was to abandon formal study of philosophy for psychology, completing his licence de psychologie in 1951. This was followed by a diploma in psychopathology and work in psychiatric institutions and prisons. His doctorate which was on the history of madness was undertaken whilst at the University of Uppsala and was completed in 1964. It must be emphasised that fifteen years was quite a normal period of time to complete a doctorate in the Faculties des Lettres (Faure,1968b, p. 94f). In his early work the influence of Ganguilhelm and Bachelard, is strong (Gutting, 1989). He certainly read Bachelard (Eribon,1991, p. 31), but a possible pivotal influence here was Althusser's teaching at the École Normale Supérieure.

Foucault claimed that reading Nietzsche in the early 1950's was not merely intellectually revealing but that it caused him to break with his life and work and, in 1955, to leave France. His overt homosexuality caused him psychological problems (Eribon, 1991) and this may also have influenced his decision to leave France; "when I left France, freedom for personal life was very sharply restricted" (Foucault 1983a). After reading Nietzsche he felt that he had become a stranger, entrapped, and never again felt able to integrate fully into French social and intellectual life. For several years in the 1950's he taught and worked abroad, first at the University of Uppsala where he taught in the French department, and later as Director of the French Institutes of Warsaw and Hamburg. It may appear difficult therefore, on the surface, to talk of him as emerging from French, especially Parisian, intellectual, aesthetic and political currents. Nevertheless he should be understood in this way, but with the notion of "emergence" understood more as defining oneself in opposition to, or across, existing intellectual traditions or currents. He was a hybrid writer, outside of the customary genres, and therefore not constrained by any one disciplinary methodology. Here the early work on madness, on dreams in Binswanger, on Roussel, and the influences of Bataille and Lacan on transgression and defining the Other must be important - see below.

As a result of his sojourn in Warsaw he was to have an abiding respect for Poland, and whilst no longer a Catholic, was to feel pride and joy at the installation of Pope John II. A member briefly of the Partie Communiste Francaise (P.C.F.) he was to leave it in 1953 and during his time in Warsaw to develop an intense dislike for Eastern European socialism. Later he was in the forefront of efforts to assist their dissidents (see Foucault 1981a, 1981b, for comments on Poland). At Clermont-Ferrand he made life intolerable for Roger Garaudy and virtually forced him to depart for Poitiers (Garaudy had been Secretary of the P.C.F.).

In 1960 he joined the philosophy department at the University of Clermont - Ferrand under Jules Vuillemin, where he stayed until 1966 when the important house of Gallimard published *Les Mots and Choses* (published in English as *The Order of Things*,1973a). It is important to note that Gallimard initially rejected *Folie et Deraison: la historie de la folie à l'àge classique*, and that it was the distinguished historian Phillipe Ariès who recommended it to Plon. Later another distinguished French historian, Fernand Braudel of *Annales* fame, was to applaud the work and Gallimard to do an unfortunately abridged edition (e.g., it was this edition which was translated into English and it excluded an important critique of Descartes - see chapter 4). After two years in Tunis (1966-68) he moved to Paris, first to the "experimental" university of Vincennes and later to a prestigious chair at the Collège de France. Jean Hyppolite was his predecessor in the chair. Foucault was to designate the position as "Professor of History of Thought", because neither philosophy, nor history of ideas, nor social history was adequate for the path which he wished to both create and follow.

Even though he was still in Tunis, there is little doubt that the events of May 1968 had an enormous impact upon him. May 1968 was "an insurrection against learning" (1974, p. 52), but the kind of 'learning' referred to above by Foucault in relation to his schooling. It was a pulling down of barriers, and "the intrusion of a new kind of learning" which he "felt rather at home in" (ibid.). But learning was not the only barrier to be dismantled (see below), and even if he said that he felt at home in this new kind of learning, there is little doubt that his time at Vincennes was personally taxing (Eribon,1991; chapter 14).

As Head of Philosophy at Vincennes he attracted some excellent junior staff, including Alain Badiou, Etienne Balibar, Jean François Lyotard, Judith Miller (Lacan's daughter), Jacque Rancierre and Michel Serres. But this was a turbulent two years and it drained him physically, for on the one hand there were the endless protests, in which the philosophy department seemed to be in the van, and on the other hand the continual attacks by the media upon the "experiment" at Vincennes.

In practical affairs he was very active in the Group d'Information sur les Prisons, whose purpose was to provide means for prisoners to speak for themselves, thereby empowering prisoners to set up their own active organisations. His actions here were perfectly compatible with what he believed to be the proper role of intellectuals (Foucault,1972a). Briefly he did not see the role of intellectuals as formulating and articulating a grand theory or of speaking for others - the great indignity. Also he debated with the working class re-iterating these points on intellectuals (Foucault,1973b). Initially he was to provide support for Ayatollah Khomeini (Foucault 1978b) but was to withdraw this support as the nature of the Islamic revolution unfolded. He was also a supporter of gay rights though, as his later philosophical position was to require, he preferred terms like "homosexual" to be applied to acts and not used to classify persons. He was himself, obviously, a homosexual: if he never wished this to be the case he was not able to hide it (Piel, 1986; *Libération*, 1984).

He appears at one level to have been a private and an impersonal human being, avoiding public debate and polemics, and anything autobiographical. Writing of Foucault, commentator and friend Alan Sheridan said:

> Foucault's imprint on his apartment seemed at first sight non-existent,but that was merely his style. It was designed by an interior decorator with clinical anonymity. Not a single object in it was worthy of attention on aesthetic grounds. Its oldest contents must have been the books that he had bought as a student. The only colour in the rooms was also supplied by the books.....he was also the sweetest, kindest of men.....(his) intelligence and humour shone from his eyes. (1984, p. 21)

Yet at another level Sheridan has "omitted" (perhaps it was another apartment and in later financial security) to mention the Picabia, the Soulages and the Magritte on the walls of his apartment (*Libération*, 1984). These would "represent" better a person always deeply involved in the arts and who worked with constant music (Piel, 1986). On this issue he said of himself: "in my personal life music played a great role" (Foucault, 1983c).

Of himself in later life Foucault was to say:

> I don't feel that it is necessary to know exactly what I am. The main interest in life and work is to become someone else that you were not in the beginning. If you knew when you began a book what you would say at the end, do you think you would have the courage to write it? What is true for writing and for a love relationship is true also for life. The game is worthwhile

insofar as we don't know where it will end. (1982a, p. 9)

The end for Michel Foucault was in Paris's Hôpital de la Salpétrière on 25 June, 1984 of neurological complications following acute septicemia, according to the medical bulletin (according to *Libération* it was cancer). Framing the bulletin were many tributes, but the lead (Said,1988, p. 1) was by the distinguished sociologist of education Pierre Bourdieu, a colleague of Foucault at the Collège de France. Ironically, this was a hospital in which he had researched for his work according to Said (1988). (His early work was done at Saint-Anne). If these were the final causes it is almost certain that he had aids (Eribon,1991, pp. 324-329: Miller, 1993 et.passim). George Dumezil had often remarked that Michel would write his obituary but, instead, it was Dumezil who was to do this for Foucault in *Le Nouvel Observateur*, on June 29 1984, in what has been said to be "the most moving essay ever written about Foucault" (Eribon, 1991, p. 328).

Foucault as Genealogist

It has been noted above that Foucault does not seem to fit easily into recognisable categories. Given that he uses historical data (though it does make some historians shudder but not leading French historians such as Fenand Braudel, Phillipe Aries, Georges Dumezil and Paul Veyne) it may be best to see Foucault as writing a different kind of history. Given the present splintering of history and historical methodology there may be something to be said for this interpretation. In what ways then is Foucault presenting us with a new or different form of history.

At one time history could have been conceived as narrative writing within the humanities, concerned with great events, great people and the emergence of our constitutions and institutions. What has come to be called "social history" has invaded this comfortable domain. Social history introduced not just a different set of topics such as the family, women and classes, but also brought with it from other social science disciplines a bewildering number of social science methodologies which were used by historians. These include economics, class analysis from sociology, and "thick" interpretation from anthropology. If historical methodology had always been disputed at the meta-level by philosophers this was a new conflict at the level of *doing* history.

Historians such as Megill (1979) interpret his work as anti-historical. These criticisms can be summarised under the following categories - I will use *Discipline and Punish: the birth of the prison* (Foucault, 1979a) to exemplify these points.

1. There is no complete history of the past in the period covered. There is no development or emergence of the "present" from earlier existing state of affairs. Thus *Discipline and Punish* commences with the execution of Damiens in 1757 and moves forward within three pages to an account of the treatment of young offenders in Faucher's reformatory in Paris, some eighty years later. The methodology here is to juxtapose upon one another two procedures which are quite dramatically different. But this is not a mere stylistic point as it has to do with the method of genealogy.

2. Historical data, from widely different sources, are suddenly inserted into the "history" but there is no apparent theory of selection as one moves from hospital to madhouse to schoolhouse..., and back again.

3. He does not advance the notion of an historical cause. For example he notes the sudden incarceration of people in the early nineteenth century, yet he gives no particular explanation even though incarceration is critical for his account of the disciplines, disciplinary blocks and the human sciences. If he identifies "spaces" in which possibilities are created it is to indicate that several outcomes were possible and that the actual outcome was not necessary - it could have been otherwise. There is no causal explanation offered of why one outcome happened rather than another.

4. In *Discipline and Punish* we are presented with a bewildering amount of data drawn from a widely differing number of sources. Details of the construction of hospitals, schools, military barracks and the prison are run together when, at first sight, these would appear to be different kinds of institutions constructed for different needs. Yet Foucault shows through his notion of power/knowledge that there are relationships between these constructions. These new relationships are based upon an analysis of *space* (space was long neglected according to Foucault, because of a philosophical concentration upon time). But why the spaces which he has selected, for the home might well exemplify power relationships (see here Phillipe Aries' (1962) account of the home, the family and the changed attitudes to the young, including the exercise of power over them). Foucault gives no rational reason for this

selection but he does indicate that his interests have always arisen from a set of problems which had preoccupied him at a particular point in time:

> Each of my works is a part of my own biography. For one or another reason I had the occasion to live and feel those things....I used to work in a psychiatric hospital in the 1950's. After having studied philosophy I wanted to study what madness was: I had been mad enough to study reason; I was reasonable enough to study madness. (Foucault, 1982a, p. 11)

And:

> ...if one is interested in doing historical work that has political meaning, utility and effectiveness, then this is possible only if one has some form of involvement with the struggles taking part in the area in question. I tried first to do a genealogy of psychiatry because I had a certain amount of practical experience in psychiatric hospitals and was aware of the combats, the lines of force, tensions and points of collision which existed there. My historical work was undertaken only as a function of those conflicts. (Foucault, 1976, p. 64)

5. Foucault gives us no teleological unfolding of reason. Indeed he argues quite convincingly that what appears as irrational to us in the twentieth century in the practice of torture is quite rational given certain assumptions of the time about guilt (here Charles Taylor (1986) says that he finds Foucault quite convincing). There is no Enlightenment future for mankind then, according to Foucault, because reason is embedded in socio-historical conditions and there is no rational unfolding of history in any developmental or improving sense. Neither reason then nor history offers us liberation or indeed a return to the abyss (if his earlier writings up to *Discipline and Punish* are pessimistic his later writings are much more optimistic).

6. Foucault is not writing history of ideas. The title of the chair which he held at the College de France was "History of Thought" and this title had been deliberately selected by Foucault so as to distinguish his methodology from the history of ideas. History of ideas tends to approach objects (as identified by concepts) as if there is a developmental emergence of these ideas in a more or less continuous and rational

fashion. Against this view Foucault shows that the concept of punishment, amongst many other examples that he uses, cannot be traced in any such manner. Instead there are ruptures and discontinuities which make the notion of punishment as a continuous object through time problematic. Hence the physical and temporal juxtaposition in *Discipline and Punish*, of disciplinary punishment and juridico-legal punishment.

7. Foucault is seen by some of his critics as not merely Nietzschean but as heralding the end of history. There are certainly Nietzschean influences upon Foucault (see 1977a and chapter one for a fuller discussion of these influences) but even so Nietzsche is adapted and made to groan.

An historian generally sympathetic to Foucault, Mark Poster, summarises these problems well:

> The flow of Foucault's texts, the way one thing is put after another, disturbs the expectations of the reader familiar with social history. There appear to be huge gaps in the narrative, silences that scream at the reader. Topics are annoyingly placed out of the normal order, disrupting one's sense of logical sequence. Levels of analysis are mixed together in irritating confusion: the difference between ideas and behaviour goes unrecognised and is violated. Simple questions of causality are ignored or appear in reverse order. The writing is thick and metaphoric and the point of view of the narrative line is often lost. The object of investigation is never quite clarified and appears to be neither individuals, nor groups, nor institutions. What is worse, things seem to shift in the course of the writing; at the beginning one issue is at stake, by the end we seem to be reading about something else. Worst of all, the author's attitude toward the topic of study never emerges clearly. He seems to take a perverse pleasure in shifting his stance, or simply in adopting provocatively an unorthodox attitude toward a topic. Finally, while much research has contributed to Foucault's studies, a great deal of material has not been looked at. The evidential basis of the texts is odd and incomplete. No wonder historians are skeptical about the value of his efforts. (1984, p. 72)

Poster sees Foucault as a philosopher of discontinuity, attempting to show how the past was strange and threatening and to distance ourselves from the cosy relationships of continuity with the past. According to Poster his concern is not to support the present by tracing lines of inevitability from the past but to cut the past off, to show that it is foreign, and that it cannot be domesticated and put to use in the glory of the present. His concern, according to Poster, is that historical writing, whatever ideological position one is coming from, tends to erase differences and justify the present. History, Foucault reminds us, is a creation or a fiction and historians should not claim to have truths about the past which they represent in writing.

Foucault rejected this strong claim. Whilst acknowledging gaps or ruptures he disputed that his historical writing was founded upon discontinuity (Foucault, 1977, pp. 111-113). This rejection is elaborated upon in chapter one.

Foucault does not develop a theory of history but equally few historians do reflect philosophically upon their methodology. Poster (loc.cit.) laments the opportunity that the 'new' social history presented for philosophical and theoretical reflection upon the basic assumptions of doing history. For him Foucault provides a challenge to historians because his later work raises "the important theoretical questions in the most forceful way".

Foucault is normally considered to have employed an (arguably) historical methodology of *genealogy* in, and after, *Discipline and Punish*, but in this methodology a general approach to concepts from his earlier work is evident; for example, in his writings on madness. This approach to concepts is derived from Bachelard and Canguilhelm (see chapter one for more detail). But the method also disrupts traditional historical form by concentrating on historical objects not normally considered to be the province of historical enquiry. The body is perhaps the most stunning example here. But the madhouse becomes the site of genealogical analysis of reason, and the prison the site of genealogical analysis of the gaze or surveillance (the only major work not of a legal kind on the prison which had arguably preceded Foucault was Ruschke and Kircheimer, 1939). But rather than continue with abstract talk of genealogy it might be more fruitful to see what one actually does. What would one do if one did a genealogical analysis? Better still what did Foucault do? Again I will stay with *Discipline and Punish*, as exemplar and whilst it is better to read the book to get a feel for the structure, I will attempt a brief analysis of the book's structure, presentation and argument in so far as these represent genealogical method.

Foucault divided the book into four sections. The first two

sections cover the "history" of punishment from savage brutality to what can be called the gentle way. The third section "generalises" the notion of discipline into several other institutional settings. The fourth section is an analysis of the function of nineteenth century prisons. The third section on discipline is the major section of the book and structurally represents a rupture or discontinuity with the earlier two sections. Similarly the fourth section, returning as it does to an almost functional analysis of the prison, represents a rupture with section three, which is concerned with the infiltration of discipline and disciplinary techniques throughout the social body. These structural breaks in presentation are important because the book itself represents in its structure the method of genealogy. There are important reasons for this associated with Foucault's notion of an author and of thinking and differently and creatively. Style was important for him. I thus disagree with Donnelly (1982) who argues that these four sections exhibit different methodologies. He argues that the first two sections involve a genealogy of the birth of the prison, the third an evolutionary account of the general diffusion of discipline, and the fourth section a functionalist account of the birth of the prison. Genealogical method is employed in the third section in the use of objects, and data, in the ways outlined above by Poster.

The first two sections should not be read as a general history of the prison. This would be mistaken for Foucault is not primarily concerned with the prison and he is certainly not trying to write as Rusche and Kircheimer did on the prison but from a different perspective. The story told of the prison is an interpretation meant to help us understand modern power. As his story is concerned more with exercises of power the basis of the selection of data is concerned with the "emergence" of the gentle way insofar as it unmasks modern power. His story is detached from the spheres of law, criminology and traditional legal and philosophical treatment of "punishment" where traditionally questions about the meaning of "punishment" and its justification have loomed large (see e.g., the collection of papers in Acton, 1963). It is also detached theoretically from juridical-legal political theory of the social contract. Foucault had called the social contract a bluff (Gordon,1991, p. 7). Finally in asking "what" and "how" questions about punishment Foucault gives new insight to those people who are interested, as philosophers, criminologists, and sociologists in punishment or its effects.

There is clearly a Nietzschean turn here (see chapter one). His concern is not to write on the emergence of the modern prison or to glorify the more humane treatment of offenders or to see this as the rational outcome of Enlightenment thinking post Cesare Beccaria's *On Crime and Punishment* (1764). In the very selection of data, and his refusal to glorify the present he exhibits Nietzschean turns. He is not so much concerned with the reconstruction of facts but with events, bracketing the truth of facts. This turn is perhaps well exemplified in *I, Pierre Rivière, Having Slaughtered My Mother, My Sister and My Brother* (Foucault, 1975a). In this co-authored book a whole number of competing discourses are brought together in one arena, so to say, as an event - the trial of a peasant boy for murdering three members of his family. The cacophony caused in this arena where these discourses intersect and "fight" to be heard shows us the complexity of events.

At the outset in *Discipline and Punish* we are presented with a very violent landscape - the public execution on the scaffold of the regicide Damiens. This is sharply juxtaposed within three pages of text with the routines of the young offenders in Faucher's House of Young Offenders in Paris some eighty years later. On the one hand we have the violent horrifying details of Damien's execution and on the other an account of what appears to be the daily routines of a caring rehabilitating institution and which seems to be a forbear of the caring society. Not so Foucault will tell us. But the contrast is not merely to shock, for it certainly does that, but to defamiliarise through showing us two ways of exercising power. Further he argues that what we find horrifying and irrational in the case of Damiens is, given certain socio-historical conditions quite rational (on this issue Charles Taylor (1986) finds Foucault "quite convincing"). His point is that what from our twentieth century perspective in which the individual is so important, is seen as so awful and irrational, is merely different. In which case the present is not more rational or has not evolved according to the promised message of the Enlightenment (see further chapter six). Changes in the form that punishment has taken should not be seen then as improvements in our thinking about offenders but, rather, as refinements in the exercise of power, and the "emergence" of modern bio-power.

This power is not meant to destroy human beings but to *make* human beings. It is not a power exemplified in public space with the pomp and "splendour" of the King arrayed but, rather, it is exercised quietly in confined spaces. Spaces come to operate differently and how they operate is pursued in section 3 of *Discipline and Punish.* There is a genealogical juxtaposition of the spaces in which modern power operates in section 3 with the scaffold of the earlier sections. In the public space of the scaffold individuals are made aware of their place in the grand cosmic order of the King, and this grand order is restored by the public execution. But spaces in the new disciplinary blocks operate differently as individuals are constituted in various ways through technologies of domination and in spaces, again private, where individuals constitute themselves through technologies of the self. Instead of being allotted their place in the grand order individuals are made, normalised on a number of parameters so as to lead useful docile and practical lives. This new form of power - bio-power - operates in the cause of governmentality of state according to Foucault (see chapter four).

The violent landscapes then which Foucault offers us depend upon the denial of more traditional approaches to historical data. In *Discipline and Punish* his choice of historical data "is choppy, disconnected, even arbitrary" (Poster, 1984, p. 95). He claims that he is not trying to supplant or deny other approaches to historical data but, rather, to show us another aspect or mask that reality wears. As in the case of *I, Pierre Rivière* he is adding another voice, competing for space, to a series of events.

Structure of the Book

Chapter one deals with some of the influences upon Foucault's thinking. It looks first at the general post world war II intellectual scene in France and second at the more obvious particular influences upon Foucault, such as his teachers, at Bachelard and Nietzsche amongst others, and at the theories and theorists whom he often defined himself against, in particular marxism and Sartre. Whilst essentially on the left Foucault was not able to articulate a left version of governmentality.

Chapter two looks at liberalism and liberal education. The former is introduced historically, including recent neo-liberal views which have been enormously influential in the "reforms" of western education systems. Liberal education is introduced through the works and ideas of John Dewey and Richard Peters. They represent what might be called a liberal democratic approach to education. Both emphasise, though in different ways, the importance of the individual and the importance of democratic principles. Neo-liberal ideas are introduced through the work of F.C. Hayek, and a form of neo-liberal education through the writings of Kenneth Strike. Strike emphasises the importance of freedom from and notes that democratic structures and procedures in education may be coercive of individuals. All however emphasise the importance of autonomy and rationality and the development of personal autonomy as an aim of education.

Chapter three begins the Foucauldean critique of personal autonomy as an aim of education. First the notion of autonomy is developed historically and the differing positions on autonomy that philosophers and philosophers of education have taken outlined. Then Foucault's critique of this as an aim of education is made explicit.

In chapter four Foucault's notion of governmentality is introduced and his account of power developed more fully. It is argued that the concept of power needs to come further onto the centre stage in education where, normally in liberal education, authority has been used to identify and describe issues of social control.

Foucault did not write much explicitly on education. Chapter five looks first at his own educational practices and evaluates them against the existing educational turmoil in France in the late 1960's. It is argued that he was a classical academic, committed to the disciplines and scholarship, and thus in his own practices far from an anarchistic iconoclast. The chapter also looks at the ways in which Foucault has been used by educationalists.

Chapter six returns to autonomy and looks at why Foucault believed that the Man of the human sciences was dead. The notion of the autonomous chooser in neo-liberal educational reforms is examined and found wanting. Finally it is argued that Foucault was not a post-modernist except in a rather weak sense of not looking back nostalgically to the past.

In chapter seven Foucault's way of doing philosophy is further investigated and his approach to punishment contrasted with the more traditional approach of Richard Peters, which comes out of traditional philosophical approaches to punishment and is exemplified in the Flew-Benn-Hart model of punishment. It is argued that Foucault's concept of disciplinary punishment is more akin to the punishment of children than the account of punishment given by traditional analytic philosophy of education.

Throughout these chapters it will be argued that whilst Foucault uses a genealogical method his interest is essentially in concepts, and to this extent it is essentially philosophical. From his early interests in madness and rationality, through power/knowledge to punishment, and latterly with the concept of the self there is an emphasis on concepts which is essentially derived and developed from the historical approach to concepts of Bachelard and Canguilhelm.

It is also a central theme of the book that Foucault's works should not be separated from his biographical details. This has not always been a fashionable thesis to argue in philosophy. For example criticisms of Rousseau's approach to education, based upon his treatment and desertion of his own children, have been defused by arguing that the man must be separated from the ideas because the latter, as ideas, can stand independently. But Foucault's own temperament, his isolation from others, his dislike of communitarian living are at the least compatible with a welcoming of the other and of an acceptance of transgression. Similarly his own early psychological instability cannot be dissociated from his interests in psychology and psychopathology, his work at Hôpital Saint-Anne, and his subsequent interest in the Binswanger translation. Furthermore, on several occasions in interviews he notes that his major works cannot be separated from his self and his problems at those times.

The critique of personal autonomy, which begins with an account of liberal education in chapter two is developed and extended through to chapter six. Chapter five represents a Foucauldean break in the argument, halting the critique to argue that Foucault was a traditional classical academic, particularly in his practices as a member of an advisory committee to government on the reforms of French education in the 1960's, and as a teacher at Clermont-Ferrand, Vincennes and le Collége de France.

It is easy enough to write *about* Foucault, but as Foucault is reluctant to tell us what to do I have tried to adopt a Foucauldean position to mount a critique, to *show* how Foucault can be used in practice, in relation to a particular issue not normally conceived in liberal education as problematic. Then, in the final chapter, I have tried to show how in practice, by looking at the concept of punishment through Foucauldean eyes, our understanding of the punishment of children, and its legitimation, can be clarified. Thus Foucault is used to mount a critique of liberal education and then it is shown how his approach to concepts is more fruitful than that of conceptual analysis, which has its normal home in forms of liberal education. The critique is twofold then - it argues that a central plank of liberal education - personal autonomy - is problematic at the least, and that analytic philosophy of education - a central form of legitimation for liberal education - is also problematic as a fruitful philosophical methodology.

CHAPTER 1

THE INFLUENCES UPON FOUCAULT

In this first main chapter we will look at some of the background influences upon Michel Foucault's development as a thinker. This introduction will be divided into two main sections - which will be entitled respectively "philosophers of the enlightenment" and the "voices of the others". These sections deal with contemporary philosophical positions when Foucault began his advanced studies - essentially they were Enlightenment thinkers - and the thinkers who took him out of these more traditional positions. Of course they overlap for, as Foucault admitted, it was reading the others, for example, Bataille and Blanchot, *against* Sartre that permitted him to reject Sartre.

Nor can connections between Foucault and thinkers who may have influenced his thought be drawn always explicitly, for in his own writing he did not always pay his dues to his forbears, and he declined usually to enter into polemical arguments with adversaries. Yet he did pay tribute to a group of thinkers, friends and mentors who encouraged him (see below). But all who were adopted were not merely adopted, but adapted and then made to groan.

Philosophers of the Enlightenment

According to Lemert and Gillen (1982) Foucault appears to come from nowhere. He appears to have no intellectual genealogy and to subscribe to no disciplinary framework or theoretical model. This is a common enough interpretation of Foucault but, it will be argued, this is mistaken. Briefly it will be argued that as with his Ph.D., where the examiners noted that he was "more philosopher than exegete or historian" (Eribon,1991, pp. 112-115), so his work should continue to be seen. However, there is a major emphasis on historical data, insofar as these relate to conceptual examinations - e.g., the concepts of madness, punishment, and the self.

In their important and generally sympathetic exposition of Foucault's work and thought, Hubert Dreyfus and Paul Rabinow (1983) state that:

> To triangulate Foucault's movements it is important to pin down precisely all three positions: structuralism, phenomenology, and hermeneutics.

They argue that Foucault's differences with structuralism and the hermeneutic quest for truth were not as simple, or as clearly marked and defined, as some might claim. Also, Foucault is clearly influenced by phenomenology in his early writing, especially in the introduction which he wrote for the translation of Ludwig Binswanger's *Dreams and Existence* (Foucault,1954a). Here there are clear influences from existentialism and phenomenology, with the major influence being Heidegger. On Heidegger Foucault (1985b, p. 250) said: "my entire philosophical development was determined by my reading of Heidegger".

In this early work and his attack upon Descartes, and Descartes' strong influence upon Western reason in *Folie et Déraison* (Foucault,1961), Foucault utters a cry for freedom from the constraints and oppression that are entailed by what he saw by Descartes as an attempt to curtail the imagination and creativity. If he abandoned what appeared to be a total rejection of Western reason in the light of Derrida's (1963) attack upon his interpretations of the history of philosophy, he never abandoned the cry for freedom.

According to Poster (1984), on the other hand, Foucault's recent works may be considered "as a theoretical response to the difficulties of Western Marxism in confronting the upheavals of the 1960's, and the new social formation which emerged thereafter". However, these works should not be seen as a continuation of a marxist tradition but, rather, as a departure from it, for whilst Foucault agrees with the Western Marxists that reason is within history, and thereby with them undercuts the notion that reason is an arbiter of reality yet, nevertheless, he parts company with them in the belief that reason can be liberating. Reason fails to liberate either through the classical Hegel-Marx dialectic and class struggle or, in the case of the Frankfurt school and Habermas in particular, the post-Enlightenment view that liberation is possible through the autonomous exercise of reason, for autonomy as normally conceived is a sham, according to Foucault. Furthermore, he does not believe in the development of a totalising universal world view, which cuts him off from many marxists (especially Sartre).

In his later life he became distressed that the left had not been able to articulate a coherent intellectual position and a book planned on the left with Pierre Bourdieu never came to fruition (Eribon,1991, p.

307).

In France, prior to World War II, marxism had not really penetrated working-class thought. However, and somewhat ironically in view of Fascism's role in Germany and Italy, it is the German occupation of 1940-44 which provides the conditions for marxism to emerge in both theory and practice in France. The French Communist Party (P.C.F.), after its very high profile in the Resistance, not only gained political and organisational control of the Left but, also, recruited a considerable number of intellectuals to join the almost solitary Henri Lefebvre (Anderson,1976, p. 37). On the out-skirts of the P.C.F. were Sartre and Merleau-Ponty, locked in an almost cat and mouse game of attack and rapprochement between existentialism and marxism. It should be added that the existentialist movement had itself gained credos in the resistance and enjoyed considerable popularity with the young after World War II. In the journal *Les Temps Moderne* Sartre and Merleau-Ponty, amongst others, adopted a general leftist political orientation, that the resistance had been betrayed (Hirsh, 1981, p. 41), and the P.C.F. was a target of their critiques for abandoning revolution.

Maurice Merleau-Ponty popularised the term "Western Marxism" (in *Adventures of the Dialectic*). Western Marxism took a shift in direction, away from the means and relations of production, towards issues of everyday life and culture. Several conditions made this shift in area of critical concern possible; some were general theoretical problems which Western Marxism had to confront, whereas others were theoretical and practical problems, some of a particularly French nature.

These moves took two forms. First there were theoretical examinations of marxist theory, in particular Marcuse and Adorno. Second, there were practical moves towards redefining the centre of attention for critical theory away from the means and relations of production towards cultural questions - e.g. in France the work of the Arguments group, so called after the appearance of the journal *Arguments* in 1956. However, both such moves prompted further quarrelsome questions; were these "new" areas of proper concern for marxists?; were these thinkers really marxists, or, merely, intellectuals of the left?

Within France the P.C.F., because of its involvement and leadership in the Resistance, was at the height of its power immediately post-war. Many intellectuals of the left, including Foucault, were members at one time or another. However his involvement was minimal, and he soon broke away (Eribon,1991, chapter 5). His membership was at the most for eighteen months with the break occurring in 1953, and by 1955 he had abandoned marxism.

The praxis of the party was dominated by Stalin from Moscow and, within the P.C.F., the intellectuals were generally subordinate to the politicians. The role of intellectuals within the P.C.F. was, then, determined from Moscow. Essentially their role was to defend the Soviet Union against capitalism and to use marxist doctrine to show the superiority of Soviet society over the West. Yet at a time of revolutionary fervour in France, immediately after World War II, when marxists "should" have been advocating revolution, the P.C.F. was restraining its militants because of Stalin's doctrines of stability for Europe and his support for De Gaulle. The first group of marxists to openly criticise Stalin's Russia and to draw theoretical conclusions was the group which contributed to the journal *Socialisme ou Barbarie* but the major members, Castoriades and Lefort, were not members of the P.C.F. It was, however, via a return to Hegel and the early works of Marx that Stalinism was seriously questioned as a valid interpretation of marxism. The groundwork for this renaissance was laid by the teaching of Alexandre Kojeve and Jean Hyppolite on Hegel, and developed by attention to Marx's Paris Manuscripts. From Hegel was taken the view that reason is not absolute but dialectical and dependent upon historical conditions in the world and, from the earlier Marx, alienation was resurrected as a fundamental marxist concept. Thereby intellectual critiques were mounted against Stalinism from marxist sources; for example *Socialisme ou Barbarie* saw Stalinism as a crude dehumanising form of capitalism (Poster,1975, pp. 202-205: Hirsh,1981, Chapter 5).

Among the intellectuals disciplined for their "sins" by the P.C.F. was Henri Lefebrve: in 1949 he was made to apologise publicly and in 1958 he was expelled from the party. The uprising in Hungry, along with news of the Gulag, the Korean War, and the revelations of the 1938-39 Moscow Trials, posed problems for those whose allotted role was to invoke the superiority of the Soviet Union.

Freed from the confines and restraints of official P.C.F. and Stalinist doctrine Lefebrve, who was also a director of *Arguments*, began to develop and explore themes concerned with daily life that he had considered as far back as 1936. He develops this concept of daily life from the earlier negative notion of oppressed ordinary existence to the notion that daily family life should form the basis for understanding alienation and human potential. Alienation was not to be based upon the relations of production, but upon the relations of daily life - according to Lefebrve man would be fully human only when daily life became a "festival" and where alienation, fetishism and lack of human satisfaction were absent. At this basic level of human life the human was discovered and created. If Lefebrve sounds somewhat romantic, in this particular account, his focus on family life is historically important as it replaces Marx's work place as the "heart" of society. Sartre and Merleau-Ponty were to write on this theme also but Lefebrve was (probably) the most interesting and significant thinker of the Arguments' group (Hirsh, 1981, p. 92).

Daniel Cohn Bendit - Dany the Red - was a student of Lefebrve's at the University of Paris at Nanterre and was certainly familiar with the ideas of Socialisme ou Barbarie. Indeed these sources are quoted widely in *Obsolete Communism: The Left Wing Alternative.* A handful of students led by Cohn-Bendit on 22nd March 1968 detonated an already smouldering student uprising which spread to the Sorbonne on 3rd May and, finally, to the Renault factory at Flins on 16th May. As academic authority was overturned in educational institutions so, also, was the authority of the capitalist owners in the workplace, as ten million workers went on strike. The stability and authority of the state were called in question. However, what was new in the May 1968 revolution was the organisational form of the action committees, representing a possible new society, though in embryonic form. What was important was that these committees were already that society living out a form of social life in which democratic decision-making underlay liberated, creative action across a wide section of social life. Although May '68 was "a social upheaval along the lines envisaged by Sartre, Lefebrve and Castoriadis" (Hirsh, 1981, p. 140) yet, nevertheless, whilst instigators were well aware of these ideas, in general the participants were not intellectuals developing theoretical forms of organisation for society(ies) but, rather, were highly autonomous people organised into effective action committees where the alienation of hierarchical authority structures and bureaucratic technology had been bypassed, if not eliminated. If Cohn-Bendit was aware of the theories which might have legitimated the "revolution" most students were not.

Of extreme importance also is that these "new" organisations and structures were independent of the existing political institutions of opposition - themselves hierarchical and conservative (especially the P.C.F.). A form of social organisation based, not upon the workplace as focus, but upon wider structures and daily living had been shown to be not merely theoretically possible but capable of realisation though not,finally, without state power.

The events of 1968 had an enormous influence upon Foucault, even though he was in Tunis at the time. He acknowledged the influences explicitly (e.g., Foucault, 1971c; 1972a; 1977c; 1983c). First he saw the possibilities of successful resistances, which did not need to be driven by totalising and encompassing theory, against oppressive bureaucracies and authorities. Second, when the Gaullists came onto the streets, Foucault saw that grasping state power, in the sense of ownership of that power, was pointless, because for him the "real" power was operating at the micro and not the macro level, if indeed it might need to be supported ultimately by state power.

Foucault directly confronts marxism. For example, in "Truth and Power" (Foucault,1977c) he accuses marxist intellectuals of paying dues to both the French academic establishment and to Stalinism (see above), and of being deaf to many questions, especially the conjoint problems of internment and the improper uses of psychiatry. Nor had marxism addressed itself to micro-power, to the mechanics of power. Marxism's notion of ideology stands in opposition to the Truth and was therefore unhelpful when the concern was to look at the effects of true (and false) discourses. Second, ideology, is associated with the notion of the subject, and hence for Foucault with a form of post-Enlightenment humanism. Finally, it is related to an over arching determining economic *structure*, a macro-phenomenon, which Foucault saw post 1968 as not being at all helpful.

Yet if Foucault broke with marxism he never broke with Louis Althusser, his former teacher (see e.g., the delightful and respectful comment in Foucault, 1967, p. 8). He shared with Althusser's structuralist marxism the notion of the decentering of the subject. Althusser's reading of Marx was an attempt to settle the score with humanist readings of Marx, in particular with "a concept of man as an *originating subject*" (Althusser,1976, p. 205). But Foucault did not agree with Althusser that Marx's work represented an epistemological break with its post-Enlightenment predecessors (Foucault,1967, p. 8).

Sartre's solution to the crisis of western marxism had been to "marry" existentialism and marxism, to introduce existentialism into a background marxism where the classical marxist premises are presupposed as broad general background rather than being stated explicitly (Barnes, 1968, p. xix). Sartre makes this point explicitly:

> Why, then, are we not simply Marxists? It is because we take the statements of Engels and Garaudy (P.C.F. Theorist) as guiding principles, as indications of jobs to be done, as problems - not as concrete truths. It is because their assertions seem to us insufficiently defined and, as such, capable of numerous interpretations: in a word, it is because they appear to us as

regulative ideas (Author's enclosure). (1968, p. 35).

In *Search for a Method* Sartre calls for a strategy of supplementation of marxism by existentialism. The author of *Being and Nothingness* - an extremely radical view of freedom in which the individual consciousness is independent but alone - now says of existentialism that it is:

> an ideology...a parasitical system living on the margin of knowledge, which at first it opposed but into which today it seeks to be integrated. (Sartre, 1968, p. 8)

Crucial to this supplementation of marxism by existentialism are two requirements, Sartre says, which Marxism itself derives from Hegelianism:

> if such a thing as a truth can exist in anthropology, it must be a truth that has become, and it must make itself a totalisation. (1968, p. xxxiv)

Sartre's concerns then seem traditionally philosophical - with truth, reality and knowledge, perhaps Truth, Reality and Knowledge - for philosophy seems to be seen by him as a super-science providing firm foundations for the natural and human sciences. In this respect he is firmly in a philosophical tradition from Descartes and Locke to Kant and Hegel, with closer affinities to the latter. But, according to Sartre, philosophy does not provide absolute Truth in the sense of a proposition, or propositions, being true for all time. Philosophies are methods by which the "rising class" becomes conscious of itself in its movements towards emancipation (Sartre, 1968, p. 6). As such philosophies have themselves been shaped by socio-historical conditions.

Totalisation is an important marxist concept and it is important in Sartre's later thought. But how can truth both become and, also, be a totalisation? In Marx's writings there is a clear belief that the individual can and should conceptualise the totality. Not only did Marx believe that the individual could grasp reality in conceptual terms in its totality but, also, he saw this as necessary in order to develop revolutionary theory and practice. Marx believed that the proletarian revolution would emancipate mankind totally, as opposed to the factional liberation of bourgeois revolutions, whereby the bourgeoisie obtained a freedom which was used to exploit the proletariat (for a full discussion of this concept see Jay, 1984).

This belief in the necessary roles of both reason and the intellectual poses problems for historical materialism, as it cedes to reason and the intellectual the revolutionary capacity and initiating power that should reside within the proletariat. Nevertheless Sartre too holds to this concept. However he rejects what he calls the apriori totalising of contemporary marxists, i.e., the determining for any object of its:

> "real" place in the total process according to classical marxist theory by establishing "the material conditions of its existence, the class which has produced it, the interests of that class .... (1968, p. 36)

Sartre rejects such totalisation because it:

> does not derive its concepts from experience - or at least from the new experience which it seeks to interpret. It has already formed its concepts.... Its sole purpose is to force the events, the persons, or the acts considered into prefabricated moulds. (1968, p. 37)

Sartre held that critical theory should contain two aspects to totalisation - an ontological, or metaphysical, and an epistemological aspect. The ontological assumption was that human society was a structural whole but one built by human beings: it was a totality of human agency. However Sartre here amends, or reinterprets, Engel's statement - "Men themselves make their history but in a given environment which conditions them" - to read: "Men make their history on the basis of real prior conditions (among which we would include acquired characteristics, distortions imposed by the mode of work and of life, alienation, etc.), but it is the men who make it and not the prior conditions" (1968, p. 87). Thus while human society was at any one time a structural whole it was a structural whole in an historical process. Thus it was both an existent being but a whole which was also becoming. In these senses then Sartre holds that knowledge is both becoming and a totality.

Foucault and Sartre were not friends or scarcely even acquaintances, though in the 1970's they combined in various protest movements. They did not meet until November, 1971. At Sartre's funeral Foucault is reported as saying:

> When I was a young man he was the one - along with everything he represented, the terrorism of *Les Temps Modernes* - from whom I wished to free myself. (Eribon, 1991, p. 280)

Of three hundred or so entries in James Bernauer and Thomas Keenan's (1988) Foucault bibliography there is only one recorded publication in *Les Temps Modernes* in 1972, and that is an interview with some maoists (Foucault, 1972c). His position towards Sartre is quite ambiguous, as on many occasions he is respectful, but in private he seemed less respectful. Thus in Foucault (1968, p. 41) he says such things as:

> I belong to a generation of people for whom the horizon of reflection was defined by Husserl in a general way, Sartre more precisely and Merleau-Ponty even more precisely.

Earlier, in Foucault (1966a, p. 14) he had paid homage to Sartre, Merleau Ponty and the "generation des Temps Modernes" and to Sartre's generation during World War II. He seemed to be directing these interviews away from a direct confrontation. In (1966b, p. 8) however, he is to refer to *The Critique of Dialectical Reason* as "the magnificent but pathetic attempt of a nineteenth century man to conceive of the twentieth century". A day after their first meeting in 1973, when someone said of Foucault in a restaurant, "There's Jean- Paul Sartre", Foucault added, "I'm not sure it was a compliment" (Eribon, 1991, p. 240).

For Foucault, Sartre was the last Hegelian and the last marxist (1966b, p. 8). Everything that Sartre stood for as an intellectual Foucault rejected - especially the attempts to totalise and to articulate for others. Foucault sternly resisted this role for intellectuals. Yet if he came to Bataille and Blanchot, the writers who were to bring him to break with the established spaces of philosophy and politics, through Sartre, they were read *against* Sartre (Eribon, 1991, p. 58).

If Foucault's works can be interpreted as a theoretical response to the crisis of marxism and, in particular, to existentialist marxism, they should not however be seen either as structuralist, perhaps as post-structuralist, but not as post-modernist. In his earlier works - *The Order of Things*, *The Archaeology of Knowledge* and "The Discourse on Language", there are structuralist tendencies. Indeed he was considered by many commentators to be a structuralist (see Dreyfus and Rabinow here) and this in spite of his denials (e.g. "...I don't see who could be more of an anti-structuralist than myself", (1977c, p. 114). And more forcefully in *The Order of Things*:

> In France, certain half witted "commentators" persist in labelling me a structuralist. I have been unable to get it into their tiny minds that I have used none of the methods, concepts, or key terms that characterize structural analysis'. (1973a, p. xiv)

Whilst a thinker can be mistaken about his own intellectual position, perhaps Lecourt is correct when speaking of Foucault's earlier works:

> As for those of Foucault, they have been the object of a strange misunderstanding since they have owed a part of their rapid celebrity to the echo they aroused in a camp to which it is clear today that they did not belong, that of "structuralism". (1975, p. 120)

Structuralism can be understood as a methodological reaction to phenomenology in trying to eliminate the Husserlian conception of a meaning giving transcendental subject. The structuralist approach attempts to find objective laws which govern human social activity and which do not depend upon a subject and meaning. In the work of Claude Levi-Strauss, the anthropologist, who applied the insights of structural linguistics to the study of social life, anthropology is said to be decentred because man as subject, as speaker, does not endow spoken words in a particular context with meaning; nor does man bestow a transcendent meaning upon words. Meaning, both in general and in particular contexts, is dependent only upon the position "occupied" by those words in the totality of words.

Finally if Foucault exhibits "structuralist" tendencies in his talk of the epistemic or structured discourses he does not employ the traditional structuralist methods and terminology.

In *The Order of Things* (1973a, p. xiv) he rejects any theoretical approach "which gives absolute priority to the observing subject ... which, in short, leads to a transcendental consciousness". Rather than a theory of the knowing subject, the historical analysis of a scientific discourse should be subject to a theory of discursive practice. Foucault is rejecting explicitly that which he refers to broadly, as the phenomenological approach. Here then is to be seen a major point of opposition to Sartre - a position which he shares with the structuralists.

But if he is against a theory of the knowing subject in *The Order of Things*, in *The Archaeology of Knowledge* (1972b) he is also against the "object", as an object of knowledge. Following in an epistemological tradition from Bachelard and Canguilhelm (Lecourt, 1975: Gutting,1989)) on the notion of rupture and discontinuity in science, Foucault argues that the notion of a transcendental meaning giving subject is inadequate for the explanation of rapid shifts in regimes of discourse and knowledge and is, in effect, the attempt to impose continuity and harmony upon what appears as rupture and discontinuity. Equally the positing of an object - for example psychopathology and its attendant "objects" seen as hallucinations, speech disorders and sexual abberations - involves the search for a continuity of thing. But the reification of such objects is equally inadequate to provide an account of rupture and discontinuity, Foucault argues, because such objects emerge, blur and are erased, and do not explain why one set of objects emerged rather than another, why they were approved of, modified, or whatever. Indeed Foucault sees the postulation of objects as but the other side of the coin of subjectivity in that they provide an alleged continuity and coherence. At best appeal to "objects" describes an emergence of categories, classifications and subsequent treatments, but it does not explain why a particular set of objects was adopted for use in a particular discourse.

If Foucault took the notion of discontinuity in scientific thought from Bachelard and Canguilhelm he certainly did not wish to stay with the notion of discontinuity as a primitive notion which was itself inexplicable. Foucault stated that he was flabbergasted to find himself described as "a philosopher who founds his theory of history on discontinuity" (1977c, p. 111). What he had wished to emphasise was that in the human sciences there had not been the smooth evolution that histories based upon continuity seemed to presuppose. There are not merely new discoveries but totally different *forms* of knowledge that have just "taken off" as modifications have taken place in the rules for the formation of statements which are to be accepted as true. Changes had taken place in the regimes of truth and, in the human sciences, a continuous view of history was, Foucault claimed, inappropriate. Hence it was a question of knowing "what effects of power circulate among scientific statements" (ibid., p. 112). Discontinuity is not then the basis for his historical approach but a notion which is itself sited in certain forms of inquiry. However, if the theory of power/knowledge was not explicitly articulated, the episteme is quietly abandoned because of its emphasis on discontinuity and its structuralist tendencies (Lecourt, 1975, pp. 187-213).

Yet Foucault seems to retain the notion of an absent cause to his own theory. The discourses/practices with their associated techniques of power seem to hover over mankind shaping individuals in certain ways according to current discourses/practices in the social sciences. Power is exercised over individuals shaping them in certain ways so as to obtain domination over them, but there appears to be no conscious puppet master intentionally driving the totality or retuning the structure.

In what we will see below as being a general attack on post-enlightenment liberal humanism, Foucault places marxism firmly into this targeted tradition:

> At the deepest level of Western knowledge, Marxism introduced no real discontinuity, it found its place without difficulty, as a full, quiet, comfortable and, goodness knows, satisfying form for a time (its own), within an epistemological arrangement that welcomed it gladly (since it was this arrangement that was in fact making room for it) and that it, in return, had no intention of disturbing and, above all, no power to modify, even one jot, since it rested entirely within it. Marxism exists in nineteenth century thought like a fish in water; that is, it is unable to breathe anywhere else. (1973a, p. 261).

Foucault, using Nietzsche, argues that this general tradition ignores, within the conditions of possibility of truth, the possibilities that there is no truth but only truths, that there are no epistemological foundations for such truths, and that historical analysis can reveal the emergence of truths by disclosing connected patterns of domination. Truth is not to be separated from power, or discourse from practice, and the identification of these conditions of possibility requires not only a selection of different historical data but a use and organisation of this data which runs counter to accepted views of what counts as history.

In traditional marxism reason becomes essentially an epiphenomenon of history. Whilst some marxists reject this view - particularly Habermas - nevertheless reason is still seen as a liberating influence which is capable of overcoming forms of domination and subjugation. Foucault opts for a more radical stance towards reason and history. It is not that reason is immanent in history but, rather, that there is no such thing as history as a form of continuity providing a background or foundation for reason, e.g., the class struggle. History is not as continuous nor as ordered, nor as capable of ordering, as historians would have us believe, he argues. Rather it is discontinuous, with breaks and ruptures between the "stories", and patterns of development and evolution that traditional historians attempt to impose. What needs to be identified in the human sciences are the historical conditions that made certain discourses (truths) possible. For example, why do we incarcerate some criminals rather than others?; why do children of the same age follow essentially the same syllabus across formal systems of education?; why do we treat the body(ies) of the insane, the deviant etc...? These historical conditions of possibility are not to be understood either as reasons for, or as causes of, the emergence of some discourses/practices rather than others ('why did we incarcerate the mentally ill at a certain period of time and why is there a move now towards decarceration?). Here Foucault challenges both the established methodologies of history and, also, of philosophy. [These points will be developed further below].

Therefore when Foucault appears to be endorsing or to be supportive of marxists, this support should be seen as support of marxism as a critique and as having served an important historical purpose. Consider this acknowledgement to Marx by Foucault:

> It is impossible at the present time to write history without using a whole range of concepts directly or indirectly linked with Marx's thought and situating oneself within a horizon of thought which has been defined and described by Marx. (1975b, p. 53)

This acknowledgement must be tempered however by Foucault's own words in the quoted text - "at the present time". Foucault admits that at the present time it is almost impossible to formulate a critique of modern society and a theory of resistance that does not presuppose the language and categories that he wishes to reject. Marxism is formulated within these general presuppositions (cf. e.g. 1975b, p. 110). Furthermore as critique it has come to occupy an important and unique historical and intellectual stance as critique against oppression, even if it seems to Foucault overly addressed to that form of domination and oppression based upon economic exploitation. Foucault (1983a) identifies three broad types of domination, all interconnected, in which economic oppression is one, but only one, and not the most basic form of oppression.

With these acknowledgements and recognitions it can be said, in summary at this stage, that Foucault sees marxism as a type of discourse/practice, as a "product" of a certain set of conditions which permitted its possibility, but one which is theoretically unable to address the appropriate questions for description and analysis of modern society which would transcend the conceptual categories and meta-ethical foundations that have permeated approaches to critical theory since the enlightenment.

Foucault should be seen as rejecting marxist approaches not only as particular theoretical approaches but as exemplifying the wrong kind of theoretical approach. Here his critique can be interpreted as involving three levels (Fraser,1985) or, so as not to ascribe any status to any one level, three *strands* of thought. At these "levels" of critique Foucault can be understood perhaps as rejecting not only Sartre and Althusser but also, more generally, most enlightenment humanist thought, with its meta ethical grounding of values in a humanistic liberal rational world view. These levels are (Fraser, 1985):

1. *Conceptual.* The post enlightenment vocabulary is deeply embedded in the Cartesian subject - object dichotomy (*The Order of Things*, *The Archaeology of Knowledge*), so that the expression of a theory which presupposes such dichotomies is deeply flawed in any attempt to address twentieth century modernity. The approaches of both Sartre and Althusser presuppose this distinction. Secondly the attempt to ground such concepts as "autonomy", "repression" and "resistance" in the liberal humanistic view of Man is philosophically mistaken, according to Foucault.

2. *Strategic.* The cries of "Liberté", "Egalité" and "Fraternité" may have once possessed considerable emancipatory force in France (and elsewhere of course). But if they were effective in relieving one type of political domination they appear to have aided and abetted in other forms of domination, e.g.s., men over women) the "normal" over the mentally ill, the "normal" heterosexual over the homosexual, etc. The appeal to legal rights, to use one of Foucault's targets of the judiciary here, is to employ a weak, if not useless strategy, in the attempt to overcome domination of groups over other groups.

3. *Ethical.* The post-enlightenment - liberal - rational approach to the alleviation of domination may not be just conceptually awry and the wrong medium in which to ground to values, attitudes, hopes and aspirations, and a poor strategy to adopt by those who wish to oppose and/or resist domination but, more strongly, it may be an ethically undesirable approach to adopt. Far from being a formula to adopt to alleviate and destroy domination it is, simply a formula which aids and abets domination, because it has the very essence of domination built into it.

These levels, identified by Fraser (1985) are neither explicitly formulated nor explicitly rejected by Foucault. Given an annoying refusal by Foucault to spell out the necessary theoretical presuppositions underlying his work it is not surprising that these turn out to be generally conflated. Nevertheless there are sufficient rejections by him of the post-enlightenment humanistic ideals at all three levels to identify positive rejectionist attitudes and tendencies.

Hoy (1981) interprets Foucault's rejectionist attitude in merely conceptual terms thereby, effectively, reducing his attacks, e.g., upon the normalising disciplines (in *Discipline and Punish*) to a philosophical rejection of humanistic ideals as providing a proper philosophical meta-ethical, or meta-theoretical, foundation for concepts like "autonomy", "liberty" and the values and practices in everyday life that they serve to underpin. Here particular philosophical targets are the subject/object dichotomy, the view that humans can be the arbiter upon truth and values as opposed to a deity, tradition or established practices, and that humans are generally improving the material and social conditions of their existence. At the strategic level he may be interpreted, e.g., as in *Discipline and Punish*, where he points out that the humanistic ideal of saving the "soul" of the wrong doer came to be interpreted as saving the "soul" by the exercise of power upon the body which, in turn, became domination over bodies so that they should be productive but docile. But in order to save the soul Man had first to be known. Here Foucault's rejection can be seen as entering its normative phase for, gaining knowledge of human beings - Man - required first wholescale incarceration and, second, the production of a particular form of discourse/practice, as power/knowledge, which was both source of knowledge of Man and, also, ground for practice and source of further knowledge and further legitimation of practices in the production of Man. But these discourses and practices involve domination. Foucault's ethical rejection then is based upon his view that these conceptions of Man presupposed domination of men and women to both formulate their concept of Man and to "construct" socially men, and women, in accordance with this conception. Insofar as domination is necessary for Man then such conceptions of Man and the production (or construction) of human beings in accordance with such conceptions are to be rejected as ethically undesirable.

The Voices of Others

In this section some more specific influences upon Foucault's work will be identified. These will include ideas of Binswanger, Bataille, Bachelard, Canguilhelm, and Nietzsche and general points on logic, philosophy and history. His "reactions" to general currents of intellectual thought have been introduced above but these need to be supplemented by the ways in which his working practices, "methodology" or "theory", were influenced by individual thinkers (at the same time acknowledging that he proclaimed no general methodology or theory). We need to look at some of the voices of the Others, because Foucault never abandoned some of his earlier positions which arose from his personal experiences, and which influence his later writings and his stances as an intellectual. He was to say, e.g. as late as 1981, that:

> My books have always arisen from personal problems with madness, prison, sexuality ... (1984d, p. 339)

A major influence here is that of history and philosophy of science and the ideas of Bachelard and Canguilhelm. This is a rich philosophic tradition which, according to Hacking (1981), predated the work of Kuhn in many ways. In particular it objected to the notion of a unified and universal objective science, progressing in a rational and coherent manner. Second, there had been major changes in historical methodology. In France this was represented by the *Annales* group, particularly by Fernand Braudel who had commented favourably on *Folie et Déraison* (it was Phillippe Ariès who had originally recommended it to the publishing house of Plon). But Foucault brought not only ideas from the history and philosophy of science towards his investigations but also Nietzsche - the Nietzsche of *The Genealogy of Morals* and *The Gay Tragedy* (Foucault, 1973c, p. 77). Foucault (1967, p. 14) gives praise to these historians and others. However, his work differs considerably, for while they may deal with new and/or forgotten histories, there is in their approach to history a search for continuity, and this represents a major point of disagreement for Foucault, versed in Bachelardian views. Nevertheless Boyne (1990) considers that Foucault and Ariès can be read together.

First we will look at Foucault's early critique of Descartes and identify the notions of difference and the Other. Then through his also early work on Binswanger and dreams, obtain some grasp of his rejection of phenomenology and his early overall scepticism towards Western reason. Then we will look at what he adopts and adapts from Bataille (and Blanchot), Bachelard, Canguihelm and Nietzsche.

Foucault's critique of Descartes centres around three poles which can be called the ontological, the epistemological and the political,though they merge and intertwine. The starting point is the juxtaposed notions of sameness and otherness, or identity and difference. These are important themes also in understanding his "evolution" as a writer (Seigel, 1990).

First, there is the ontological point. At issue is the interpretation of "is", or the copula as it is known in logic (Descombes,1980) for there are essentially two broad interpretations. If the distinction between a priori and synthetic judgements is accepted, there is an interpretation of the copula which is essentially analytic. This is to interpret the "is" as the "is" of identity which, if this interpretation is adopted, receives its clearest exposition in analytic propositions of the form, "a is a". Propositions of form, "a is b" ("John Major is the Prime Minister of Great Britain"), and "a is F" ("John Major is a conservative"), are inferior in form to "a is a", but "aspire" to this form, in essentially asserting *identity* between the two terms on either side of the copula "is". This meaning and priority can be traced at least to Hume (Marshall, 1973) and to Kant. Post-Kantian, and recent French approaches, deny this interpretation of *identity* between subject and predicate. Instead *difference* is introduced into the very definition of *identity*, so that a certain *non-being*, or difference, or otherness, is introduced into the very notion of *being*; non-being becomes interior to being. Here Descombes quotes Kojève (1969):

> Parmenides was right in saying that Being *is* and that Nothingness *is not*; but he forgot to add that there *is* a "difference between Nothingness and Being, a difference which to a certain extent *is* as much as Being itself *is*, since without it, if there were no *difference* between Being and Nothingness, Being itself would not be".

Essentially difference is then a part of that which is.

But the concept of difference is not merely concerned with a conceptual difference - Deleuze is careful to make this distinction (Deleuze,1968). Conceptual difference, or mere conceptual difference, is given by different concepts such as man and women, which are both specific concepts within the generic concept human being. Conceptual difference gives us *diversity*. The concept of difference, however, permits us to think *differently* within identity, *within* the concept of woman *or* man. If one thinks of what is *given* by different concepts such as woman or man, the concept of difference however is a condition of the very being of the givens, woman *and* man. In relation to the concept of difference then, difference is not the diversity given by woman and man, but a very condition of both of those givens; difference is contained in both of the concepts, as both woman "contains" the other and man "contains" the other. But what is "contained" in woman is not man but other than woman, and what is "contained" in man is not woman but other than man.

Another way to think about this notion is available through Boolean algebra. Suppose we consider a universe of discourse A, and within that universe a concept W - say woman - and a concept M - say man. Let us assume further that these concepts do not overlap and are genuinely diverse. In order to draw the Boolean circle W, I must know what counts as a W and what is a not-W. In other words to define W, I must know where the other lies in the universe of discourse; I must know what is not-W, or what is different from W, but not perhaps included in other diverse concepts such as M. Without this knowledge, or without a decision procedure, I cannot draw the circle.

Now, following Kant, if we say that the concept is what is identical in several representations, it becomes tempting or habitual to overlook the necessity of difference *within* an identity. The most authentic instances of difference then would be when thought deliberately introduced such differences into the concept, challenging the notions of a generality of representations or, to stay with the Boolean algebra mnemonic, how to draw the circle.

Talk of the other then is not talk of others, man as opposed to woman say, but talk within the concept woman of *otherness*. This is important in Foucault's discussion of modern subjectivity.

In *Folie et Déraison* (though not in the abridged English version - *Madness and Civilisation*, 1973d), Foucault's critique of Descartes is to be found. Here Foucault critiques the logic of the Western world in which the possibility of being mad is excluded, and is part of the other for the rational thinker. Yet if non-rational must be part of the rational then it too must have a voice. Effectively madness was philosophically excluded, as being part of Nothingness; but if the argument above is correct then this is philosophically mistaken. For Foucault this mistake opens up the logical possibilities of other forms of reason, and historically, he shows, that the voice of unreason was allowed a voice in the medieval era and into the Renaissance (here I follow Boyne's (1990) account and his sources from Foucault,1961). The total rejection of Western reason in this work is to be abandoned later as a result of Derrida's (1963) critique.

At the epistemological level Foucault contests Descartes' arguments in the *Meditations* for the rejection of the possibility that he, the sceptical doubter, might be mad. Foucault's concerns are not with the arguments per se - he is not engaging in internal critique of Descartes - but with the outcomes for Western thought of the emergence of the rational subject.

Foucault saw that Descartes was presented with three possible reasons for doubt: that he was deceived by the senses; that he was dreaming; that he was mad. Descartes argued against the first two possibilities by claiming that we can only be mislead in both cases if a certain relation to the real world and "true" perception is maintained. As Foucault says:

> Neither the images created in sleep, nor the certain awareness that the senses can be deceived, can take doubt to the extreme point of its universality; suppose we are asleep; truth will not entirely escape into the night. (1961, p. 57)

However, as Foucault rightly protests, Descartes treats madness quite differently. Here Foucault points out:

> It is not the permanence of a truth which guarantees thought against madness, as it would permit truth to detach itself from error or to emerge from a dream; it is an impossibility of being mad not to the object of thought but to the subject who thinks. (loc.cit)

Effectively Descartes is declaring that he, the thinker, cannot be mad.

But Foucault does not interpret this as a preemptory dismissal by Descartes. Rather there is an important shift from a relationship in the case of sense illusions and dreams from the *object* of thought to, in the case of madness, the *subject* of thought. In the former cases there are analyses of the objects of thought; in the latter case of madness the assertion that if the argument is to continue then the saneness of the arguing subject must be presupposed. The state of madness is then epistemologically excluded as a basis for knowledge.

But already in the *Meditations* Descartes has assumed the validity of certain ideas (I exclude here the role of God). These are 'logical' -

the law of non-contradiction - and causality. But if this is now seen in relation to the philosophical exclusion of madness by reference to the epistemological priority of the rationally thinking subject, it can be seen that it is the subject as intellect as source of truth that has been inserted as an epistemological base by Descartes. It is this subject which will feature pre-eminently in the post-Renaissance world.

Boyne (1990, p. 43) claims that Descartes is involved in a double dismissal of otherness. First, as we have seen, Descartes rejects any possibility that madness, insofar as it exemplifies unreason, has anything to offer the thinking, rational subject. Second, Descartes "constructs" God as a more perfect and rationally thinking subject than humans. But construed in this manner God is the same as humans, and not a member of, or part of, the Other (Fifth *Meditation*). There is a sense then in which Descartes twice denies Otherness in his construction of the thinking subject, thereby according primacy to the rational meaning giving subject.

At the political pole Foucault's objection to this pre-cursor to the Enlightenment programme takes two forms. First:

> unreason is plunged deeper under the ground, there no doubt to disappear, but there also to take root. (Foucault, 1961, p. 58)

This is to lead in his later writings to the themes of the suppression of other discourses (Foucault,1979a), his critique of the role of intellectuals in purporting to speak for others (Foucault,1972a; 1973b; 1980b), and his general support for oppressed groups.

Second, the pole of the political operates at another level. Foucault does not attribute the consequences directly to Descartes of this form of reason's dominance of the western world in the twentieth century. Rather he talks of governance (Foucault, 1979b), of policing (1980a), and of modern power (et. passim.). In *Discipline and Punish* (1979a), for example he talks of the development of knowledge in disciplinary institutions in which people are individualised or normalised. There is little doubt however that it is such exclusionary practices as that of the category of madness, and the associated treatment by confinement, that have permitted us to advance the "cause" of modern power (or bio-power). This is not just a question of oppression by exclusion and treatment but, rather, the development of individualisation and normalisation practices which, if they can have positive effects (Foucault, 1983b), can also lead us to useful, practical and docile forms of life in which the threshold of political resistance may be very low.

Always in Foucault there was a certain insubordination and an early fascination with writers such as Bataille who talked of transgression, of the limit experience. It was Bataille and Blanchot who permitted him to make the break with phenomenology and marxism (Eribon,1991, p. 58). In Bataille's case it was the notion of the forbidden and transgression of the forbidden that seemed to fascinate Foucault. Miller (1993) makes much of this in relation to Foucault's personal life.

Another early influence upon Foucault's work was Ludwig Binswanger. Not only was this an early influence but, also, it had long term effects. In his early work from his study of Binswanger, his response to this work, and his work in psychiatry and psychology in general is to be found the theme of freedom.

Associated with freedom for Foucault is a notion of a freedom "defined" by not accepting dogmas and of withholding judgement upon beliefs which, in turn, impose restrictions upon ourselves and upon our lives and our thought. There is no need to carry forward an intellectual "baggage" a particular view of reason, riddled with dogmatic assumptions. The freedom to be sought by Foucault is a freedom to *think* differently and to *be* different.

This general thesis is to be found early in his work in the foreword to Binswanger's, *Dream and Existence* (1986). In this "foreword" he takes a radical if not revolutionary stance to the role of dreams in our conception of human being and of reason. Foucault argues that dreams, far from being peripheral to rationality, are a central and crucial aspect. Here he "follows" Heidegger and Binswanger on the notion of what it means to be a human being. Heidegger's *Being and Time* poses the existential question of the meaning of *Being*. Binswanger takes up this existential question to concentrate upon the dream as being a definite mode of human being.

This represents an important epistemological break with the Western tradition on dreams. Nowhere, perhaps, is this Western position on dreams more clearly expounded than by Descartes. Descartes relegates the dream to the periphery of thought and perception, as an inferior and seriously flawed mode of perception. Dreams, according to Descartes, could not be considered seriously as a contender for the grounding of objective thought upon perception. At best, for Descartes, the dream acts as a foil for his account of perception in consciousness and scientific thought. Dreams, on this traditional view, are relegated to the very margins of human experience. At best they represent pale shadows of the real and integral aspects of human experience; they have little or no value in and of themselves.

To a certain extent Freud had resurrected the dream. He had interpreted dreams as being the outcomes or effects of unconscious desires, and whilst some philosophers have been interested in Freud's work, in general, this has not led to a philosophical statement of the importance of dreams to explicating the nature of human being. But Binswanger and Foucault do accept this challenge.

The challenge is to seek to ground a basic epistemic function in the dream. The claim is that far from the dream being merely an aspect of the imagination, and an epistemically inferior aspect at that, the dream serves as a very condition of the imagination. Imagining depends upon the dream ; it is epistemically grounded in the dream. This is a much more radical thesis than that of Freud. If Freud had reinstated the importance of the dream he had not advanced a complex theory of meaning based upon the dream.

Foucault departs however from Binswanger in "Dream, Imagination and Existence", the title he gave to the foreword. Represented in Foucault's departure are, at least:

(i) a rejection of phenomenology as a method;
(ii) a continuation of his challenge to Descartes and the Western philosophical tradition; and,
(iii) a "cry" for freedom.

Foucault thought that phenomenology concentrated on the individual subject, existing now, and disregarded the history of the subject. Here his target would seem to be Husserl rather than Heidegger, for Heidegger attempted to ground *dasein* in an historical world, dispensing with the 'subject' of Cartesianism. Binswanger followed Heidegger, but Foucault's contribution seems to be directed at Husserl (Hoeller, 1986). According to Foucault, Binswanger:

> rejoined a tradition left unclarified by a 19th century psychology that Freud did not always succeed in transcending ... Freud thus restored a psychological dimension to the dream, but he did not succeed in understanding it as a specific form of experience. (1986, p. 43)

By psychologising the dream, in the way that he did, Freud deprived the dream of "any privilege as a specific form of experience" (loc.cit.). This was because the dream, for Freud, was the outcome of unconscious desires, and therefore dependent upon the pre-established meanings of conscious intentions.

It is interesting to note here that already Foucault is appealing to early historical examples of discussions of the dream. He returns to the Greco-Roman notion that the early morning dreams have validity; if a dream occurs in the early morning it has valid meaning as opposed to those dreams disturbed by the digestive vapours:

> morning dreams ... like the dawn they proclaim a new day, with a depth to their clarity that the wakefulness of high noon will never know. (loc.cit.)

Foucault tracks this important point on the imagination and dreaming through the western tradition, including Spinoza, to Binswanger's classical reaffirmation of the epistemological importance of the dream. But, according to Foucault, Binswanger stops short. It is not enough that the dream should be *part* of the imagination but, rather, that it should *ground* the imagination:

> placing at the heart of imagination the meaning of the dream, one can restore the fundamental forms of existence, and one can reveal its freedom. And one can also designate its happiness and its unhappiness ... (Foucault, 1986, p. 75)

Hence even in this early work, written before his Ph.D., there is a cry for freedom. I do not understand how Pignatelli (1993a) can say that no one except Rachjman had noticed this cry for freedom in Foucault's writing. No one who has read Foucault could have missed this - it stands out like a bolt from the blue and perhaps the commentators have therefore ignored, what I see, as the obvious. In these earlier writings it is a cry for the legitimation of the imagination, based upon the dream as a valid grasping towards experience, as a possibility or epistemological ground for valid experience. It is not to be an experience validated itself by "exterior" canons of rationality which in turn structure the validity of the dream (as in Freud), but, instead, a valid form of experience necessary for the grounding of other experiences including perception, even if, in itself, it permits only possibilities and not verites. It is at this early moment in his thought that Foucault attempts to open up the possibility of freedom, which is to be a freedom from control, objectification, and subjectification by the "rational" human sciences. This general theme is never abandoned by Foucault.

But Foucault's meeting with Binswanger was important and for another reason. Whilst he was later to express dissatisfaction with existential anaylsis and with phenomenological psychaitry he took from his meetings, and discussions with Binswanger about his work, the general notion that there was some reality underlying madness (Eribon,1991). Foucault was to say later that this had been important to him because it helped him:

> limit and better define what it was about academic psychiatric knowledge that was heavy and oppressive. (Trombadori, 1981, p. 41. Quoted in Eribon, 1991, p. 47)

Another influence upon Foucault was the philosophy and history of science. The work of the philosopher of science, Gaston Bachelard, is especially important here. There are several ideas in Bachelard which Foucault seems to adopt and, of course, adapt (compare his treatment of Nietzsche). For whatever reason, Bachelard's work on philosophy of science predated discussions in Anglo-American philosophy by several years. For example, Thomas Kuhn, to a certain extent, was old hat in French intellectual thought (Hacking,1981). (On Bachelard and to a certain extent Canguilhelm I follow Gutting,1989).

Given that Foucault is rather remiss in acknowledging his intellectual forebears (apart from in his inaugural lecture at Le Collége de France, and interviews (such as Foucault, 1967; 1968; 1982c; 1983c), and in engaging in critical discourse with them, it is important that Bachelard's ideas, insofar as they appear to have influenced him, be identified.

Foucault did not fully partake in the intellectual pattern followed by so many in France. This was essentially existential and phenomenological philosophy combined with marxist political and social thought, and when this began to founder, structuralism. On the contrary Foucault saw himself as connected to the "network" of the historical critique of reason represented by Bachelard and Canguilhelm (Foucault, 1983c), and traceable to Jean Cavaillès who was shot as a member of the Resistance. Althusser, his friend and teacher, must have encouraged him here.

Bachelard argues that there are no viable accounts of rationality except those that have or can be derived from scientific reason. And scientific reason is to be known and understood through reflection upon the history of science. He was particularly concerned to reject a priori philosophical ideals of rationality because, he believed, these continued to be contradicted by historical scientific developments and achievements. For Bachelard then reason is immanent in the historical practices of scientists, in their *actual* employment of reason. This cannot be a fixed and monolithic rationality, for Bachelard believed that there were breaks and discontinuities in the history of science. Corresponding to these breaks, gaps, or ruptures, were changed conceptions of rationality. Furthermore, Bachelard argues that strictly speaking there is no such thing as *the* history of science. Rather there are various histories of the various areas of science. If there is no one unified science then there can be no one unified and totalising form of rationality.

The philosopher must work then from the concrete developments of the sciences. Central to this project must be an account of scientific change. Bachelard proposes a model of scientific change which is built around four key epistemological categories (Gutting, 1989, p. 14) : epistemological breaks, epistemological obstacles, epistemological profiles and epistemological acts.

There are two senses to the notion of an epistemological break. First science splits off from common sense. Scientific knowledge is not merely different from common sense experience and beliefs but it also contradicts commonsense. Scientific knowledge is a distinct cognitive realm for Bachelard (cf. Stephan Körner, 1966). According to Bachelard:

> Scientific progress always reveals a break (rupture), constant breaks, between ordinary (commune) knowledge and common sense. (1953, p. 207) (quoted in Gutting, 1989)

Science breaks with these common sense beliefs by first placing objects of commonsense under new categories that reveal "new" relationships and properties. Second, new scientific concepts are needed to explain familiar facts of our experience; for example, Lamark's futile attempt to explain combustion by relying on immediate phenomenal experiences. Lavoisier, according to Bachelard, had already shown these to be inadequate for understanding combustion. If science does use common sense terms these are often metaphorical, or they are tacitly redefined so that they are totally different. Here he refers to the notion of the "water-drop" in Bohr's model of the atom. Finally, science breaks not merely with commonsense but also with earlier scientific thought.

The notion of a break implies that there is a resistance or an *obstacle* obstructing or preventing the break. Obstacles are theories, concepts or models from previous ways of thinking which may include commonsense experience and beliefs. Often these obstacles may be implicit for those constrained by them. Bachelard saw a need for a "psychoanalysis" of reason so that what was implicit could be made an object of conscious awareness.

The notion of an epistemological profile is closely related to the notions of obstacles and the psychoanalysis of reason. The notion of a profile is that of a personal record of a "scientist's" thought. In one sense this can be seen as a personal history of the obstacles which constrain the thought of a thinker. Bachelard (1969, pp. 36-38) provides a profile of his own concept of mass; this, he claims, is dominated by the eighteenth century notion of mass. This can be seen in his own case as an obstacle to the understanding of more recent concepts of mass. But these obstacles in the profile carry with them a certain validity, because they contribute to the philosophical complexity "to obtain the complete notion of a particular piece of knowledge" (ibid., p. 42). In this realm there may be non-scientific notions, indeed poetic notions, and they are a necessary complement to scientific knowledge according to Bachelard.

Finally the notion of an epistemological act provides the leaps, or jumps, or transcendences, that permit the introduction of new ideas and provide the impetus for scientific advances. The acts counterbalance the obstacles and permit scientific progress. It is not just change that he is talking about but positive scientific progress.

For Bachelard science has *progressed.* The science of the present is, in his view, vastly superior to ancient or even classical science. He insists upon a history of science that "starts from the certainties of the present and discovers in the past progressive formations of the trut" as "recurrent history" (Gutting, 1989, p. 19).

This is not an objective neutral history, or even a history written from a particular theoretical position (e.g. a marxist perspective on schooling which is not neutral but which may be "objective" relative to the theoretical assumptions). Nor was it an attempt by Bachelard to reinterpret ancient and classical science in terms of present day concepts and theories. The past must be represented in its own terms. The history of the science of the present is "a selective projection of light on the past" (Canguilhelm, 1977, p. 22).

Whilst Bachelard is insistent that science progresses he is also insistent that all scientific achievements are open to revision. Whilst a particular break involves a rejection of past science it is also a preservation of certain aspects, as old ideas are reformulated or accepted as correct under certain conditions. His example here is that of Euclidean geometry. Whereas the development of non-Euclidean geometries refutes Kantian type claims about Euclidean geometry representing the whole truth about the description of space, Euclidean geometry remains true as exemplifying one set of a more general set of geometric postulates. Thus Bachelard believes that he is able to deny the *continuity* and "progressive" development of science but still argue that it *progresses*. Built into this notion of progress are the retention of old errors and old norms. These are the obstacles of the past reformulated and accommodated, preserved in a rectified form. They are not seen by Bachelard as errors and abberations, or mistaken paths that are to be discarded. On the contrary errors have an essential role.

Bachelard then rejects totally any general a priori application of philosophical theory(ies) to the progress of science. Indeed he sees them as groundless speculation about what there is, and what, and how, we can know about what there is. Instead, the nature of the world and how we know about the world is to be understood through the study of the successful actual applications of reason in the world. Philosophy then is a form of reflection upon the sciences, but is not part of science itself.

Inherent in his position then is a severe critique of foundationalism, particularly Cartesian foundationalism (Bachelard, 1984: Chapter 6). Descartes' notion of certainty, based upon indubitable truths, is quite at odds with the epistemological notions of gaps, revision and progress that are to be found in Bachelard. Gutting (1989) summarises Bachelard's critique of Descartes' project of attaining clear and distinct perceptions thus:

> The requisite *clarity* would require a degree of self-awareness that is not available, and the requisite *distinctness* a likewise unavailable simplicity of the intuited object.

Bachelard's critique of the Cartesian subject is important. He stresses that in order for the subject to be certain of its intuitive judgements of certainty, the subject must itself be able to filter out any potentially distorting feelings, biases and prejudices. Bachelard believes, contrary to Descartes, that such reflective transparency is simply not available to the subject as it cannot see and assess all that it, the subject, brings to the alleged certain intuition. Bachelard's point is that we cannot examine the depths of the self and that therefore there may always be unexamined assumptions that distort any intuitions.

Canguilhelm was an historian of science rather than a philosopher of science. But he was an historian who was extremely sensitive to philosophical issues. Unlike Bachelard, who took physics and chemistry as historical examples of scientific rationality, he took as his major sources, biology and medicine. It could be said that in selecting biology and medicine, and in rejecting great scientific events such as the Copernican Revolution, that he forged a change of course in French History of Science. These sciences were not as rigorous as physics and chemistry and are inextricably intertwined with non-discursive practices. Foucault is to extend this displacement further to the human sciences.

Whereas Bachelard is concerned with scientific change and scientific rationality, Canguilhelm's concern is with the history of concepts. His history of concepts is not the history of ideas. Nor is it a history of terms, of phenomena, or even of theories. Perhaps his position can be explained best by first eliminating these other possible contenders.

A history of terms, if indeed there is such a thing, would concern itself with tracking through the use of a term, perhaps in modern usage, from its historical antecedents. Thus whilst the term "atom" is in current use in modern science it was also employed by the pre-Socratics. However whilst the same term or word was used by both pre-Socratics and contemporary scientists, the referents of these terms have little or nothing in common. Whether or not such a history has any intellectual significance is not so important here as the fact that such a history is clearly not on Canguilhelm's agenda. He was concerned with a history of concepts.

Nor is this to be identified with a history of phenomena. For example someone might produce a history of volcanic eruptions or a history of earthquakes, say in San Francisco. What is crucial here for Canguilhelm is not what is observed - the phenomena - but the interpretation of those phenomena. It is not enough then for someone to observe and describe phenomena no matter how new, or unexpected (perhaps as the result of a Baconian experiment), for that person to have a scientific concept, or to be doing science, or to be writing the history of science. For Canguilhelm the history of science is not the history of phenomena in the sense identified above. Nor is it sufficient, as in the case of Priestly, who had attempted to explain combustion in observational terms (when Lavoisier had already shown this to be inadequate). For Canguilhelm Priestly did not have the concept of oxygen, whereas Lavoisier did.

Canguilhelm insists upon the separation of concepts from any theories which may "use" those concepts. Thus he does not believe that concepts are imbedded in theories, that they either derive their meaning from associated theories or that their meaning is to be fully explicated by those theories. For Canguilhelm concepts permit one to identify data in a scientifically meaningful and useful manner: theories *explain* the data and/or phenomena identified prior to explanation by concepts. Concepts permit scientific questions to be formulated and theory(ies) provide(s) scientific answers to those questions. Furthermore he claims that concepts are "theoretically polyvalent" (Canguilhelm, 1977, p. 6). This means that a concept can occur in quite different theories and be the same concept. In this manner he wrote histories of concepts, e.g., of the reflex arc, which occur in different theories. These concepts may become reformulated and transformed between theories but still retain an underlying fundamental scientific content. Because of this continuity of content this was not to regress to a history of terms.

Canguilhelm believes then that the history of science is not the history of the discovery of phenomena. It is rather the history of concepts as outlined. He is claiming that there is a close relationship between concepts and phenomena and, if he is rejecting the distinction sometimes claimed between (neutral) facts and theories, he is not doing so in any simplistic fashion which claims that there are no observed facts apart from their theoretical interpretations. His position is more complex as he makes distinctions between terms, concepts and theories. Concepts which are theoretically polyvalent identify phenomena, not necessarily or merely theories. Instead theories explain those phenomena identified prior to explanation by concepts.

Clearly Canguilhelm does not view the history of science as itself possessing scientific status. Such a view of the history of science would see it in positivistic manner as presenting already constituted objects from the past of science to be scrutinised by the historian of science, just like any other data in a laboratory. What is wrong with this approach is Canguilhelm's insistence that history of science is normative. Here he would seem to be following Bachelard in believing that the historian's judgements of the past are informed by the present. This involves a form of epistemological analysis which furnishes to the historian the principles for informed judgement of the past. Clearly there are normative notions associated with the evaluation of science's achievements and progress.

Finally, the objects of the history of science are very different from the objects of science. Science arrests time, construing its objects as non-temporal, as not having a history. The full reality of the scientific object is in principle available to the scientist in the present. It is of course true that these objects exist in time and change through time. However the objects of history of science are regarded themselves as part of an historical development which has not yet finished. The objects of history of science are incomplete. Whereas the objects of geology can be treated as complete, as "givens" open to analysis, the objects of history of science cannot, as their value and meaning are determined first by an epistemological and normative judgement and, second, are always in principle open to re-evaluation as to their value and meaning in accordance with the progress of science.

Both Bachelard and Canguilhem have influenced Foucault. This is not simply in Canguilhem's case as being an earlier teacher at the École Normale Superiéure, and his Ph.D. examiner. Foucault acknowledges the close reading given by Canguilhem to his Ph.D. thesis (Foucault, 1961; preface), but Foucault was too much of a rebel, even early in his school days (*Liberation*, 1984), to merely accept ideas because they were those of his teachers, or to become a disciple of others. Therefore their ideas are not simply adopted. As in his "use" of Nietzsche, who is made to groan (Foucault, 1971d), Foucault adopts but also *adapts* and uses these ideas for his own purposes.

Although Foucault did not write extensively on the natural sciences his view is essentially Bachelardian (Gutting, 1989, p. 52). Furthermore many of Bachelard's views on the philosophy of science are transferred by Foucault into his investigations of the human sciences. There is the nature of a break or a rupture, though it is not clear as to how much weight Foucault placed upon this notion, as there are passages where he rejected the ascription of historian or philosopher of discontinuity (see e.g., Foucault, 1977c, p. 111). Indeed he seems to follow Canguilhem in looking for continuities where breaks or ruptures seem pre-eminent. Thus the apparent break in the treatment of offenders in *Discipline and Punish*, between the awful spectacle of Damiens and the scaffold and the young offenders in Faucher's reformatory, appears to represent a major break in the forms of punishment. Yet Foucault "uncovers" an underlying continuity concerned with the exercise of power.

It is this underlying power/knowledge which could or might be linked to Bachelard's psychoanalysis of knowledge. At one point Foucault talked of trying to identify:

> an autonomous domain that would be that of the unconscious of science, the unconscious of knowledge (savoir) which would have its own rules, just as the unconscious of the human individuals also has its rules and determinations. (1968, p. 21)

This leads to Foucault's position on philosophical a prioris. In insisting that these reflect our unwillingness or inability to see that these merely represent a re-ification of socially and temporally contingent categories, he clearly follows Bachelard.

Foucault launched several attacks upon grand philosophy, insofar as it attempted to produce totalising theory, e.g., in commenting on Sartre (Foucault, 1968), and insisted upon the importance of local theory(ies) (Foucault 1972a). Similarly in attacking the role of the intellectual as being that of the production of totalising theories for others, he is rejecting the idea of grand totalising theory. If there can be no such things as grand theories, then it is clear that there cannot be any production role for intellectuals. In asserting that the oppressed are perfectly able to formulate and articulate their problems and their solutions, he is not only asserting the primacy of local or regional theory but also he is rejecting any sharp distinctions between theory and observation and science and non-science. On rejecting the latter of these two distinctions he can be seen as following Canguilhelm and not Bachelard.

The clearest influence of Canguilhelm upon Foucault is to be seen from Canguilhelm's insistence upon the primacy of concepts. Foucault's analysis of notions such as madness, illness and punishment, for example, reflect the primacy of the concept over theory. In *Discipline and Punish* there is a clear and unequivocal rejection of penal and legal theory, and of the general enlightenment improvement thesis about the more humane forms of punishment. Instead, historically, Foucault looks at who gets punished and *how* they are punished; it is the actual practices of punishment that determine the concept and theories about punishment. Indeed his notion of disciplinary punishment is established in this way (though it can be elucidated by conceptual analysis (Marshall,1975).

If Foucault's 1954 publications, *Maladie Mentale et Personalite* and the introduction to *Dreams and Existence*, have been said to have involved Heideggerian analyses of the world of the mad, and a form of marxist analysis of the social reality which caused this world, the later works are different and, according to Gutting, whilst Foucault departs from Canguilhelm something like his history of concepts occurs in *Folie et Déraison*, *Birth of the Clinic* and *The Order of Things* (Gutting, 1989, p. 54).

In "Nietzsche, Genealogy, History" Foucault (1971d) expounds Nietzsche's rejections of certain ways of doing history. In particular the notion of history as an emergence in any developmental linear form from some kind of origin. In *The Order of Things* he is to assert the futility of the search for the origins of man. This is a fruitless exercise he claims. In Canguilhelm we are presented with the futility of the search for precursors. Canguilhelm points out the logical implications of the search for precursors - science ceases to have a history as all science "originates" in some golden age. Foucault's point on the origin of man is different however. In relation to man his origin can only be found in something different, *other* than man. The futility rests therefore not so much in the golden age but in seeking that which can only be the other.

In summarising the influences of Bachelard and Canguilhelm upon Foucault, Gutting says:

> None of the above is meant to suggest that Foucault was a mere disciple of Bachelard and Canguilhelm. His work developed from his own distinctive agenda ... (Foucault) extends, adapts, and transforms their ideas and methods. (1989, p. 54)

Foucault began to read Nietzsche in 1953 (Eribon, 1991, p. 52). At one point he had claimed that he had wanted to be a Nietzschean communist (in Trombadori, 1981, p. 30). A little earlier he had began to read Blanchot and Bataille.

> I read him (Nietzsche) because of Bataille, and Bataille because of Blanchot. (Foucault, 1983d, p. 24)

But he was not a French Nietzschean though he took Nietzsche seriously, as presenting a challenge, as a means of displacing himself philosophically from marxism, phenomenology and existentialism (ibid., p. 31). It was Nietsche's thoughts on truth, the history of truth, and the will to truth that had initially interested him (ibid., p. 32) and which he was to "use" in his genealogical approach (usually said to be post-*Archaeology of Knowledge*). Perhaps, also, reading Nietzsche was an act of transgression (Bataille) against those who dismissed those "rather strange, witty, graceful texts" (ibid., p. 33). He was to say elsewhere that:

> Nietzsche was a revelation to me. I felt that there was someone quite different from what I had been taught. I read him with a great passion and broke with my life, left my job in the asylum, left France: I had the feeling I had been trapped. Through Nietzsche, I had become a stranger to all that. I'm still not quite integrated within French social and intellectual life. (1984, p. 13)

Foucault's reading of Nietzsche is to be found in "Nietzsche, History, Genealogy" (Foucault, 1971d). There he asserts Nietzschean themes on the nature and role of history. Instead of history reaching outwards for objective truth for Foucault it turns inwards, becoming something which is to be used in the present and in the future. History is not something which purports to capture reality in any total form.

Two Nietzschean concepts are developed in this paper. These are the concepts of herkunft or *descent*, and estehung or *emergence* and they are contrasted with the notion of origin. As we have seen genealogy does not seek origins.

Descent is not a continuous and uninterrupted notion as there are a multiplicity of factors which must be unravelled from lowly sources and subjugated knowledges that will play havoc with notions of continuity. There are errors and accidents to be discovered which will disturb notions of order. The concept of descent then is not a search for firm foundations: on the contrary it discovers moving sands, fragmented and incoherent events, warts, faults, errors and ommissions, as well as faulty appraisals and evaluations and pious claims and aspirations. For Foucault's reading of Nietzsche "historical truths" rest upon complex, contingent and fragile ground.

The concept of emergence captures the present, but not in any final way, as a result of historical development and as a stage in the warlike confrontation between opposing forces in the quest for control and domination. In that paper historical developments are conceptualised as manifestations either of stable mechanisms of governance, or as exercises of power to restore stability, or as out and out contestations or struggles. Emergence concentrates on domination/subjection relationships as exemplifying the underlying balances of political forces. We look at historical developments then not as culminations of historical processes, intentions of great actors, or hidden political designs but, instead, as manifestations of the balance of power of people over people.

Genealogy, as we have seen, acts to disrupt traditional historical form.

CHAPTER 2

LIBERALISM AND LIBERAL EDUCATION

In this chapter we will look at the notions of liberalism and liberal education. The former will be discussed historically as a doctrine which initially was progressive politically and socially. More recent neo-liberal views, which have been enormously influential in the restructurings of Western educational systems, will also be discussed. It will be argued in the ways in which the individual/society nexus is construed, that there are at least two major strands to liberalism: particularly in the ways in which they construe the individual/society nexus: one of these is a socially progressive doctrine, whereas the other is inherently conservative.

Liberal education will be introduced through the ideas of some major philosophers of education. There will be no sustained attempt to explore or critique the positions of these philosophers in detail however, as considerable exposition and critique is available elsewhere - particularly in the cases of R.S.Peters and John Dewey. The other philosopher of education to be introduced will be Kenneth Strike. These philosophers of education represent liberal-democratic and neo-liberal views on education. The neo-liberal views on education of economist F.C.Hayek, representing the conservative strand of liberalism, will also be discussed. But first we will look at liberalism.

The political term "liberalism" is Spanish in origin (Schapiro,1958). It came from the name of a political party ('liberales') which early in the nineteenth century advocated constitutional government for Spain. Later the term was taken over into other countries to designate governments, parties, policies, opinions, or people who advocated freedom as opposed to authoritarianism.

Whilst the advocacy of freedom is still a central plank in liberal theory the nature of this freedom is in dispute. Is freedom to be construed merely as negative, as freedom from constraint, or is it to be construed positively, as requiring certain provisions to be made for it to exist, or to be exercised? Within a liberal framework some thinkers, e.g., Hayek, construe freedom as freedom *from*. This leads to comments such as those by Jules Guesde (quoted by Foucault,1983e, p. 161): "free foxes in free henhouses". On the other hand, it is argued, freedom cannot just be construed negatively as freedom from, but should be seen in a positive sense, as some positive power, or capacity or ability to *do* something. The problem is acute in education where often we remove some impediment preventing people from obtaining an education - the provision of free secondary education for example - without actually providing the opportunity for some people to participate - for example those who live in remote rural areas. This view was expressed clearly by T.H.Green:

> If I have given a true account of that freedom which forms the goal of social effort, we shall see that freedom from constraint, freedom in all the forms of doing what one will with one's own is valuable only as a means to an end. That end is what I call freedom in the positive sense.... When we speak of freedom as something to be highly prized, we mean a positive power or capacity of doing or enjoying something worth doing or enjoying and that, too, something we do and enjoy in common with others. (1889, p. 370f)

Given this fundamental difference, at the very basis of liberalism and the differences that will be identified below, it may be better to see liberalism, not as a set of basic ideas or principles but, rather, as an attitude of mind.

Nevertheless, in all versions of liberalism, there is a deep and fundamental concern for the freedom of the individual from authoritarianism, be it church, state, or political party. However, the individual is construed (s)he is of moral worth and to be accorded essential and absolute dignity and worth *as* a human being. A central notion is then that the interests and concerns of individuals should have precedence over the interests and concerns of the state and church. This is essentially the Kantian notion that every person is to be treated as an end in itself and not as a means to advance the interests of others. Therefore individuals must be granted autonomy to both formulate what is in their best interests and to pursue their interests and chosen activities free from constraints. According to Hobhouse:

> Liberalism is the belief that society can be safely founded on this self-directing power of personality, that it is only on this foundation that a true community can be built...(and) there is no limit that we can place to the extent of the building. (1913, p.123)

In Locke's thought the freedom of the individual required the notion of voluntary association. Any such association would be concerned with the advancement of the legitimate interests of the group. In Locke's version of the contract, there is government by the consent of those governed (Locke,1690). This notion of voluntary association was not to be found in Hobbes, for within *Leviathan* the contract is almost compulsory, as people seem compelled to enter into a contract to avoid a life in the state of nature that is nasty, brutish, and short. Certainly Hobbes saw a need for strong and extensive government (and education) to ensure obedience to the Sovereign. There are elements of compulsion and coercion here, including education, that are not found in later liberal writings. Thus whereas Mill is to argue in *On Liberty* (1859) that all children should receive an education and that the state was to ensure that they did, this was not to be a state controlled education. Another important idea in liberalism is that of equality. If Hobbes conceived equality as the equal ability people had for killing one another, Locke conceived it as equality before the law. Human beings, because they are human beings, had equal rights before the law:

> Men (sic.)...by nature free, equal, and independent, no one can be put out of this estate and subjected to the political power of another without his own consent... (Locke, 1690, p. 164)

In part this call for equality is an unceasing war against privilege of any form which hinders or blocks the development of others. But whereas for Locke equality before the law could march hand in hand with considerable inequality of property, an emerging welfare and/or socialist strain in Rousseau (but present in Locke's times with e.g., the Levellers), was to demand positive welfare rights for human beings over and above narrowly conceived Lockean property rights. According to such people as Hayek this interferes with freedom which, some liberals argue, is of prior and more fundamental importance than equality.

Rationality plays an important part in liberal thought. First there is the notion that humans are essentially rational. Second there is the notion that all beliefs, authority structures and social institutions should be subject to rational scrutiny. Historically this has led to changes in authority structures and the exercise of authority, from charismatic or traditional authority, to what Weber was to call legal rational authority. Tradition and position were no longer sufficient or even necessary to be an authority or to exercise authority. Structures, social institutions and authority, must be shown to be required as a result of critical rational inquiry. What cannot stand this form of test, no matter how well established and how powerful the authority figures and power behind it, is to be rejected. Liberals are no lovers of tradition and vested interests masquerading as "the way the world is".

Liberals have then an abiding faith in the ability of rationality, rational processes and rationally construed decision-making structures to ameliorate, if not improve, the human condition. In general they have been rationalists and in many cases, perhaps, over-optimistic in their alignment of rationality with scientific method. Some would say that they have been treading the positivist path that Weber claimed would be an iron cage, and of our own making. Dewey is especially optimistic and remiss here - as will be seen below. This alignment of liberalism with progress has resulted not only in an abiding faith in rationality and science to improve the lot of human beings but, also, an abiding faith in education. Improvement will come about through the advancement of knowledge thereby producing personally autonomous people, who will continue down the path of progress that the earlier liberals had foreshadowed. This optimistic picture has become somewhat tarnished in the twentieth century.

Associated with liberalism is individualism. However even this doctrine has several strands to it. Initially individualism represented a wholly different conceptualisation of the world from feudal and Catholic Europe (Hall, 1986, p. 39). Feudal status and the divine order positioned people within a structure with defined duties and responsibilities. Stripped of these fixed and pre-ordained relationships individuals became atomistic and materialistic, endowed with certain attributes which would permit duties and responsibilities to be redefined. Thus human nature was set in opposition to God and the traditional fabric of society. But there were different views of human nature.

Hobbes had advanced an earlier view of human nature in a form of pre-social life in which human beings were seen as essentially egoistic, and concerned with their own self-preservation. In this state of nature, forced to compete for scarce resources and equally capable of killing one another, life was nasty, brutish and short. The only "solution" to this state of affairs was for people to enter into a contract with the Sovereign whereby they surrendered their rights to punish transgressors in return for the protection of the Sovereign. In return they were obliged to obey the Sovereign. This obligation was to be achieved by considerable Government constraint, including an education which would bring people to understand why it was necessary to obey the Sovereign (Marshall,1981). For Hobbes obedience was to be obtained "ex disciplina" (De Cive).

Hobbes can be seen as a pre-liberal then on two issues. First, he believed in considerable government interference in the affairs of individuals - including education. Second, society was held together by an imposed collectivity. Further, it is arguable whether liberalism need be committed to an egoistic view of human nature where individuals are seen as essentially self-interested and aggrandising of resources. Even neo-liberals such as Hayek protest at this type of ascription (Hayek,1960).

Individualism, later in liberal theory, sees human beings as possessing inalienable rights - life, property and liberties - and civil society as being formed by voluntary association; it is a collectivity formed by voluntary association and is not compelled. Civil society in the realms of the family, the market, and free and voluntary association was raised by liberalism over and above the State (and Church), and represented a privatising of those areas from earlier forms of thought and constraint, where duties and responsibilities were defined by feudal structures and the divine order.

However the economic theory which accompanied this liberal political theory may still have had some roots in Hobbesian human nature (Hall, 1986, p. 43). Some versions may have had, but Locke's hedonism descended not from Hobbes, but from Gassendi (Aaron, 1955, p. 257).

Whilst Locke's hedonism asserts that what is good has to be felt as pleasant, not all pleasure is morally good. Eating is a natural pleasure and is to be distinguished from a moral good which is objective and ordained by God (as in the Christian hedonism of the Gassendists). Although Locke does not explicitly affirm that human beings can determine God's divine will rationally (Locke,1690; e.g., at 11,xxviii, pp. 5,8), according to Aaron this is the essence of his teaching, as he argued for a science of morals (ibid.,IV,iv, pp. 7-8). Whilst there are strands of both hedonism and rationality in Locke the hedonism is not the materialistic hedonism of Hobbes, because for Locke there is no formal equivalence between pleasure and the good and the hedonism is part of God's purpose.

Stuart Hall (1986) argues that from its very inception liberalism exhibited an historic tension between progressive and conservative forces. This tension has offspins into different versions of individualism. Liberalism was always *opposed* to something - the old order and traditional society - and *aligned* to something - the new emerging social order. This tension can be seen below in the differences between Hayek's account of individualism, where there is an emphasis on tradition, an opposition to the potential of rationality to liberate mankind and an emphasis on Lockean property rights, and the strain of individualism which has emerged through Rousseau, where there is an emphasis on rationality, on new forms of social life, and on welfare as opposed to property rights. But these different accounts of individualism need now to be identified.

Underlying the economic thought of F.A.Hayek who has influenced Milton Friedman and other economists on the "new right" is the first form. I will use Hayek's own work to identify this, and the second form which can be traced to Rousseau. As the British philosopher Richard Norman said (1982, p. 83): "(Hayek is)...the intellectual inspiration of our rulers". Hayek says some disastrous things about education also, (O'Hear,1986), and his influence can be seen in the world wide neo-liberal/economist "reforms" of education (Marshall and Peters,1990;1991).

The form of individualism which Hayek says that he wishes to defend (Hayek,1947, p. 4) descends, according to him, from John Locke, David Hume, Adam Smith and Edmund Burke. This version of individualism is contrasted with that "represented mainly by French and other Continental writers" with Rousseau an outstanding representative (loc. cit.). This latter version he terms rationalistic individualism and claims that it always tends to develop into the opposite of "true" individualism, namely, socialism or collectivism.

True individualism is said to be primarily "an attempt to understand the forces which determine the social life of man (sic.)". These forces are those which direct the behaviour of individual actions towards other people. It is not in the first instance a political theory, and in particular it is directed against individualistic notions which posit some directing mind or general will. Social relations and institutions arise from individual actions as unintended effects. Quoting Adam Ferguson (*An Essay On the History of Civil Society*) approvingly he says:

> nations stumble upon establishments, which are indeed the result of human action but not the result of human design. (op. cit., p.7)

The fundamental difference between true individualism and collective individualism is that order is established by the unforseen results of human individual actions, whereas in the latter, all discoverable order is traceable to deliberate design. In the former case the place which reason plays in human affairs is rated rather lowly. Man is only partly guided by reason which, in individuals, is very limited and imperfect. In collective individualism, on the other hand, reason is "always fully and equally available to all humans and that everything which man achieves is the direct result, and therefore subject to, the control of individual reason" (ibid., p. 8). The former is an attitude of humility toward the anonymous and impersonal social processes by which individuals have created things greater than they know, whereas the second assumes that individual reason is capable of rationally designing our social structures and institutions. According to Hayek this is an "exaggerated belief in the powers of individual reason" (ibid.).

Hayek traces the design theories of social institutions to Descartes. In his view Cartesian rationalism has "proved a grave obstacle to an understanding of historical phenomena" (ibid., p. 10). This anti-historical attitude of Descartes has led to beliefs in inevitable laws of historical development, and perhaps modern fatalism. In Hayek's view John Stuart Mill and Herbert Spencer have been as much influenced by the Cartesian-Rousseau version of individualism as by the English tradition. The major difference for Hayek is:

> While the design theories necessarily lead to the conclusion that social processes can be made to serve human ends only if they are subjected to the control of human reason, and thus lead directly to socialism, true individualism believes on the contrary that, if left free, men will often do more than individual reason could design or foresee. (ibid.)

Adam Smith's main concern was that there should be as little chance as possible for men to do harm. How this is meant to operate in the free market conditions is far from clear however. Certainly Hayek protests at the charges of selfishness and blatant self-interest delivered against him. His response is that the individual must care for his immediate family and friends (ibid., p. 13), and presumably in the limited market exchanges with those individuals with whom one bartered. But far more important than this moral problem, Hayek argues, is the indisputable fact of the limitations of individual men's knowledge and interests. As a matter of fact his limited knowledge must limit his ability to influence anything beyond the immediate and known sphere. Therefore:

> the real question is ... whether we can allow him to be guided in his actions by those immediate consequences which he can know and care for or whether he ought to be made to do what seems

appropriate to someone else who is supposed to possess a fuller comprehension of the significance of these actions to society as a whole.

This is of course an improper presentation of the collectivist position. No doubt there are problems of the intellectual limitations of man and hence of being able to make such decisions. However, Hayek argues that the main practical conclusion from true individualism is the demand for a strict limitation of all coercive power. The target is not collective action per se, for he seems to support Lockean voluntary association, but coercion to collectivism, or to accept the reason of others. This is not to assert an anarchistic position but to argue for limits to coercion so that it should be at a minimum. Essentially coercion should be limited to ensure the proper functioning of the free market in which the individual must be free.

The third strand of liberalism, again descended from Locke, is to be found in the writings of Robert Nozick (1974). According to Nozick human beings, qua human beings, have rights, and they possess these rights simply by being human beings. His central idea is that a person is an agent capable of acting upon intentions and purposes. Persons have aims, purposes, or goals, and deliberate upon them so as to achieve desired ends. If human beings are to be of worth they must be free to pursue their aims and goals. Human rights, according to Nozick, are an implication from these fundamental assumptions about persons. In order for humans to fulfil their aims they must be able to appropriate and control portions of the external world. Without the fundamental right to freedom to acquire property persons would not be of worth because they could not pursue their aims and goals. Although this view is based upon the moral notion of the rights of the individual, all rights essentially become property rights. Even the right to be a person, to have one's integrity as a person preserved and protected in what is for Nozick a minimal state, is essentially a property right, as this right itself can be construed in terms of self-ownership.

Property rights in Nozick lead inevitably to a market society in which individuals are entitled to keep full control of their property provided that it was acquired justly in the free market. There is no suggestion that a person merits or deserves anything and what "emerges" in terms of property ownership is *just* provided that no other individual's rights were violated in the market exchanges. The welfare state and welfare rights are unjust because they do not appeal to the fundamental rights of persons, that is to property rights, but essentially to utilitarian premises which extract resources from certain individuals. Indeed from this position to claim a welfare right may be to commit a logical fallacy, given the basic construal of all rights on the basis of property rights.

The role of the state is then minimal for Nozick, as it is for Hayek. For both it is to defend freedom, but whereas for Hayek it was to defend the freedom of the market forces to operate, for Nozick it is to defend the freedom of the person to acquire property. Whilst both support a minimal state so as to maximise freedom their reasoning is different. Reason plays an important role in determining Nozick's position, whereas Hayek's is "perceived" almost intuitively as a fundamental axiom. The lowly position which Hayek accords to reason in his argument for the minimal state is not countenanced by Nozick. Rather reason's role is fundamental to his position.

According to Schapiro (1958, p. 22) there was a great upsurge of liberal political thought in the period 1815-1870, but the educational views had been shaped earlier. If as Hobhouse says "liberalism is the belief that society can safely be founded on this self-directing power of personality" ... (of which) ... the rule ... is just the application of scientific method", then we could expect that a fundamental aim of a liberal education would be to produce self-directed rational people who reveal their rationality by their use of scientific method. In contemporary language we are talking about the notion of an autonomous person, where the notion of being autonomous becomes identified with rationally autonomous, and being rational with applying scientific method. This is a "strong" position on personal autonomy and one which not all supporters of personal autonomy as an aim of education would wish to defend or support (see chapter three).

The goal of the rationally autonomous person was nowhere better expressed than by Voltaire (1773) in his *Treatise on Tolerance*:

> Do I propose, then, that every citizen shall be free to follow his own reason, and believe whatever this enlightened or deluded reason shall dictate to him? Certainly, provided he does not disturb the public order.

Voltaire, who was not to see the Revolution, put great strength in reason:

> Reason is gentle and humane. It inspires liberality, suppresses discord, and strengthens virtue; it has more power to make obedience to the law attractive than force has to compel

> it...reason...which slowly, but infallibly, enlightens men. (ibid.)

Whilst Voltaire does not equate rationality with scientific method Condorcet, the one prominent eighteenth century philosopher who lived to become prominent in the Revolution (and who himself was to cheat the guillotine only by suicide), did;

> Man, by using reason and facts will attain perfection. Nature has set no limits to the perfection of the human faculties. The perfectibility of mankind is truly indefinite...this progress...will never retrograde... If man can predict with almost complete certainty those phenomena whose laws he knows...why then should this principle be less true for the development of the intellectual and moral faculties of man than it is for the other operations of nature... Beliefs based on past experience under like conditions constitute the only rule according to which the wisest men act.

Condorcet chaired a major committee on education and reported to the Legislative Assembly in 1792. The "Report on the General Organisation of Knowledge" is an important document in the history of liberal education for it stresses the importance of education in the promotion of welfare and the progress of mankind (see excerpt above). As expressed in the Report the aim of education was:

> in short, to cultivate in each generation the physical, intellectual, and moral faculties, and thereby contribute to the general and gradual improvement of the human race - which should be the final aim of every social institution. This likewise should be the object of education, and it is for the Government a duty imposed on it by the common interest of society.

Such an education was said to be for government "an obligation of justice" in "the ever increasing progress of enlightenment" (loc.cit.).

The French Revolution represents a watershed in Liberal thought (Dunn, 1979, p. 29).

It was a break for the French with the past but also, after the terror in which liberals such as Condorcet were to die, liberals were not to be so trusting of change and the future. Value was to seen again in tradition and the continuity of the past. Whereas Voltaire could assert the slogan, "Ecrasez l'infame", liberalism reverted to its more conservative side.

On the conservative side some liberals who believed in science as the guarantor of progress, equated the scientific ability to predict the development of the intellectual and moral faculties with social Darwinism. For example, Herbert Spencer argued that the progress of civilisation was to be equated with the notion of the survival of the fittest. Furthermore Spencer included in the notion of fitness, that of economic fitness. According to him nature exhibits a stern discipline which, "is a little cruel that it may be kind" (Spencer, 1851, p. 323). Thus Spencer strongly opposed Government intervention on behalf of the poor - welfare - on the grounds that the role of government was a negative one to protect the right of a citizen's:

> freedom to do all he (sic.) wills, provided he infringes not the equal freedom of any other man - this is the special purpose for which the civil power exists. Now insuring to each the right to pursue within the specified limits the objects of his desires without let or hindrance, is quite a separate thing from insuring his satisfaction.

Here Spencer foreshadows Hayek on several issues. In spite of the general discrediting of social Darwinism Hayek also adopts it (for a critique of Hayek on this point see O'Hear,1986). Second, Hayek follows Spencer in construing freedom in the negative sense of freedom from constraint. Third, they both believe in a minimal role for Government even though Hayek does not seem so harsh as Spencer, who said that "widows and orphans should be left to struggle for life and death" for such fatalities should be "seen to be full of the highest beneficence". By beneficence he means the culling out of the economically sick along with the diseased and debilitated (Spencer, op.cit.). Perhaps Hayek should not have dismissed Spencer so summarily and relegated him to the camp of collective individualism, which was opposed to true liberalism and akin to socialism (Hayek, 1947). We will return to this conservative strand in liberal thought below.

If the most advanced ideas on education in the eighteenth century were advanced by Condorcet those who sought to create self-directing personalities were already strongly influenced by the educational and philosophical writings of John Locke and Jean-Jacques Rousseau. In

Locke's case *Some Thoughts Concerning Education* ran to forty-five editions and was translated into fifteen other languages. But it was not so much the *Thoughts* that has had influence on modern liberal education but the *Essay Concerning Human Understanding*. In the *Essay* Locke argued that there are no innate ideas, though there may be innate faculties, and that all ideas are derived from sense experience. Essentially a child comes into the world with a mind like a blank tablet of wax, or a tabula rasa, and knowledge is the effect of sensations received from the "external environment". This empiricist epistemology claims that knowledge is acquired by the reception of sensory impressions which are "treated" by the faculties of the mind. In Locke's case these faculties were not themselves derived from sense experience. This empiricist doctrine was to be adopted and further extended by the French sensationalists in the eighteenth century; particularly Condillac, Helvetius and La Mettrie, but including Condorcet. They argued that mental faculties such as discrimination and association were themselves derived from sensations. These extended ideas were the basis of Helvetius' educational thought and practice.

As we have seen above Locke's views on human nature were similar to those of Gassendi - a form of psychological hedonism instilled and validated by a well intentioned and rational God. Rousseau dispenses with such religious notions, arguing for an optimistic view of human nature. According to Rousseau in a pre-social state human beings were neither good nor bad, as these were concepts dependant upon the context of a social society. In the state of nature human beings act towards other human beings with general feelings of sympathy or empathy. Society destroyed these natural tendencies. Therefore in the education of the child it was necessary to separate the child as much as possible from the bad socialising effects - intellectual, moral and social - of society. In *Emile* these ideas are worked out. In modern liberal educational thought these are the notions that education should be aligned to the child's "true" nature, with the tutor acting in a shadowy capacity organising practical experiences so that the child learns *from* nature. Arguably the tutor in Rousseau, as a "clone" of *The Social Contract*'s Sovereign, acts in a highly manipulative manner.

If the account so far has been correct we can identify two strands of liberal thought. In general they bifurcate over the conceptions of individualism and the role of rationality. The conservative strand of liberalism which permeates Hayek, Freidman and recent educational "reforms" is fiercely individualistic, wants government out of the lives of individual citizens, and claims that Government cannot know what is good for the collective, placing too much emphasis upon rationality and rational planning, ignoring the forces and traditions of the past. This is part of the conservative backward looking face of liberalism which has been identified by Stuart Hall. Liberalism had to define itself against something in the past, but for these "modern" neo-liberals it is not to overcome some features of the past but to attempt to preserve certain features of it.

As has been argued above in Hayek's case this leads to a very conservative view of education - very ably critiqued by O'Hear (1986).

The strand of liberalism which comes from Rousseau (and Voltaire) places greater faith in rationality and the social construction of the individual (to improve society), and the reform of society through the rational explanation of the General Will. It was Robbespierre who tried politically to identify the General Will and, it might be argued, the ideological and lived contradictions of the French Revolution, spelled the end of the possibility of the Enlightenment thesis.

On the topic of the individual, and the relationships between individual and society, Dewey was very scathing about the conservative strand of liberalism, arguing also that the applications of concepts in social and historical settings different from their original uses and applications was fraught with danger. He said:

> Such thinking treats individualism as if it were something static, having a uniform content. It ignores the fact that the mental and moral structure of individuals, the pattern of their desires and purposes, change with every great change in social constitution. Individuals who are not bound together in associations, whether domestic, economic, religious, political, artistic or educational, are monstrosities. It is absurd to suppose that the ties which hold them together are merely external and do not react into mentality and character, producing the framework of personal disposition. (Dewey, 1962, p. 81)

The atomistic individualism of Hayek does indeed treat ties to others as external and non-necessary. They are treated as non-necessary because they *must* be voluntary. But from Dewey's position there must be these ties as they are part of the very essence of being human. For him to talk of the individual and society is to invoke yet another of the many dualisms which he detested. One can talk of these separately in thought, but not in reality, for they are both intertwined in his thought and necessary for understanding the development of mind and personality. Individuality and society or community are two sides of the same coin for Dewey. Indeed the opportunities for individuals to choose and develop depended upon the community in which they lived. On laissez-faire liberalism he said that there was:

> no doubt in my own mind that laissez-faire liberalism is played out, largely because of the facults of its own policies. Any system that cannot provide elementary security for millions has no claim to the title of being organised on behalf of liberty and the development of individuals. (1946, p. 132)

Liberal Education

In what follows the ideas of three liberal educators will be introduced. Dewey should be seen as a major ally of the progressive rationalism of the French philosophers, though he differs in many ways on epistemological and metaphysical issues. Peters is a liberal in the British philosophical tradition - there are influences from both Hobbes and Locke - but there is little doubt as to where he stands on rationality, and an accompanying liberal view on the development of mind by the structuring of consciousness through established public forms of life, or public traditions to be found in shared forms of language and beliefs, and cultural hopes and aspirations.

At the other end of the liberal spectrum on education is Hayek. It is clear that his ideas, or ideas very close to his, can be found in many of the proposals to "reform" public education systems in Western capitalist societies. However, a much better formulated view of education from a neo-liberal perspective is available in the writings of Kenneth Strike. Perhaps he would not wish to be classified or described as a neo-liberal conservative. Yet, in effect, his ideas and their entailments are conservative. It must be emphasised that there is no suggestion that Strike and Hayek, and Friedman, and....present any unified conservative or neo-liberal front. Strike presents a coherent liberal position in which he is opposed to democratic imposition upon others of a majority view (or views), or a centralised view which, in representative democracy, may not be a majority view or representative of anything like the General Will. Strike, as we will see, talks of thick and thin languages and cultures, where the thin turns out to be what can be agreed upon, or shared, or lived with. This means that, in effect, Dewey's views on the extension of shared interests through the schooling system, are rejected. According to Strike this would be to impose upon some people and that is not acceptable to his version of liberalism.

Richard Rorty (1982) sees similarities between Dewey and Foucault (but see Marshall, 1995d). But Foucault too, saw the importance of this liberal form of critique of the reason of state, and would side with Strike in rejecting the role, rights, and spheres of control of centralised state governments. In this respect he was more like Strike, Nozick and Hayek, than Dewey. Whilst sensitive to the force of the liberal critique against the excessive forces of government, Foucault did critique neo-liberalism and had no great love for it (Gordon,1991, p. 47).

R.S. Peters is very explicit about his liberal democratic position. Indeed his philosophical work on education is predicated upon presuppositions that are both liberal and democratic. This is not the place to develop and critique his work in full, or to examine for example his concept of education. There is already a considerable literature on such matters. The point to be made here is that the leading figure in philosophy of education for nearly two decades in Great Britain is writing from within a liberal democratic framework, and in his emphases upon freedom and personal autonomy, is open to Foucault's critique.

Peters is in no doubt that democracy is a form of social control and the preferred form of social control. In the Anglo-American version, he says the democratic way of life:

> amounts to the determination to settle political matters by recourse to reasonable discussion rather than by recourse to force or arbitrary fiat .... (it) is to be understood by reference to principles which have to be interpreted in the light of the practices; it cannot be spun out of the purely abstract concept of 'the rule of the people'. (1966, p. 299)

These principles are those of fairness, equality, freedom, consideration of the interests of others and respect for persons. These principles represent the ideas of liberalism outlined above; namely fairness, equality, a belief in rationality, a belief in rational decision making and a form of individualism. Peters believes that people can participate in democratic structures and institutions, because they are capable of rational decision making.

But he makes his liberal positions very clear when he says:

> government is at best a necessary expedient and that acceptance of it is conditional. Authority is necessary but it must be

> constituted in such a way that it does not unduly oppress the individual. It is subject to moral appraisal and must safeguard the rights of individuals and minorities .... (op. cit., p. 297)

Peters sees this Anglo-American view as different from Rousseau's conception of Government as the expression of the General Will of the people. For Peters this notion is quite alien to the Anglo-American tradition, where the political practices became formulated into procedural principles to avoid force or arbitrary fiat. If government is a necessary evil and there is little or no part in the Anglo-American tradition for governments to promote the common good then it can be seen that there are similarities to a neo-liberal position, in the Locke, Smith, Burke, Hayek, Nozick tradition rather than the Rousseau, marxist tradition.

But it would be mistaken to interpret Peters in this way. He does believe in rationality, he emphasises the important Kantian principles of consideration for the interests of others and respect for persons. For Peters the political is the moral writ large. There cannot be moral anarchy in a democracy. *Ethics and Education*, and the philosophy of education within it, are written from a traditional liberal standpoint.

For Peters education becomes essentially the development of mind through the search for truth, essentially in the traditional academic disciplines. As the title of one of his papers reveals Plato nearly got it right: what needs to be added for Peters are the sciences. For Peters autonomy is to be obtained through immersion in the rational disciplines.

In thinking rationally a person thinks on their own, autonomously. This person, the autos, is the source of the law, the nomos. But to think rationally is to employ concepts, to follow procedures and methodologies, to seek standards and tests for the truth. These are to be found as the historical products of the various disciplines. To be rational then is to adopt the canons of disciplined enquiry in the public forms of knowledge.

According to Peters both Descartes and the British empiricists were correct in identifying consciousness as the hall mark of mind (1966, chapter two). This emphasis has gone hand in hand, Peters claims, with the development of individualism as a social movement. However they disagreed over the nature of knowledge, with the British empiricists rejecting any notion of innate ideas. But where the empiricists were wrong, Peters argues, is that consciousness does not develop because of ideas or impressions from sense experience but, rather, it is the outcome of the initiation of an individual into shared forms of life, or public traditions, "enshrined in the language, concepts, beliefs, and rules of a society".

To be conscious is to be conscious of some thing - there must be an object of consciousness. These are first and foremost objects in a public world and they are identified and individuated by a public language into which the individual young are introduced. As Kant has shown us the perceptions and conceptions which we have of these objects in the word go hand in hand:

> His (sic) consciousness, as well as his individuality, is neither intelligible nor genetically explicable without the public world of which he is conscious, in relation to which he develops, and on which he develops his own individual style and consciousness. (op. cit., p. 50)

For Peters the development is more that the acquisition of such things as spatio-temporal and causal categories and principles, and requires further differentiation by immersion in the Western intellectual inheritance (at the least). The development of mind therefore requires immersion in different, differentiated, and public forms of thought such as, science, history, mathematics, religions, and other aesthetic, moral and technical forms of thought and action.

In the hands of his former colleague, collaborator and co-author, Paul Hirst (1965), this general position is "sharpened" into a basic claim that there are different *forms* of knowledge - Hirst identifies some seven or eight (compare Phillip Phenix, 1964). For Hirst then a liberal education entails initiation into these forms of thought, and whilst he claims that his forms of thought should not be identified with the established academic traditions, nevertheless the use of such names as "mathematics", "science" and "history" invites this identification.

To be free then, or to be autonomous, is to be on the inside of these forms of thought. One acts rationally insofar as one accords with the public standards and criteria, inherent in these public forms of thought. It is the laws and principles of these forms of thought which become the "nomos" or laws, which constitute the autonomous person. But more of that below.

But it is also these forms of thought which structure the individual's identity, for personal identity post-Descartes and Locke, has come to be identified with consciousness. Indeed Locke put this point very forcefully when he said:

> For it being the same consciousness that makes a man be himself to himself, personal identity depends on that only.... (Locke, 1690:II, xvii, p. 10)

Peters' well known analysis of education arrives at this position (Peters, 1966, p. 45). Education:

(i) implies the transmission of what is worthwhile to those who become committed to it;

(ii) must involve knowledge and understanding and some kind of cognitive understanding, which are not inert;

(iii) at least rules out some procedures of transmission, on the grounds that they lack willingness and voluntariness on the part of the learner.

Peters is quite explicit that this concept is normative, i.e. that it sets criteria which learning and teaching activities have to meet if they are to be educational. Not any teaching and learning can count as education. Activities can fail on each of the criteria which he has identified through philosophical analysis. Thus, for example, bingo is not a worthwhile activity, mere facts do not introduce people to knowledge and understanding as what is required by Peters is some kind of conceptual schema which makes "sense" of the facts, and indoctrination for example abuses the criteria of rationality which should structure the development of mind.

If we assume that this general position can be philosophically defended and some content given to what is really a formal definition (for example what is a worth while activity ?), then it would seem that we have a powerful normative concept which could be used to appraise people, practices and institutions. However what he didn't do was to turn to schools and attempt a similar analysis of the concept of schooling.

On the contrary he seems to assume that schools are more or less educating. Even though he discusses the role of the school in such matters as selection and social control he does not see schools as in any way like Foucault's disciplinary blocks. Yet, Kevin Harris (1977) argues there is in *Ethics and Education* an implicit account of schooling which is very different to the formal abstract account of education given by Peters, and which is more like the schools that function as disciplinary blocks for Foucault. Authority talk masks the power relations in schools and this, it will be argued, is a major defect of the liberal view of education (see Chapter four).

Peters was well aware that his concept of "education" was indistinguishable from that of "liberal education". There was he said a good reason for this and it was associated with freedom:

> If the demand is made that a man (sic.) should be free to do what he wants or allowed to do what he wants freely, this does not imply that he should do anything else; rather it implies that restrictions on or impediments in the way of doing what he wants should be removed. (Peters, op.cit., p. 43)

This means Peters continues that liberal education can be interpreted in a negative manner by use of the three criteria of education to not restrict the education system to narrowly vocational aims or to restrain knowledge and understanding to a highly specialised area. Liberal education then can be conceived as lifting restrictions which might act as impediments to people learning what they want to learn.

But in Peters' case, as we have seen, talk of the lifting of impediments becomes lost when talk of the development of mind takes over for to realise freedom we must be able to think within established modes of thought and freedom now in the case of children is suspended for greater freedom later. But during this suspension and through inculcation in the disciplines and in the development of mind the autos "emerges", whilst education aims at personal autonomy.

One of Dewey's major works is entitled "Democracy and Education". The opening lines of the preface read:

> The following pages embody an endeavour to detect and state the ideas implied in a democratic society and to apply these ideas to the enterprise of eduction .... the philosophy stated in this book connects the growth of democracy with the development of the experimental method in the sciences, and the industrial reorganisation, and is concerned to point out the changes in subject matter and method of education indicated by these developments. (Dewey, 1916)

Dewey opens the book with a discussion of the continuity of social life, through a process of transmission like the biological transmission of the species. This transmission occurs:

> by means of communication of habits of doing, thinking, and feeling from the older to the younger. Without this transmission ... social life could not survive .... this renewal is not automatic. Unless pains are taken to see that genuine and thorough transmission takes place, the most civilised group will relapse into barbarism and then into savagery. (op.cit., p. 3)

Teaching and learning are therefore necessary for the transmission of social life and the school is necessary for this transmission first, because modern social life has become too complex for individual parents to ensure a proper transmission and, second, such transmission may be haphazard, and reflect only personal interests rather than the interests of society.

But, he continues in stronger vein:

> Society not only continues to exist *by* transmission, *by* communication, but it may fairly be said to exist *in* transmission, *in* communication. (loc.cit.)

Communication binds a community into a shared form of public life. The aims, beliefs, aspirations and knowledge are what binds a community, what constitutes it, and communication ensures participation into the public, shared forms of life. Further, all communication is educative, because it involves an enlarged, modified or changed experience.

Not only then does society require communication for its very existence, but by the very fact of living together in communication, the very process of living is educative, according to Dewey. In other words if we live together then we must necessarily educate one another - the progress of human beings is ensured by the very fact of living in communities. And for Dewey, shamelessly an acculturationist, *shared* communication. To the degree that societies share interests then they are more or less democratic, in Dewey's view.

Further, Dewey believed in the intellectual and practical superiority, in solving all forms of problems, including social problems, of scientific method. Dewey had an idiosyncratic view of scientific method. If it came in part from C.S. Peirce, it was certainly not a forerunner of the hypothetico-deductive account of scientific method, even though he stresses the importance of formulating a general hypothesis, its rigorous empirical testing and its reformulation in the light of testing and new data. Only if such an hypothesis could be accommodated in the total holistic set of hypotheses could it become universal and be counted as knowledge. Hypotheses arose in what he called the indeterminate situation, when a state of intellectual confusion was caused in individuals because, with their existing set of hypotheses, or habits in his technical and practical sense of the term, the outcomes from the situation were not clear, or there were several possible outcomes. For Dewey the psychological distress suffered by the organism must be removed by enquiry - the problem had to be solved by the use of scientific method. The indeterminate situation was resolved then through enquiry: new meaning was imposed upon the situation which permitted a satisfactory outcome; new knowledge and habits acquired; and control in the future made more certain because of revised knowledge and new habits. But the new meanings which were applied as the result of enquiry had to be subject to two criteria:

(i) they had to be consistent with existing knowledge (or in an extreme situation existing knowledge has to be restructured so as to remain consistent); and,

(ii) such new meaning had to be submitted to the scrutiny of the scientific community. To put it briefly the individual could be outvoted by that community. And in this area of meaning (John Dewey, *Logic, the theory of Inquiry* (1938a), which he said was his most important work), as well as in his darker, conservative side to Dewey.

Dewey believed that societies should structure themselves democratically because the solving of problems according to scientific method, where agreement or consensus was what guaranteed warranted assertion - he did not use the term "truth" (a consequence of his general pragmatic position). According to Dewey then it is the community that accepts the hypothesis and the individual's hypothesis, if sufficient support cannot be found for it, will be discounted: 1,000 Americans can't be wrong; but one can! And if that person persists then, presumably (s)he will be declared mad.

At this stage then what can we identify in Dewey's work that would place him in a liberal-democratic framework? First, the notion of a liberal democratic society is a fundamental assumption in Dewey's thought. Rather like Peters he sees the discussion, resolution and solution to problems as lying in rationality. (He does of course have a different view of what that was and its areas of application). Equally, clearly, he is convinced of the improvement of human beings through the application of scientific rationality. Not only is there the appeal to the enlightenment notion of improvement but also the view that trust for the direction that this improvement is to take, is to be placed in the insights given by the emergence and development of scientific methodology.

Second, in this emphasis upon holistic thought, his view that the continued life and evolution of society depended upon the education of the young, indicates that he believed in the importance of rational habits in the young, so that they could lead responsible lives as decision makers within a democratic society. Here his emphasis is not at all on an anarchistic and highly individualistic person tied to other humans externally, for Dewey considered such persons to be monsters, but rather upon one whose social wants, needs and desires, if not structured by society, at least were not widely in contradiction within that society. This is not to say that a person should be constituted by that society, and thereby determined as to wants, needs and interests, for he argued that the constitution of the individual must permit that person to move out of their social, political and economic milieu of upbringing. Dewey wants an homogeneous society, that was the major problem that he saw America facing in a period of rapid expansion and immigration of people from Europe with widely different, ethnic and cultural backgrounds, but in his commitment to social equality he seemed to see this as coming through the education system which would, he thought, provide equality of opportunity. Even his marxist critics concede that Dewey had it right about education in a liberal-capitalist democracy (Bowles and Gintis, 1976): perhaps what he had wrong was that America was not a democracy. What is clear here, however, is that society has a more important role in constituting the individual in Dewey than in Peters. Furthermore, he thought that, essentially, the good guys were in charge of the constitution of individuals. This was Dewey's optimism which must cause us some concern. We do not need a Foucault to identify this mistaken optimism.

Like Peters, Dewey sees the construction of mind as crucial to liberal education, the development of thinking, and the constitution of the individual self. To be a person is to have a mind, and to have a mind is to be able to think in various ways - in traditional mainstream philosophy of education, this means initiation into the traditional disciplines, for that is the only way(s) in which we can think. In Dewey's case it involved in particular an introduction into scientific thinking (his version of problem solving). Again many liberal educators would not be happy with Dewey's reductionism of all forms of rationality to scientific rationality.

Dewey's notion of individualism differs from what we have introduced above. First as a holistic thinker it is neither individual nor the community which has metaphysical priority in his thinking. Any reductionist tenancies of society to a collection of individuals are not possible for Dewey, but nor is the opposite tendency to assert the community over the individual. Any such moves would be dualistic and antithetical to his holistic views. Whilst he places emphasis upon the interests and needs of society, he places importance upon individual problem solvers *working together* in a scientific community. Society exists in, through, and by communication, and the individual's mind and personality is developed by interaction within such a community. Even if the individual problem solver is an important linchpin in Dewey's educational thought, this is not to be an isolated discoverer in a vacuum. On the contrary individuals are to work together, as a "scientific" democratic community, sharing their problems, their proposed solutions and, jointly, constructing knowledge. At the same time the individual is also socially constructed; minds are constituted as meanings are applied to situations which, of course, include self-knowledge and thereby personal identity.

Dewey can be interpreted as advocating quite strong measures of social control, both in the constitution of the individual and in the development of democratic "structures" (e.g., for problem solving). There is little doubt that he gets himself into considerable confusion in a discussion of freedom and social control (Dewey, 1939b, Chapter four). He believed that social control was acceptable in a community operating with shared purposes, because the individual would willingly and knowingly subsume any personal preferences in the desire to participate. In a passage that is far from satisfactory, he uses analogies of games and following the rules of games, in which there must be umpires, concluding that:

> Those who take part do not feel that they are bossed by an individual person or are being subjected to the will of some outside superior person. (op.cit., p. 53)

Thus he believes that freedom is not violated because of the need to participate in forms of life.

In this passage there is no distinction drawn between power and authority but he does talk of authority. This is the authority which comes from the activities being pursued, and he believes where *direct* authority has to be employed by the umpire this is in the interests of the group, to permit participation and the activities of the group to continue. Authority therefore is rational and in the interests of the participating group and, therefore, in the interests of the individuals within that group, in Dewey's thinking.

Where he does mention power, it is negatively, in opposition to this positive notion of authority, and is clearly not seen by him as being in the interests of individuals or the group. It involves actions that are not fair, and that attempt to impose personal wishes and dictates upon others. Power is seen by him as involving personal views, not representative of interests of the community, whereas authority is general or universal, and involves legitimation from the shared forms of life, the practices and activities that constitute that community. In a well structured school then Dewey sees no place for power - it is emphatically off stage.

Here he shares much with R.S. Peters. Authority is necessary in education, it is the correct concept for the discussion of social control, and it is not contrary to the interests of the young who are being initiated into forms of life. On the other hand power acts contrary to the interests of the child and should not be needed in education. In chapter four we will see how Foucault mounts a powerful, if not disturbing critique of this liberal position on power in education.

At this point we will turn to the liberal views of Ken Strike. Strike's (1982) version of liberalism treats three aspects of liberalism, from those identified above, as central to liberal thought. These are said to be: "rational autonomy, liberty and equal rights" (op.cit., p. 1). And, he claims, "these doctrines are central in the liberal tradition".

In relation to rational autonomy he says that liberalism "assumes that it is possible and *obligatory* to think for oneself", and he clearly thinks that not only are people capable of thinking for themselves, but that also they are in a position to judge for themselves, and, therefore, must not "presume to assume that *duty* for another" (loc.cit., my emphasis). If anyone is to have authority over me, therefore, it must be as a result of my consent and it must always be provisional. It cannot be compelled as in the case of Hobbes. Essentially people do not need the supervision of their betters.

What is being asserted here is that people must have liberty, but if we turn the concepts slightly to talk of freedom what we are talking of is negative freedom, or freedom *from*. According to Strike liberals insist that government authority is limited and that people must be able to make their own decisions and, he claims, "the exercise of authority has to be justified....(as)..... an area (of) legitimate public concern" (op.cit., p. 3). In other words there must be a clear distinction between the public and the private, and the private is no concern of governments (for an excellent discussion of how this distinction has been insidiously invaded in the United States see Christopher Lasch (1979) or, in France, Jacques Donzelot (1980)).

The outcome of this is that people must have equal rights so that their views, interests, and well being cannot be over-ridden by others. Knowledge is not the province of an authority, however benign, and as people have the competence and duty, equally, to acquire knowledge, and act rationally, they must be equal before the law (insofar as there are laws).

Strike, in summary, says these are the central ideals of liberalism (op.cit., p. 3):

(i) liberals assume that knowledge is a function of experience, not authority, and that individuals have the competence and duty to be rationally autonomous;

(ii) liberals assume that there are limits on social authority and that there is a private sphere of beliefs and conduct over which the individual should exercise authority;

(iii) liberals assume that social privilege and authority are neither natural nor inheritable, as social position must be earned and authority must be justified.

While this is clearly a liberal position it seems to be closer to Locke than Rousseau. Strike has picked up one strand of liberalism, ignoring the strains of fraternity and the General Will (and of educating accordingly). "What's in a name?" Well a lot, the answer *should* be, because naming things, *makes* things. What I don't find in such neo-liberal accounts is Peters' positive concept of respect for persons and considerations of the interests of others - at least in any positive affirmation of the importance of these notions, and only perhaps in the negative sense of leaving others alone. What is missing is the third aspect of the French Revolution's cry - fraternity. Strike's emphasis is on individualism and privacy, on doing one's own thing: it is not on the group, on the necessity of shared forms of life, on the necessity of group decisions for the welfare of all (and thereby for the good of the individual), and of the necessity of ties to the other which are not merely external because they are constitutive of individuals.

At its extreme this can lead to the abstract individualism of Hayek or Friedman, though Strike's position should not be reduced in this manner. Nevertheless, his emphasis is on freedom *from*, as opposed to freedom *to*, his emphasis on equality is equality before the law, as opposed to social equality, and freedom from is seen as over-riding any thrust towards social equality. This places him in what I would prefer to label as a neo-liberal position which is not in the tradition of Dewey.

I would call this "neo-liberal" because it revives certain liberal doctrines that, at a particular time, in a particular set of social and historical conditions were progressive. But it is not at all obvious that these doctrines will be progressive in a vastly different set of social and historical conditions. Dewey made his views on this issue quite clear in 1929 - see above. Indeed far from being progressive their implications for education are inherently conservative.

If it is obligatory to think for oneself then presumably the education system must be such as to foster independent thinking - personal autonomy must be a central aim of a neo-liberal education such as Strike's (though it does not seem to be an aim for Hayek). If this aim is to be effective than such an education must be open to charges of the construction of personal identities. This is a problem for both democrats like Peters and Dewey, and "liberals" like Strike.

The important point to be brought out here, from each of these liberal writers, is the moral, epistemological and metaphysical importance of the individual. These writers see that independence or autonomy depends upon certain ways of inducing the young into adult society. Dewey stands apart however, on how to construe these moral, epistemological and metaphysical assumptions.

Regardless of these differences, and they should be seen as enhancing rather than debilitating to liberalism, within the liberal framework there is a certain view of human beings and society, which permits a general view of education to be articulated, formulated and put into practice. In many cases, in practice, schooling is a compromise; in others one faction of liberalism triumphs over another - at present negative conceptions of freedom, methodological individualism, and equality before the law. In summary then we can see that within liberalism and liberal education there is a very strongly espoused thesis about the centrality of rational autonomy, that in order to be independent and not under the authority of others, the young need to be inducted into ways of thinking that promote rational autonomy and independence. This involves induction into the rational disciplines, especially scientific thinking and problem solving. But this is also to structure the mind, and insofar as consciousness and personal identity are closely intertwined, to structure people in certain ways.

This post-Enlightenment view, especially as supported and abetted by the human sciences, is not at all liberating according to Foucault. The promised independence and liberty masks the ways in which we have been made unfree and docile, according to Foucault, in the march of modern power. The following chapters will develop his critique of this notion and his objections to an education which purports to "produce" free people of this kind.

CHAPTER 3

PERSONAL AUTONOMY AS AN AIM OF EDUCATION

Education has been justified traditionally, though not exclusively, by the notion of freeing people from the authority of others - be it state, or church or other forms of authority. Freedom has been highly valued since, at least, early references to it in the writings of Athenians in the 5th century B.C. More recently, it is often claimed, to be free is to be personally autonomous. Such persons are said to be in charge of their own lives, because they can determine for themselves, especially with the help of reason, the nature and content of their beliefs, attitudes and emotions, and the purposes and nature of their actions. In being a person of this kind one is freed from the dogma and/or authority of others - one is *independent*. But one can also be freed from the passions, or at least in control of the passions in some sort of Platonic form of control over those things human which are "lower" than reason. To be in control of oneself is to be independent of others and, thereby, autonomous. Hence the freeing of people through education has often been interpreted as positing personal autonomy (often rational autonomy) as an aim of education.

It is almost taken for granted in Western education and schooling that self-determination, or standing on one's own two feet, or determining one's own life projects, that is to say personal autonomy, is an educational ideal. In many pedagogical theories this is a fundamental premise. In much pedagogical practice it is also presupposed - in independent work, judgement and examination, as examples. But to believe that personal autonomy in modern times is liberating is mistaken - according to Foucault. In this chapter we will develop the notion of personal autonomy, why it may be flawed theoretically, and why its pursuit leads to unfreedom, according to Foucault.

Colin Lankshear (1982) argues cogently that many who wish to advance personal autonomy as an educational aim are also prepared to argue for considerable constraints upon the young. As the young are not yet rational human beings, considerable constraints need to be placed upon them. Somewhat paradoxically it would seem, if they are to be free eventually, then considerable unfreedom must be imposed upon them in their formative years. Educational philosophers such as R.S. Peters, R.F.

Dearden, P.H. Hirst and J.P. White, all of whom may be interpreted as supporting this aim for education, believe that states of unfreedom are necessary for the young. The main issue that prompts this conclusion is the inability of the young to reason, especially to make "proper" choices about their own needs and interests, and for these reasons, until they become rational, they cannot either be seen as autonomous or permitted to act as if they were autonomous. This is a mainline position and there are dissenters within the liberal tradition.

But that position presupposes a link between being rational and being autonomous. It might be said to the contrary that autonomy was merely doing one's own thing, doing what one wants to do, being spontaneous and creative, as opposed to being confined to the calculations of (cold and hard?) reason. From this second point of view then there is no necessary link between being autonomous and being rational. One can be autonomous, that is independent, without being rational, and one way that this might occur is through the emotions. No doubt this is what D.H. Lawrence is urging within a liberal tradition when he says: "be a good animal, true to your animal instincts" (*The White Peacock*). Furthermore, within the neo-liberal framework, Hayek (1960) attacks the "inflated" aspirations of reason, urging people to trust in tradition because of the limitations of reason, and the ability of many people to reason.

When reason is further unpacked, and concrete educational proposals are countenanced, it usually turns out that for the young we are talking about inculcation into the disciplines or into established, traditional forms of thought. The problems here, and which Rousseau clearly perceived, are that the established forms of thought carry concepts which structure the perceptions and understandings of the young so that they may become confined within traditional forms of thought and life (see Lankshear, op.cit.). How, under such conditions, can creativity, originality and initiative flourish? Even Dewey, with his notions of problem solving and learning through experience, has problems here, because he talks of the judgements of the "scientific" community and the totality of knowledge determining, or controlling meaning, and thereby what counts as a solution to a problem in the indeterminate situation (Dewey,1938a). Thus this determines how the child "constructs" the world. Not everything goes for Dewey.

In this chapter some of the views on autonomy will be introduced briefly. In particular it will be argued that the notion of autonomy originally held political connotations as opposed to the ethical connotations that permeate the educational literature. From Foucault's perspective the political has become *masked* and the true nature of this alleged autonomy, and its role in governmentality, hidden. Several issues on autonomy will then be posed before turning to how, through what techniques, we come to believe in ourselves as being autonomous and, thereby, as being free persons. The chapter will close with a summary of why Foucault believes that we are not freed by pursuing this notion of autonomy.

Autonomy

Initially the concept of autonomy was applied in a political rather than in an ethical, or even educational context. It was city states that were said to be autonomous, or not, according to their independence from more powerful adjoining cities or kingdoms. But gradually this notion was applied to the individual person (if Plato's *Crito* (53c) may be taken as representative, but it is clearly in Rousseau and Kant).

There are two aspects or components to this concept: the autos and the nomos; that is the individual or the self, and the law or the laws which govern the individual or the self. Whilst Plato (op. cit.) can be interpreted as extending the notion from city states to the individual (Dearden,1975), it is still the laws and institutions of the state which are held to govern the individual. Hence personal autonomy, though associated with virtue, was not a purely ethical notion as it retains its connections with the policies and institutions of the state.

The subsequent major thrust, particularly in educational writing, has been to divest the concept of its political overtones and to represent it essentially as an ethical notion (Lankshear,1982). It will be argued that this has led to the masking of the political, because the autos or self has itself been "constructed" politically, post-Enlightenment, by what Foucault calls modern power (or power/knowledge). In other words there are questions which need to be asked about the nature of "the autos" which sets or adopts the laws and the nature of "the laws" which are adopted or set thereby. Questions such as: are the autos and the nomos independent?; can a self, a private self, "set" laws; if the autos can set laws then does it have something like an *essence*? But first this general notion of autonomy needs further explication and development.

There is little doubt that the term "autonomy" in ordinary usage, and even educational usage, is used in a wide variety of ways (Dearden,1972, p. 453). At best, it has been said, it is used as a synonym for being independent (Lankshear,1982, p. 96). But there is little doubt that Kant's influence on educational thinking, especially upon philosophy of education and moral development (Piaget and Kohlberg), has been strong. First, historically, Kant applies the concept of autonomy unequivocally to individuals. "Autonomy" in the *Groundwork* is formally defined as "the property the will has of being a law to itself". In the *Critique of Practical Reason* it is described as the fundamental law of practical reason: "So act that the maxim of your will can always at the same time be valid as a principle making universal law". Here, in this second formulation, the connection between being rational and being moral is clear. According to Kant then the self makes the law which it then obeys; the self is not merely subject to the law but must be conceived as making the law. Acting autonomously in accordance with the law, is not *caused*, but is "the spontaneous activity of the will". In this sense then the autonomous person, self legislating in accordance with a universal moral principle, is said to be free because (s)he is not under the causal compulsion of desires and of principles of mere expediency. Baier (1973) argues that Kant is fundamentally mistaken here. It does not follow, Baier argues, that in an autonomous state, individual members of the state are also autonomous, that is, *self*-legislators. Here Rousseau wrestled unsuccessfully with the notion of the general will, which was designed in part to deal with the connections between individual self-legislations and the legislation of the Sovereign.

These must remain here as problems. The major educational point however is that Kant is aligning what we might think of as acting on the basis of good reason with that of acting morally. For Kant the autonomous person cannot be immoral. Yet, it can be argued, Satan (Milton's in *Paradise Lost*) acted autonomously by reversing the notions of "good" and "evil". Others, for example Dearden and Hare (1975), see autonomy as involving essentially independent judgement, of which moral judgement is but a part or aspect. In other words for those thinkers there is no necessary connection between thinking autonomously and thinking morally (and between autonomous and moral action).

For Dearden (op.cit.) the essence of autonomy is forming one's own independent judgement on the basis of criteria which are themselves not fixed or absolute, but are the outcome of other independent judgements. Whereas Kant seems to identify freedom with the spontaneous and unconditioned autonomy of the will, Dearden sees freedom as a necessary condition of the exercising of autonomy; they are not identified. A further point here is that we may be capable of thinking independently on a matter, that is exercising our autonomy, but that our autonomy may not have developed in a free environment. As Dearden says: "A.S.Neill was not himself brought up at Summerhill". Dearden denies therefore that freedom is a necessary condition for the *development* of autonomy. To this extent he should be seen as opposing child-centred educationalists who seem to believe that granting freedom to young children furthers the development of the true nature (autonomy) of the developing child. Yet "psychological" questions must be asked here: whether or not autonomy is part of human nature, waiting only to blossom; or whether it is in part socially "constructed"; or whether it is the effect of social structures; or whether it is constituted by discursive formations (Foucault)? Insofar as it is seen as an educational ideal, questions as to which kinds of environment further the development of autonomy must be asked. Unfortunately these questions may not be straightforward, as the notion of the developing child in psychology is somewhat problematic (Henriques,et.al.,1984). Briefly the question we should ask is whether the environment in someway *structures* and *constructs*, or *constitutes* "the developing child"; that perhaps the developing child is presupposed in the construction of the very environments in which the developing child is supposed to "emerge". In which case "emergence" seems to be guaranteed.

Within educational literature Robin Barrow (1975), amongst others, reasserts a Kantian type link between autonomy and morality. For Barrow a problem of the autonomous but immoral person *cannot* arise. According to him (1975, p. 131) personal autonomy presupposes three things besides being simply free from external control: first, the autonomous person must be subject to reason, rather than to the emotions; this reasoning must be authentic and not merely acquired, or borrowed from someone else; and that person must have the strength of will to act as reason *dictates*. An autonomous person then acts on judgements through reflection, calculation and decision making, so as to organise and govern behaviour.

Barrow then goes on to argue that the reasoning which dictates to actions must achieve certain standards if a person is to be said to be autonomous. Here he is criticising Dearden. Barrow objects to the notion that a master criminal could be autonomous (Dearden's own example) because no "moral rectitude or an ability to produce the right answers is written into the concept of personal autonomy". It is not enough, Barrow argues, that people should think for themselves because "they should think well" (op.cit., p. 137). He therefore adds another assumption to the notion that people should think - they must also think *well.*

And for Barrow to think well is guided by his concern that people *act* well, and ultimately *morally* (along utilitarian lines for him).

Though Barrow does not enlarge at this point upon thinking well it is clear that there is no disjunction between being autonomous and being moral.

Another position on autonomy can be identified in the writing and thinking of the existentialist, Jean-Paul Sartre. In his earlier work (*Nausea, Being and Nothingness*) Sartre disconnects the nomos from the autos in emphasising that existence precedes essence, that there is nothing logically necessary about existence (it is as Sartre puts it - "de trop"), and, because human beings are always displaced from their goals, there are both the necessity of choice and the importance of *authentic* choices. The agent must choose, but if such a choice is to be authentic, it cannot be made in accordance with moral *laws* or with what is expected by society, for there are no criteria which can be brought in advance to make the choice. If Sartre's choices are criterionless then it would seem that authentic choice is not based ultimately upon principles or laws, though one can choose to follow principles or laws. Here the emphasis seems to be on the spontaneity of the choice, and a spontaneity which is beyond the realm of reason. The outcome of such choices is anguish and suffering, for human beings must believe or feel that they have acted correctly but, unfortunately, there is no way to judge that this is so. One can choose therefore to be a self of a certain kind and to follow laws and principles, but this is always a choice. However to act merely in accord with universal laws and principles, because that was expected, would be to act in bad faith or inauthentically (see here Taylor (1991) on authenticity, where he argues that for an authentic choice, the chooser must engage with significant thought).

In spite of appeals to notions of universality in *Existentialism is a Humanism*, Sartre appears to hold an almost anarchistic position (but this changes, in e.g., *The Problem of Method*). If there is an autos and a nomos then for Sartre there is no connection between them, and no necessary essence for the autos. Yet in the more traditional doctrines identified above humans tend to have the capacity for autonomy because of their rational nature. Often rationality is taken as part of the definition of human being - its essence - and therefore the development of autonomy becomes a matter of developing this essence of rationality. But Sartre will have none of that metaphysic nor its "dependent" psychology.

Whether this brief interpretation of Sartre is correct is not so important as to articulate a particular position on autonomy. The concern for now is merely to note this interpretation of his earlier position and return to it below in relation to Foucault. The general point for Foucault would be that whatever the connection between "autonomy" and "morality", which has permitted two general approaches towards autonomy, *both* forms are essentially embedded for Foucault in a particular post-Enlightenment view of human nature and a particular *historical* conception of freedom.

At this point then we can summarise from the established literature (the tradition?) several possible positions on autonomy:

(1) that autonomy and morality are necessarily connected in the Kant (or Barrow) sense;

(2) that autonomy is independent *but* rational judgement, with no necessary links to morality as in Dearden and Hare (moral judgement is but one form of independent judgement);

(3) that being autonomous is part of human nature;

(4) that to be an autonomous person is the outcome or effect of some form of social "construction";

(5) that the "development" of autonomy presupposes freedom;

(6) that the "development" of autonomy is compatible with considerable unfreedom;

(7) that for the autos to "accept" a nomos - to be an individual self governing in accordance with universal laws - is to be free; and,

(8) that to act in accordance with universal laws is to be inauthentic, or to act in bad faith, and not be free (Sartre).

How, from the reading of Foucault offered here, would he answer these questions? Briefly, at this stage, the answer would start from (3) and (4). If there were to be any such thing as an autonomous person, in some sense as outlined above, then for Foucault that person would be the effect of some form of social "construction". Certainly in the strong sense of (3), Man is dead for Foucault. (Note that by "Man" Foucault means post-Enlightenment and humanist conceptions of human being, and is not simply writing in unacceptable language; I will continue to use "Man" in this sense). He denies (3), as at best 'human nature' is a socially constructed entity: but he does not therefore fully endorse (4).

There is something misconceived, and fundamentally false, about the post-Enlightenment conception of Man according to Foucault. What is constructed or constituted under (4) is not a *free* person but one who is governable. Why does he see things this way?

The "development" of autonomy in this liberal Enlightenment sense does not presuppose freedom for Foucault. On the contrary this development (of a particular form of autonomy) which takes place in disciplinary blocks (see below) is both a negation of freedom in the developmental processes themselves, and a denial of freedom as an aim or outcome of such processes, by those who bring power/knowledge into existence. But if, in the earlier writings, freedom is not presupposed as a necessary condition for the "developmental processes" to proceed, in his later (1983a) work it is. Human beings can only be the bearers of power/knowledge if they are free agents, and able to resist (Foucault,1983a). Thus the deterministic and fatalistic nature of *Discipline and Punish* becomes mellowed by notions of resistance, freedom and hope.

The morally autonomous person is a leading variant of this conception of Man, but Foucault denies that there is any such thing as autonomy, insofar as it involves the acceptance by an independent self or subject (Man) of "external" universal laws, be they moral or otherwise (Kant and Barrow as opposed to Dearden and Hare). One reason is that he does not believe in universal laws or totalisations from specific cases. Here the influences of Bachelard and Canguilhelm are to be seem. Just as there is no one history or philosophy of science so there are no universal principles to be used in all cases of independent judgment. In other words for Foucault there is no nomos to be accepted, if by that is meant to accept *universal laws*. Here he seems to agree with Sartre's earlier existential position: but he does not stand with Sartre on the possibility of Grand Theory (Foucault, 1972a) and the role of intellectuals in the formulation of totalising grand theory (Sartre, 1973). His disagreement with Sartre will be developed more fully below.

But if he attacks the nomos he also attacks the self and the notion of a self which is able, in principle, to accept the nomos. This is in itself a form of social "construction". The notion of a self able to deliberate upon and accept laws so as to act autonomously as opposed to following laws heteronomously is a fiction, foisted upon the Western world post Kant as the basis for moral action but, for Foucault it has been used in the cause of governmentality (see Chapter four). Such a self regulating person is governable; laws are accepted even if they are critiqued and not accepted uncritically. Here the traditional liberal distinction between morality and mores, and the notion that mores are always open to critical evaluation presupposes just anther "higher" level of generality to which appeal is to be made. But such general abstract higher level "laws" are also fictions.

It is not just that he is objecting to persons accepting the nomos, because there is something suspect about the nomos that either leads to subjection, or unfreedom but, rather, that accepting the very *notion* of the autos, as being independent of the nomos, and thereby of some form of social construction, leads to unfreedom. It is not then a question of rejecting the nomos but that of entry into any notion of an autos which *polarises* the options in any such manner. It is not a question of an autos accepting laws - set X on sexuality say - and then rejecting them. This would be too simplistic. It cannot be represented as either a person a accepting X or not X, but rather as an a, already contaminated by both X and not-X, accepting X or not-X. Here what he had to say on freeing oneself from sexual repressions is very apposite; freedom was not to be gained a là California, by rejecting all that oppressed one.

In summary then the pursuit of the morally autonomous person involves the social construction (i.e., (4)) of something which is destined to fail. From the very outset this liberal and Enlightenement conception involves falsehoods. The particular falsehood to which he objects most is that such a conception implies the possibility of freedom. It doesn't, because stripped of its political connotations, it masks the fact that the constitution of such persons is a major political act. Consequently whilst we believe ourselves to be free, to be acting autonomously, in general, we are not. This is not to say that freedom does not exist for Foucault. Quite to the contrary for he should be interpreted as exploring to the full this notion both academically (and personally, if we follow Miller, 1993). Foucault is not arguing that the conception of the morally autonomous person involves, necessarily, a falsehood for all conceptions of objects involve norms (Bachelard and Canguilhelm), but that this particular conception involves governmentality, which is hidden and masked.

In what sense then is the pursuit of the (morally) autonomous person, as an aim of education, a political rather than a morally appropriate aim? To understand this we must first understand how Foucault sees the self as being constituted. In the terminology adopted above this would be to talk about the autos, but for Foucault there is little or no distinction between the auto and the nomos. In particular there is no self (autos) independent of the behaviour and principles (nomos) that classify or objectify that self as being an individual of a certain kind.

Power/Knowledge

The general answer is that the self is constituted in two ways; first by what can be called technologies of domination and, second, by what can be called technologies of the self. In order to make sense of how these technologies produce certain effects, we need to make some preliminary remarks about his concept of power. These will not be concerned with the wider notion of governmentality which is discussed in Chapter Five. Our concern in this chapter is with the effects of power in the construction of the self. Why such selves are necessary for wider notions of governance will be developed later. Foucault sees two main technologies as constituting the self - technologies of domination and technologies of the self. First we will consider technologies of domination.

Foucault is not interested in Who or What questions about power. Rather his question is *How*: how is power exercised? His concern is with the extremities of the political system, at the micro-level, and it is with the *exercise* of power at these "lowly" levels. Indeed the state can only operate according to Foucault, "on the basis of other, already existing power relations ... (i.e.,) a whole series of power networks that invest the body, sexuality, the family, kinship, knowledge, technology and so forth" (1977c:122). But this poses considerable problems for Foucault (Poulantzas, 1978: Walzer, 1986).

In his earlier works power is treated as *repressive* and there is talk of the hostile engagement of warlike forces in the domination of individuals, groups, etc. Foucault reverses Clauswitz's assertion that war is politics continued by other means to read, "power is war, a war continued by other means" (Foucault, 1977a, p. 90). At that stage in his thought he was contrasting repression with oppression, which is said to be the result when power extends or exceeds its legal limits and becomes an abuse, as in contract theory. Whilst also a form of domination, repression is not an extension or abuse of legal powers but, rather, is a continuation of a perpetual relation of forceful domination, not by manifold forms, but exercised within society at a capillary level and by each and every member of that society; on "the underside of the law", as he calls it. Repression is not an extension of legal power because it is itself usually legitimated - or is at least in those areas of discretionary justice - by knowledge which has, in itself, been produced by this power, i.e., by experts in the appropriate disciplines. There is therefore a very close affinity between power and knowledge (true discourses) for Foucault. He develops this idea as follows:

> ... we are forced to produce the truth of power that society demands, of which it has need, in order to function: we *must* speak the truth; we are constrained or condemned to confess or discover the truth. Power never ceases its interrogation, its inquisition, its registration of truth: it institutionalises, professionalises and rewards its pursuit. In the last analysis, we must produce truth as we must produce wealth ... it is truth that makes the laws, that produces the true discourse which, at least partially, decides, transmits and itself extends upon the effects of power. In the end, we are destined to a certain mode of living or dying, as a function of the true discourses which are the bearers of the specific effects of power. (1977a, p. 93f)

The particular type of truth that Foucault is concerned with, is not, e.g., that children with learning difficulties can be identified within the first year of formalised instruction but rather with the regimes of discourse/practice or power/knowledge which permit such statements to emerge and be legitimated as truth. As Ian Hacking (1981) notes Foucault's concern is more with a rather Kantian question about the conditions of knowledge in general. But Foucault locates these conditions in socio-historical contexts which he referred to as an epistémè does not give a set of transcendental Kantian conditions for knowledge in general but rather the conditions for particular knowledges. If in *The Order of Things* (Foucault, 1973a) his space for the identification of these conditions is restricted to language, in the later book *The Archaeology of Knowledge* (Foucault, 1972b) this space has been extended to cover technical and institutional conditions - what he refers to as discourse/practice.

So the power/knowledge which is his concern is the underlying power/knowledge or set of conditions that permit and legitimate certain particular claims to truth. For example the notion that to function in modern society, i.e. be governable, one must be literate, *might* be one of the conditions underlying the legitimation of the above statement on early identification of learning difficulties. This general proposition clearly carries with it the power connotations.

In later writings Foucault is to drop the concept of repression, because "repression is quite inadequate for capturing what is precisely the productive aspect of power ... (and) this (repression) is a wholly negative, narrow skeletar conception of power" (1977c, p. 119), though the warlike metaphors are retained as late as 1983.

Technologies of Domination

How is this power exercised? How do we come to be subjects in the sense of being people with a certain view of ourselves and as subjects who are *subjected*? It is in *disciplinary blocks* that power/knowledge was developed and is exercised according to knowledge which has itself been the product of the exercise of power. It is a particular type of power *and* knowledge, for Foucault identifies the two, and it has immense educational implications.

Foucault's very use of the terms "discipline" and "disciplinary block" is but another example of "landscapes emerging from earthquakes" to quote his colleague, the historian Paul Veyne (quoted in Goldstein, 1984). In *Discipline and Punish* (1979a) for example, he is talking about such people as doctors, teachers, psychiatrists, psychoanalysts, warders and the military; about the practices which these people pursue; and about institutions in which these practices are pursued. We would normally use terms like "professional" or "profession", where Foucault uses "discipline". This is part of Foucault's strategy, viz., the defamiliarisation and reconstruction of our ordinary everyday life (Goldstein, 1984). In particular the term "discipline" captures aspects of power and knowledge which are normally masked. (He is probably following Lacan's original position here on the deliberate ambiguity of terms such as "subject"). Also Foucault is drawing together those two senses of the term discipline where, in education in talking of a subject area and its conceptual structure, talk of discipline, i.e. subjection and obedience, has tended to be downplayed and drained away into the concept of discipline associated with social control.

"Power" designates relationships between partners where certain actions modify the actions of others. This power is to be distinguished from that power which people have as abilities or capacities for modifying, using, consuming, or destroying things. It is also to be distinguished, as a relationship, from relationships of communication which transmit information by means of a language or symbolic medium, though the production and circulation of meanings and knowledge can have as their objectives certain results in the realm of power. This is not to say, however, that there are three separate and diverse domains; a domain of things which can be transformed by abilities, a symbolic domain,and a domain of power relationships. On the contrary these domains are closely interconnected and cannot be dissociated.

In the disciplines their connectedness and mutual dependence can be seen. Disciplines are "blocks" - disciplinary blocks - in which the adjustment of people's abilities and resources, relationships of communication,and power relationships, form regulated systems. For example, in schools, children learn to read and write in an ensemble of regulated communications (lessons, questions, answers, orders, etc.) in enclosed spaces, close supervision, reward and punishment, etc Some disciplines may emphasise the power relationships; others those of communication; whereas others may concentrate on changing capacities and/or abilities. Prisons emphasise the first, apprenticeships those of communication, and ballet schools the changing of abilities and capacities. Schools exercise all three though, in their history in the Western world, in varying degrees.

In order for power to be exercised in a disciplinary block a number of conditions must be fulfilled. Essentially these are concerned with the organisation of space, time and capacities. First individuals are allocated to spaces. The key idea here is that of the monastic cell - indeed Foucault "traces" the origins of the spatial block to monastic, and earlier, origins. The main idea here is that of self-contained units contained within larger units. The larger enclosure prevents distractions or invasions from the outside whereas the smaller partitioned unit permits *any* individual to be placed under surveillance at *any* time. The ideal model for surveillance was given by Bentham's *Panopticon* (Foucault, 1977d; 1979a). Cells (desks, beds, etc.,) are assigned according to a rank which has been established by grading, assessment or examination. As a result of classification people are assigned to their "cells". The purpose of the cell and the organisation of space is to prevent imprecise distributions of people, uncontrolled disappearances, and diffuse and dangerous circulations. Spatial organisation aims at knowing, mastering and using.

Second, activities are then planned for individuals according to a time-table, which is also of monastic origin. The principles here are those of prescribing those activities appropriate to the discipline and establishing set regular rhythms for these activities. These two principles are applied not only to the general activities but also to the particular activities of the body within the general activity - for example within the military marching is seen as an important activity which is planned to occupy certain periods within the week or day and, within such periods, times are allocated carefully for planned activities.

Third, activities are broken down into stages so that particular skills, abilities or capacities can be developed in a given time through constant exercise. For example, if a given time unit is an academic year then certain activities will be designated as appropriate for that stage, depending upon the previous stage, the examination and classification, and the next planned stage(s). What activities are appropriate to any particular stage will depend essentially upon that discipline's "true" discourse, i.e., the knowledge of people, processes and activities which has been established through the exercise of power within that disciplinary block. Examinations, classifications, promotions and remedial treatments establish "normal" patterns of expectations. This knowledge developed through the exercise of power is used in the exercise of power to produce what Foucault calls *normalised individuals*.

Finally, as cells may need to be moved within the larger cells, and as individuals need to "work" with maximum efficiency at activities, intricate systems of commands and instructions are required. Whistles, bells, and other more sophisticated devices signal the times for changes in cells and other moves "within" the timetable.

The activities which are planned for individuals depend upon knowledge which has been built up within the disciplines from the observance and examination of past cases, whereby normal patterns or expectations have been created. Foucault sometimes uses the term "calculable", almost interchanging it with "normalised" in reference to individuals. Calculable should be understood in terms of governance of controlling the outcomes of behaviour. Power is exercised in the disciplinary blocks for certain outcomes - individuals who are subjects and who will lead useful, docile and practical lives. The norms which are established, the examinations and classifications, the promotions, remedial treatments and, where necessary, the disciplinary punishments, are all part of this notion of governance. The examination occupies a key role also in that it lays bare to the individual his "true" self.

Technologies of domination then essentially act on the body,classifying and objectified individuals. But insofar as these objective classifications are adopted and accepted by individuals so their selves are also constructed.

In *Discipline and Punish* Foucault places the school firmly in the disciplines:

> (t)he organisation of a serial space was one of the technical mutations of elementary education. It made it possible to supersede the traditional system (a pupil working for a few minutes with the master, while the rest of the heterogeneous group remained idle and unattended) ... By assigning individual

> places it made possible the supervision of each individual and the simultaneous work of all. It organised a new economy of the time of apprenticeship. It made the educational space function like a learning machine, but also as a machine for supervision, hierarchising, rewarding. Jean-Baptiste de La Salle dreamt of a classroom in which the spatial distribution might provide a whole series of distinctions at once: according to the pupil's progress, worth, character, application, cleanliness and parents' fortune. (1979a, p. 147)

Adding:

> (i)t is this disciplinary time that was gradually imposed on pedagogical practice - specialising the time of training and detaching it from the adult time, from the time of mastery; arranging different stages, separated from one another by graded examinations; drawing up programmes; each of which involves exercises of increasing difficulty; qualifying individuals according to the way in which they progress through these series. For the "initiatory" time of traditional training an overall time, supervised by the master alone, authorised by a single examination, disciplinary time had substituted its multiple and progressive series. A whole analytical pedagogy was being formed, meticulous in its detail (it broke down the subject being taught into its simplest elements, it hierarchised each stage of development into small steps). (ibid, p. 159)

Technologies of the Self

In Vol. I of the *History of Sexuality* (Foucault, 1980a) the key to the technology of the self is the belief, now common in Western culture, that it is possible to tell the truth about one's self. It has almost become a basic tenet of Western culture that with the help of professionals "truth" about one's self can be discovered through the self-examination of consciousness and the confession of one's feelings, attitudes, desires, thoughts and acts. The belief that the body and its desires reveal the deepest truths about one's self has become almost commonplace. These truths are embedded in what Foucault calls sexuality. By telling the truth about one's sexuality, where the deepest truth is embedded in the discourse and discursive practices of sexuality, the individual becomes an object of knowledge both to himself and to others. In telling the truth one knows oneself and is known to others in a process which is both therapeutic and also controlling. But if sexuality structures the deepest truths there are other areas in which we tell the truth. These discourses and the set of discursive practices associated with them are part of what Foucault calls the human sciences: they penetrate and "inform" e.g., medicine, psychiatry, psychology, the law and education.

The examination and the confession are the principal technologies for the construction of the self in *The History of Sexuality*, Vol.1 (1980a). These technologies are developed "from" medical models in parallel clinical methods in the 19th century. Certain clinical and psychiatric examinations required the subject to speak and an authority trained in observation and interpretation to determine either the truth of what the subject said or an underlying truth of which the subject may not even have been aware. What was needed for the construction of sex as the deepest underlying "truth" about ourselves and of sexuality as a discourse and discursive practice, were the "proper" techniques to elicit and to interpret confessions.

A fundamental shift in clinical methods took place according to Foucault. First there was a shift in tasks from the strict medical clinical model. In that model the patient "confessed" to the doctor as part of the examination and the attempt to classify *objectively* the medical problem which needs correction: in the "new" model the confession and the examination are part of a process of constructing the sexuality of subjects so that their discourse is controlled and they become individuals of a certain fort. The "truth", or "knowing one's self" is essentially therapeutic:

> [S]poken in time, to the proper party and by the person who was both the hearer of it and the one responsible for it, the truth healed. (Foucault, 1980a, p. 67)

The thrust towards knowledge of oneself could not have been sufficient from the apparent great desire to talk about one's self. Foucault is fascinated by the desire in modern culture to tell the truth about one's self. Indeed he says often (e.g.) that, "there has been a very strong incitement to speak of sexuality". Part of the cause of this incitement, he believes, was the negative power effects of various sexual prohibitions. If power is conceived as merely repressive, he argues, then to talk about sexuality would necessarily be a liberation. At the times in the 19th century when there were sexual prohibitions there was also a burgeoning discourse on sexuality caused, in part, by the need to create a scientific structure to explain sex and to train "scientists". This structure and discourse meant that eventually the subject could no longer understand what was being said and could no longer therefore be the arbiter on the deepest "truths". This role fell to the authority, the "scientist" not only to incite the "truth" and to interpret these deep truths but also to reconstruct the subject's experience of sexuality, and discourse and, thereby, control the subject. In knowing one's true self one has not only to tell the truth in the confession but also to *speak* the truth in the concepts of the discourse on sexuality: in speaking this truth, in knowing one's true self one constructs the experience of sex, and one reconstructs one's self by adopting new descriptions and hopefully new practices. The therapy comes about; from telling the truth, which can itself involve vicarious pleasurable and liberating effects; from thereby knowing one's self through speaking the truth; and thereby liberating one's self from the repressive aspects by the acts of speaking and reconstructing the self.

In addition in speaking the truth one does not merely describe oneself but one "*makes* it so" because of the performatory feature or function of language. Just as the judge makes the alleged person guilty be a declarative performance of guilt so, also, in speaking about ourselves in the new and refined concepts of the social sciences, do we construct ourselves, our very identities, in those acts of speech. Through the performatory function of speech then we begin to construct ourselves.

In *Discipline and Punish* the emphasis was on the production of the self by the human sciences through processes of classification and objectification - the techniques of domination. However Foucault becomes increasingly interested in how "a human being turns him - or herself into a subject" (Foucault, 1983a, p. 208). Whilst this issue was addressed in *The History of Sexuality* (Vol.1) his emphasis there rests with how the self is objectified by "the increasing valorization of the discourse on sex" (Foucault, 1980a, p. 23). According to Foucault this change in direction towards technologies of the self was suggested by his reading Christopher Lasch's *The Culture of Narcissism.* Technologies of the self:

> permit individuals to effect by their own means or with the help of others a certain number of operations on their own bodies and souls, thoughts, conduct, and way of being, so as to transform themselves in order to attain a certain state of happiness, purity, wisdom, perfection or immortality. (Foucault, 1982a, p. 18)

They differ from the techniques of domination and power discussed above and which, Foucault considered (ibid.), he may have concentrated too much upon.

Foucault's starting point for technologies of the self is the perceived oddity in Western culture of the association of prohibition and strong incantations to speak the truth. In sexuality this association was particularly important for the emerging discourse on sexuality was critical for a period when the fostering of life and the growth and care of populations was a central concern for the state. His later project then becomes that of a history of the link between the obligation to tell the truth and prohibitions against sexuality. His question became: "how had the subject been compelled to decipher himself in regard to what was forbidden" (Foucault, 1982b, p. 17).

If the problem in *Madness and Civilization* was how madmen were controlled the new problem is how one "controls" oneself in relation to sexual behaviour. So *The History of Sexuality* is not a history of morals or behaviour or sexual practices, but the way in which pleasures,desires and sexual behaviour were problematised, reflected upon and conceived in relation to a certain art of living. By "problematisation" he means how a totality of discourses and how discursive practices introduces something into discourse as an object for thought. It is through problematisation, reflection and conception that we "construct" ourselves in relation to sexual behaviour by "telling" the truth about ourselves.

According to Foucault the Delphic maxim, "to know yourself" has taken over from the other notion of Greek antiquity, "to take care of yourself". He argues that the "need to take care for oneself brought the Delphic maxim into operation" and that the latter was subordinated to the former. This is *not* the case in modern Western culture, he claims, as the notion of caring for oneself has come to be seen as an immorality, a means of escape from rules and respect for law. Given further the Christian inheritance that the road to salvation lies through self-renunciation to know oneself seems paradoxically the road to self-renunciation and salvation. Secondly, he argues, theoretical philosophy since Descartes has placed ever-increasing importance upon knowledge of the self as the first step in epistemology. His conclusion is that the order of priority of these two maxims has become reversed; "know thyself" has priority.

The Critique of Autonomy

But what is the point of returning to Antiquity, to the Greeks and Romans, and to early Christianity, apart from the historical project on the link between the obligation to tell the truth and prohibitions against sexuality? Apart also from the obvious resort to genealogical method, it is for Foucault, a question of morality and liberty: "...for what is morality, if not the practice of liberty, the deliberate practice of liberty" (Foucault, 1984c, p. 4). In the greco-roman world, he says, care for the self, was the manner in which individual liberty considered itself as ethical. From Plato to the later Stoics "the theme of care for the self has truly permeated all ethical thought" (ibid.). In order to behave properly, to practice freedom properly, it was necessary to care for the self not merely to know one's self but also to improve, to surpass and to master one's self. Caring for the self would prevent one being a *slave* (of another city, or authority, or of family, friends and colleagues, and of one's own passions). This was a very important notion not only for the Greeks but also for Foucault.

The theme of domination by others is a constant theme in Foucault. The human sciences in classifying and objectifying individuals turn people into (*subjected*) subjects. If the shift in emphasis from "care of one's self" to "know thyself" is bad enough it is a self which is now to be known through the human sciences. To care for one's self in the twentieth century has come to be to fit oneself out, retail, with a set of "truths" which, by being learned, memorized, progressively put into practice, construct a subject with a certain mode of being and a certain visible manner of acting. Foucault believes that this modern self is *not* free because insofar as it is the outcome of the human sciences, political control and not freedom has been the aim.

One way of understanding Foucault at this point is to see him as advocating a rejection of the human sciences as a basis for truth when one "talks" to oneself. What is crucial for Foucault is what one takes as the relevant truths to internalise, what we take from "outside", as authoritative. His problems with the human sciences are that they each posit a view of man, a "real" view of human nature, and that all such views involve a fundamental misunderstanding.

Valerie Walkerdine (1986) illustrates this well in her discussion of the developing child. Her point is that if an environment is structured in certain ways which in themselves presuppose the existence of the developing child, then don't be surprised to see the emergence of *the* developing child. In other words if we return to the autos/nomos distinction from the start of the chapter, developmental psychology, which in various ways assumes some such distinction - the real human nature (autos) waiting to adopt certain laws (say of Piagetian development) - really structures the autos, so that it cannot but adopt the nomos of the developing child. Walkerdine's works shows clearly how this apparently fundamental distinction breaks down *in* the human sciences.

Essentially what has happened is that certain acts or behaviour which people *do* have become "pathologised", so that these acts become part of the real nature of people. If we take the ways in which children think about such things as space, time and physical objects - the Piagetian stages - this behaviour is taken as evidence for certain cognitive structures. What was an act or behaviour becomes internalised as something about the real nature of human beings.

Foucault notes the changes in ethical concerns from acts in the time of the ancient Greeks, to desires with Augustine, to intentions with Kant and to feelings in modern times. He argues that the substance of ethics during this period has not changed overmuch - for example sex between men (and boys) is a continuing part of the substance of ethics - but it is problematised differently. In ancient greece it was a problem of acts, whereas now it is a question of feelings, or to rephrase the difference, what were acts of a certain kind have become reified and internalised into a being a person of a certain kind - a homosexual. This term purports to say something about the real nature of the person to whom it is ascribed, but, Foucault argues, this is at best a catch word used to describe a number of acts; there are actions or behaviour which might be described as homosexual *acts* but there are not homosexual persons, if by that is meant they are persons who have a particular human nature.

In education we are very adept at pathologising behaviour. Ability talk is an excellent example, as we seem very confident in talking about abilities. We say that Susan has mathematical ability, or that John has musical ability. Ability talk *reifies* abilities as entities. But if so they are murky metaphysical entities (Tuck, 1984). What we do is infer from certain behaviour or performances, say on tests, to an ability. But this inference is surely questionable (and the way in which such talk is used to make predictions about future behaviour, even more questionable). To ask the question as to what type of entity an ability is, to ask how abilities are to be individuated and identified, is to be on the path to demystifying such talk, and to seeing how it has been misused - e.g. in allocating children to particular life chance programmes, on the basis of prediction from "identified" abilities.

After abilities there are a host of other educational examples: the developing child; the deprived child; the slow learning child; the gifted child; the hyperactive child; the at risk child; to mention but a few.

If we continue with the autos/nomos categories it can be seen that in each case there is an invasion of the autos by attributes, or characteristics, or general behaviour which properly belong to the category of nomos. In this way we socially construct people. We make them homosexuals by saying that they are homosexuals, by objectively classifying them as homosexuals. If we are in a privileged position as professionals in institutions or, as Foucault would put it as therapists in a disciplinary block, then we speak the Truth about people. But these are the truths of the human sciences, manufactured and legitimated in institutions, themselves like Piaget's developing children. Classifying people as being people of certain kinds leads to particular individualised programmes for people so that they become normalised.

If this reading of Foucault is correct the autonomous person has an autos which is permeated by the nomos. The earlier questions about the nature of this self that sets the laws and the laws which are set are shown by Foucault to be crucially important. For Foucault the very notion of independence is false, because the autos is contaminated by aspects of the nomos. The notion of deliberation upon the substance of a particular ethical issue is misconstrued, because the autos itself has been constituted by the nomos. It cannot "deliberate" independently upon the laws or set the laws because it, itself, has been in part set by the laws. The autos can deliberate, true, but only in certain ways which have been determined by the infiltration of the autos by aspects of the nomos. It is an autos, or self, *contaminated* by the laws and principles of the nomos. What price independence?

It might be thought that in rejecting (7) above that Foucault is in part supporting (8) and, thereby, aligning himself, at least on this issue, with Sartre. That would be a complete misunderstanding of both Sartre and Foucault and the intellectual debates and issues in which they found themselves.

Foucault believed that the replacement in priority of the Greek maxim, to care for thyself, with the maxim, also Greek, to know thyself, was fundamentally mistaken. Part of his critque is that this second maxim has been over-riding since the time of the Enlightenment and has been involved in the constitution of subjects who are governable and not free. Here Foucault's critique of the liberal education ideal of the development of personal autonomy is important.

A New Approach to Personal Autonomy

It is interesting therefore to see an emerging liberal critique of personal autonomy as an educational aim in the work of Stefaan Cuypers. Cuypers (1992) argues that a notion of caring for the self should replace personal autonomy as a fundamental educational aim. It is not so much that personal autonomy is mistaken but that it should not have educational priority. Educators are not fundamentally mistaken in aiming at personal autonomy but rather they have gone astray in considering personal autonomy "as the fundamental structural condition of education". Instead a principle of caring about oneself should be given educational priority. At first sight his position may seem to have affinities with Foucault through the notion of caring for the self. But on closer inspection this is not the case. Whilst welcoming this critique of personal autonomy as a fundamental aim of education, it remains, in my view, subject both to Foucault's general critique and to have some other difficulties. This is because of the way in which he construes the notion of caring for oneself. Cuypers has developed this notion from the work of Frankfurt (1988). According to Cuypers Frankfurt has two incompatible accounts of self-identification which in turn are related to Dworkin's (1981) notion of a hierarchy of personal autonomy. This is a sophisticated account of personal autonomy and is based upon a hierarchy of desires. At the first level according to this hierarchical account one can desire certain things, and at a second higher level one can desire (or not desire) to desire those things. What is important for an account of personal autonomy is that there be reflection and evaluation of the first level at the second level, and that any such reflection and evaluation be independent and not influenced by "alien" forces, processes or evaluations. A person then is autonomous when (s)he identifies on reflection with desires, goals and purposes, and when that refection is procedurally an independent process.

Central to this concept of personal autonomy is the notion of a person capable of self-consciousness and mental reflexivity, and the notion of "motivational or volitional structure"; in brief we have a will and we reason, we have desires that move us to action, and we reason about, or reflect upon, those actions. If a person cares about the self then (s)he reflects upon which desires should be effected by the will. Insofar as the person accepts certain first order desires and effects them by acts of the will so that person has a certain identity. Identity changes then when a person, in reflecting upon first order desires, amends or rejects some of them. Depending upon what sort of person one wishes to be, one tries to induce new desires or to amplify, weaken or reject existing desires. A person exercises freedom of the will when (s)he effects first order desires which that person desires to desire. This accords with what is meant by autonomy; first there is the autos or the self which controls desires and is in turn constructed by those desires, and second there is the notion of the nomos or regulation by laws. But this regulation must be independent and not influenced by other persons, or by attitudes or principles "alien" to that person. Thus the second order evaluation of desires must be *independent*.

Cuypers notes problems with this account and in particular the possibility in the hierarchy of an infinite regress in that further levels of desire may be deemed necessary in order to justify the second order. Also he notes the potentially passive aspect of personal identification - one cannot legislate for one's desires and therefore it may be illusory to imagine that one is in full control of one's self identifications. This second criticism of the Dworkin-Frankfurt position is turned by Cuypers into his positive account of caring about oneself.

Whilst Frankfurt adopts this position there is also in his work, according to Cuypers, an implicit account in which self-identification occurs at the primary level by appealing to the notion of caring about something at that first level. It is this first level notion of desire, of what one cares about and thus desires, which Cuypers then develops and which he opposes to personal autonomy as an educational aim:

> When we care about something, it's about *us*, our own personal projects and ideals or certain individuals and groups to which we are particularly attached. These objects of care are of a more personal kind in the sense that they give some sort of guidance to a caring person in what he does with his own life ... guided by such objects of care as, for example, a professional career, a family tradition, a dear friendship, a political party or a religious community.

Now if this first level caring is long-term then life will be integrated and personal identity constituted through time. Furthermore, caring about something may not always be under voluntary control. One cannot *help* caring about some things and one cannot bring oneself to will contrary to those objects that are cared about. First order desires become associated with these objects. This is not so much a brute force but it is a necessity, and is referred to by Frankfurt as "volitional necessity".

The essential differences between Frankfurt-Dworkin and Cuypers are that self identification occurs in the first position at the second order level and is an active process, whereas in the second position, self identification occurs at the first level and is essentially a passive affair. Cuypers then argues that the evaluative criteria which a person uses to evaluate what he cares about must necessarily be social because of what is almost a necessary desire of persons for recognition by other people. Persons seek recognition of themselves as persons which necessarily involves social interdependence, or a shared form of life, and some general agreement on what one should care about.

Education as an initiation into a form of life should therefore concern itself with what one cares about, and with initiation into what people have cared about, so that they become "devoted and sociable people" with secondarily, a degree of autonomy compatible with what one cares about. Personal autonomy is desirable but subsumed under what one cares about, which in turn is subsumed under what society cares about.

A major problem which Cuypers is tackling, and commendably, is that whatever we do we cannot but fail to initiate our children into a form of life. What they come to care about, at least initially, will reflect a certain form of life, a certain language, a certain way of doing things. This cannot be avoided and I have no answer to my child who demands to know why he isn't French. Of course we care for and love our children (well most of the time). That sense of care I understand and I understand in parallel the notion of volitional necessity. When asked as to whether he defended justice Albert Camus replied: "I will defend my mother before I will defend justice". And whilst torn from context I can understand that also. And I can understand Wittgenstein's desire to do philosophy in the way in which he thought there was philosophy - and I can care about that. But the sense of "care" has now shifted. Even if Wittgenstein cared about philosophy in almost as intense a state as Camus (apparently) cared about his mother I cannot care in the same way about Wittgenstein's views on philosophy - nor, clearly did he care for jazz, in the way that I might. Caring about Wittgenstein's views on philosophy is an acquired and educated form of "caring". Precisely so would Cuypers respond (I think?), and that is why education is concerned with developing care for oneself, in constructing an identity in which philosophy is desired. But Wittgenstein didn't seem to think it was much value or use to people - they would be better off if they didn't pursue it, at least academically, in his view.

I have tried to identify two ways in which we care. The first is a "psychological" type of bonding, love perhaps, or volitional necessity, and which is of the first level of desires, which may not be restricted just to human relationships, and the second is an acquired, "educated" form of caring which may never be as intense as the former, which is certainly the result of second order reflection upon first order desires, and if it becomes a first order desire it differs from that desire expressed by Camus about his mother. These are not passively acquired desires but one's which may have to be actively promoted.

Now the really interesting philosophical question is: in which sense of "care" are we to understand the notion of caring for oneself? Is it the former, in which case, are we going down some narcissistic trail, or is it the latter, in which case questions about independence of evaluation must arise? An argument can be developed that it cannot be the former because for that first meaning to be developed there had to be an object of desire, one to which notions of volitional necessity apply. But how can the self have as its object of desire the very same self? Is this care for the self the result of a passive acquisition of a desire? Is such a notion coherent? For these reasons I will turn to the second possibility.

Caring about oneself, reflecting upon first order desires, evaluating them in accordance with other people's evaluations, and identifying as a person with certain first order desires, is essentially constituting one's own identity. Cuypers is talking about, in Foucault's terminology, techniques for the constitution of the self. The criticisms which Foucault raises against the constitution of personal identity are available here.

First Cuypers seems to be saying that human beings have some form of essence - for example that persons have motivational systems, including a desire for social recognition. What if this motivational system was itself socially constructed? Care for the self as an educational aim in a society, because of the very desire for social recognition and social approbation, which depends upon certain social and general mores, would then be justifiable only if a society's value systems were themselves capable of justification. First, how is a person ever to be free from the social milieu into which (s)he was born. But, second, these forms of social evaluation have become heavily tainted with the human sciences - with their claims to knowledge and with their techniques and technologies. Foucault believes that far from freeing us we have become *subjects* (in his sense of the term).

The "solution" to this problem for Foucault was to work very actively on the self - to refuse ascriptions, to push limit situations, to explore the Other. On the part of individuals this required a very active form of resistance, quite alien to the often passive form that caring for the self seems to invoke.

The problem with passivity of self formation which Cuypers seems to invoke is that it makes it difficult to understand how one could ever "escape" the social milieu into which one was born. That has been an aim of education for many educators, including John Dewey. How are we to meet the demands of a neo-liberal like Ken Strike who asserts the primacy of freedom from interference in one's own life projects when passively many of first level desires may have been constructed through passive volitional necessities. If we are all loving caring parents and live in a "nice" society then not too much may be at stake. But this is not the case for many millions of people, and for many disadvantaged in those "nice" societies. How could we induce the first level desire to reject the evaluations of my society when I disagreed with them. It couldn't be a first level desire arrived at passively.

The problem which I am moving towards is what I see as a certain conservatism or preservation of tradition. Cuypers is right to see the importance of first level passively acquired desires, and that the quality of these is important educationally. But I have problems in seeing how these are to be amended, rejected, whatever, yet held with the same strength. If we pursued care of oneself as an educational aim would we emphasise the importance of community and fraternity over freedom and truth, over the right not to have my self identity determined from "alien" sources?

Another difficulty which I have with the account is that the distinction between first level desires and second level desires, seems to be a distinction between what happens to me in practice, and what I want to think "actively", about those passively acquired first level desires. There seems to be a split between thought and action, between judgement and practice, and between theory and practice. There is a notion that things happen passively to people, and desires are acquired, but that these can be reflected upon and action amended so that certain things are no longer reinforced or no longer happen. But things do not just happen to people - even to young children. Dewey reminds us to watch how young children learn, as to how they interact with their environment, when they learn. It is not just passive. Briefly if we take Dewey seriously on these matters, which I do, the learning of a desire for social recognition is not a passively acquired desire but one elicited by both the parent and the child in a mutual demand for social recognition and approbation. Equally if we take Dewey seriously that there is no distinction between judgement and habit (in his sense of the term), and that thinking is not merely "in the mind" then the notion of a first order desire, passively acquired as a matter of volitional necessity and only able to be judged at a second order level, becomes rather odd. Are we back to some old dualisms that have their genesis in Descartes, in mind and body?

In relation to the eight possible positions on autonomy identified earlier in the chapter Foucault would have answered as follows. First, autonomy and morality cannot be related in any meaningful sense as the notion of autonomy in the liberal literature is itself seriously flawed. If by morality is meant any universal or objective law like form of morality then, equally for Foucault, it could not be linked to anything because it also is flawed. Much the same applies to the second less strong position as in Dearden and Hare. Third, being autonomous could not be part of human nature as Man is dead. Autonomous people are the result of constitution, both social and personal but this presupposes considerable unfreedom. And, finally, to act in accordance with universal laws would be to ignore the particularity of every event or situation and the potential power relations which exist and which could be brought into play.

CHAPTER 4

EDUCATION AND POWER

In the previous chapter the emphasis was upon the notion of personal autonomy, why this notion is misconceived, and the techniques through which attempts are made to develop such persons. It was argued that what appears as an ethical and educational ideal is a masquerade for the political aim of constituting selves as subjects of a certain kind. This is done through technologies of power.

In this chapter it will be argued that power, which is essentially "off-stage" in education, particularly in philosophy of education, needs to be brought onto the "centre stage". The reasons for this are to be found in Foucault's accounts of bio-power and governmentality. First, Foucault's account of governmentality will be introduced. Then his account of power will be developed more fully than in chapter three, and against what will be called liberal theories of power. Finally it will be argued that power needs to be more fully on the educational agenda than it is at present. Power talk is excluded and suppressed by the liberal framework because of its conception of power and the propensity of liberal theorists to talk about authority.

Technologies of domination and technologies of the self, introduced in chapter three, are to be distinguished from technologies of production and technologies of sign systems (Foucault, 1982b, p. 18). Whilst they hardly ever function separately the latter two are usually associated with the study and applications of the sciences and linguistics. Technologies of domination are concerned with defining and controlling the conduct of individuals, submitting them through the exercise of power to certain ends so as to lead useful, docile and practical lives. Technologies of the self, on the other hand, permit individuals "to effect certain operations on their own bodies, souls, thoughts, conduct and way of being" (ibid.), so as to reconstruct and transform their selves to attain certain states of wisdom, perfection, purity, and even, happiness. But these technologies are not just associated with constituting the self but, also, with *governmentality*.

Foucault's works can be seen as a history of the organization of knowledge with respect to both domination and the self' (ibid.), though they can be read and interpreted in other ways (e.g., by Megill, 1979). The contact, or conjoint effects of these two technologies, he refers to as governmentality. In various sources, though particularly in the article

"Governmentality" (Foucault, 1979b), he develops the notion of governmentality, as the art of government or, as sometimes referred to, "reason of state". This notion "refers to the state, to its nature and to its own rationality" (Foucault, 1982c, p. 150). Foucault sees the technologies of domination and self as being the techniques used "to make of the individual a significant element for the state" (ibid: 153). These new political technologies of power were originally given the name "policing".

By "government" Foucault should be understood as meaning something close to "the conduct of conduct" (Gordon,1991, p. 2). And by this should be understood a form of activity which attempts or aims at the conduct of persons; it is the attempt to shape, guide, or affect not only the conduct of people but, also, the attempt to constitute people in such ways that they can be governed. In Foucault's work this activity of governance could cover the relations of self to self, self to others, relations between institutions and social communities, and the exercise of political sovereignty. By "rationality of government" he means the "art of government as activity or practice" (Gordon,ibid.). It is thus a way of thinking about what is involved in governing, and about who or what should be governed. The worrying feature of the practice of government in the Western world, for Foucault, is the concern to both totalise and individualise. This concern is exemplified in his notion of bio-power, which is a form of power directed in a totalising manner at whole populations and, at one and the same time, at individuals so that they were both individualised and normalised. Here the human sciences and their "truths", and the institutions or disciplinary blocks in which these truths have been developed, played and continue to play a crucially important role.

According to Foucault:

> the history of the West cannot be dissociated from the way its "truth" is produced and produces its effects. (1977c, p. 112)

By this he does not mean that this would be a history undertaken by established or academic, institutionalised historians because, even if they deal with feelings, behaviour and the body, they would be dealing with effects of truth, and not with *how* such "truths" are produced. What is needed, according to Foucault, is a different approach to "history". His approach, adopted and adapted from Nietzsche and influenced by

Heidegger (Foucault,1982a, p. 12), is essentially genealogical and well exhibited by structure and content in his book *Discipline and Punish* (Foucault, 1979a). This methodology has been discussed above in the introduction and in chapter one.

In the quotation above he summarises his position that, in the West and essentially post-Enlightenment, we have produced and disseminated various discourses and associated practices which, whilst professing their aim to be the pursuit of truth, in fact mask their true function. It is *not* the will-to-knowledge but Nietzsche's will-to-power. Professing to be advancing truth in the development and circulation of such discourses, specific powers are attained and used to produce certain effects. His particular target is the discourse(s) of the human sciences, and sometimes referred to by him as "humanism". Perhaps an example will help make this position clearer.

In "The Dangerous Individual" (Foucault, (1978a) he discussed the "emergence", or insertion of psychiatric medicine into the French penal system in the 19th century and particularly, the development of the notion of monomania or homicidal mania. A series of apparently inexplicable and monstrous murders, not open to existing explanations by psychiatry, is suddenly described by an entirely fictitious entity. "Monomania" is used to describe a crime for which there is no apparent cause or reason and which is believed to be caused by a form of insanity for just that reason. By inserting this concept into the medical field psychiatry was to define its specificity in the field of medicine, to ensure its recognition among other medical practices, and to insert itself into legal and criminal practices, claiming people as "its own" in denouncing medical and legal practices and decisions in courts, and publishing studies and reports on monomania. Only the trained expert could identify monomania and thereby through the effects of observation by the trained eye, *produce* monomaniac patients. Foucault comments:

> Nineteenth century psychiatry invented an entirely fictitious entity, a crime which is insanity, a crime which is nothing but insanity, an insanity which is nothing but crime. (1978a, p. 132)

And whilst monomania was to disappear after some fifty years the outcomes had been the insertion of psychiatry into the law not just because it applied a new medical rationality to mental or behavioural disorders but because psychiatry now "functioned as a sort of public hygiene" (ibid. p. 134). But it is a cross which we still have to bear for: "the play between penal responsibility and psychological determinism has become the cross of legal and medical thought" (ibid., p. 140).

Foucault is interested in "the history of the West" because the political and social processes by which Western European societies were structured and ordered have been obscured, or perhaps forgotten, or become part of the habitual. They are a part of our most familiar landscape, and we don't perceive them any more (Foucault, 1982a:11). It was his reading of Nietzsche that brought revelation (ibid., 13). A revelation that caused him to feel trapped, to leave France and never to feel properly integrated within French social and intellectual life (ibid.). The idea of man and society which he was rejecting was:

> this idea of man (which) has become normative, self-evident, and is supposed to be universal ... [This] humanism ... presents a certain form of our ethics as a universal model for any kind of freedom. (ibid., p. 15)

Between social history, history of ideas and more formal analyses of thought there is a narrow path, Foucault believes, where he, as an historian of thought, can tread a wary path and defamiliarise our familiar and comforting landscapes.

How does Foucault believe that we have become entrapped? How do we come to believe that we are rationally autonomous individuals free to make certain choices when, as he says, "there are more possible freedoms ... than we can imagine". There are two general answers that Foucault gives and they are not disconnected, even though they carry with them differences in the analyses of power and appear to be "disconnected" in time. The answers are to be found in his analyses of the technologies of domination and technologies of the self, discussed in chapter three. The temporal differences between *Discipline and Punish: the birth of the prison* (Foucault, 1979a) and Vols. II and III of *The History of Sexuality* (Foucault, 1985a:1990). Vol. I of *The History of Sexuality* (Foucault, 1980a) sits uneasily between the interests and emphases of Vols. II and III and the earlier *Discipline and Punish*.

The connecting thread between these technologies is the exercises of power upon the body; the body and its powers and capacities which are to be transformed in the processes of individualisation, and the body and its desires which are to be transformed in the construction of the self. In the former case the discourse and practice of power/knowledge developed in the disciplines produce normalised individuals, objectively classified, and politically dominated. In the second case individuals turn themselves into subjects. These technologies of domination and of the self produce as effects the modern individual who, in Foucault's eyes is far from being free. Instead he or she is governable. But what are these technologies of governance? This is the story that Foucault tells.

At times he uses the terms "technique", "practice" and "technology" as though they are interchangeable (Foucault, 1982c, p. 153). His interest in techniques, technologies and practices arises from his typical "philosophical" orientation, which is to bypass questions of the nature and legitimacy of, e.g., power, and to ask questions about *how* individuals have come to be significant elements of the state. He is not interested in the role of the state - its institutions and forms of decision-making - or in theories or ideologies which have been developed in order to justify the state. Rather his interest is with *how*, in the emergence of the modern state, individuals become utilised by the state to live, to work, to produce, to consume and, sometimes, to die.

It is techniques, technologies and practices of a political kind that have made individuals into utilisable elements for the state. These have been developed in the general framework of the reason of the state which involves a new form of political rationality from that, as e.g., previously advocated by Machiavelli. The aim of this new form of rationality is not to reinforce the power of the Prince but, rather, to reinforce the state, itself (Foucault, 1979b).

Built into this "new" notion of the state is a notion of the art of government which is concerned with ensuring the right distribution of "things", arranged so as to lead to an end convenient for each of the things that are to *be* governed. For Machiavelli's Prince "things" are the territory and its inhabitants with the emphasis on the former. In the new form of the state, government does not bear upon the territory per se but, rather, upon the complex unit of human beings in all of their relations and their links with property and culture in the widest senses, including accidents and misfortunes such as famines and war (Foucault, 1979b, p. 11). For this a new form of rationality or reason of state is required, one which reinforces the state and not the sovereign; one which "refers to the state, to its nature, and to its own rationality" (Foucault,1982c, p. 150). It is about how to govern and not about the legitimation of the state. Foucault is not discarding traditional political philosophy where major concerns are with the legitimation of the sovereign, but he is certainly saying that such theories and concerns do not tell the sovereign *how* to govern.

First, if the state is to be strengthened the state's capacity and the means to enlarge it must be established. For this a form of political knowledge different from political theories about the nature of the state and its legitimation, is required. Governance required then more than implementing general principles of justice, wisdom and prudence. A certain concrete, precise and specific knowledge became necessary.

From the beginning of the 17th century states began to enter into competition so that strengths and weaknesses became important *historically* as each state faced an indefinite future, locked in struggle and competition with other states. Political knowledge and the utilisation of individuals becomes critically important in preserving, if not in reinforcing, the state. Included in this political knowledge, if individuals are to be utilised to reinforce the state, must be knowledge of individuals, of the propensities, abilities and capacities to be utilised. Individuals on this view become instrumental to the ends of the state. Justice, welfare and health are important for individuals, not because they are good in themselves for individuals, though they may be, but because they increase the strength of the state. Investment in health and education are instrumental investments *now* in the individual, but later to be cashed in by the increased strength of the state.

What Foucault is concerned with are the ways in which these new individuals came to be produced. His answer is that it was through a new form of power - bio-power - which is to be identified through the ways in which it is exercised. It is in reference to these ways of exercising power that he uses the terms "technique" and "technology". Furthermore he identifies a particular technology as that of *police*. By this from the early 17th century he means "specific techniques by which a government in the framework of the state was able to govern people as individuals significantly useful for the world" (Foucault, 1982c:154).

Jacques Donzelot (quoting von Justi (1768), *Éléments généraux de police*, which was a source also used by Foucault (1982c), defines "police" thus:

> [T]he purpose of policing is to ensure the good fortune of the state through the wisdom of regulations, and to augment its forces and its power to the limits of its capability. The science of policing consists, therefore, in regulating everything that relates to the present condition of society, in strengthening and improving it, in seeing that all things contribute to the welfare of the members that compose it. The aim of policing is to make everything that composes the state serve to strengthen and increase its power, and likewise the public welfare. (1980, p. 7)

Foucault identifies three general forms that this technology of policing took: as ideal, dream or utopia; then as a real practice or set of practices, or rules of some actual institution; finally as an academic discipline, perhaps developed from practices and knowledge derived from such practices, in institutions.

In the first form - police as dream - he identifies writings early in the 17th century of the forming of opinion (Foucault, 1982c, p. 154). The notion of police was that of techniques so that "a government in the framework of the state was able to govern people as individuals significantly useful for the world". In this respect the task of *the* police was to foster civil respect and public morality. Foucault (ibid.) notes explicitly that in the writings of Louis Turquet de Mayenne (1611) education was seen as a central responsibility of the police, determining very precisely each individual's aptitudes and tastes by testing from the very beginning of life. According to Turquet: "The police's true object is man".

If these earlier writings were utopian, a century later there existed in France a police manual giving in systematic order the regulations for police. The domain of police is clearly set out in Foucault's reports: "from religion to poor people, through morals, health liberal arts, and so on... apart from the army and justice and direct tax the police apparently see to everything" (Foucault, 1982c, p. 156). In brief the police see to *living*.

Foucault sees this overt systematisation of administrative practices as important for several reasons. First there is an attempt to classify needs, not as in older philosophical traditions, but in terms of utility scales for individuals and the state. Dealing with peoples' needs and, thereby their happiness, is no longer seen as an effect or as an outcome of state policy but is seen as a condition or requirement for the survival and development of the state.

Finally policing becomes a discipline in the academic meaning of the word, and was taught in various universities, notably at Goettingan. Here von Justi's work, for example, becomes a text for students. He sees police as having a positive task and not the merely negative one of protecting the state against internal or external enemies through the vehicle of the law. In its positive role police govern not by the law but by a specific, a permanent, and a positive intervention in the behaviour of individuals. Von Justi's originality here may lie in his seeing population and environment in a perpetual living interrelation which the state has to take care of also. So it is not only humans as individuals but also humans as a population that the state has to see to. Policing becomes than an actual governmental technology.

Foucault suggests that by the end of the 18th century we have a political rationality linked with a political technology; a conjunction of reason of state and science of police. The latter involves interventions into the life of individuals through observation, surveillance, examination, classification and normalisation. These techniques and technologies are deeply enmeshed or embroiled in the emergence and development of the human sciences.

Although Foucault refers often to Hobbes and Walzer (1986), for example, sees Hobbes as Foucault's antagonist, there is a sense in which Rousseau should be seen as his major antagonist, as a theorist concerned with the reason of state, and as a precursor of the Enlightenment and the attempt to live the General Will in the immediate aftermath of the Revolution. The emergence of reason of state had not done away with the problem of the Sovereign, because that problem had re-emerged in even more acute form. Rousseau, in *The Social Contract*, had posed notions concerning human nature, contract, and the General Will as general principles of government, which permitted both a juridical principle of Sovereignty, and the basis for the definition and the characterization of the art of government. Later in *Emile* and *Sophie* he articulates the role of education in the art of government - certainly Emile and Sophie were governable (in Foucault's sense). But as Lankshear notes after considerable discussion of Rousseau's educational proposals:

> The whole educational schema proposed by Rousseau looks much more conducive to heteronomy than autonomy. (1982, p. 161)

Foucault saw Hobbes as a "17th century jurist" concerned merely with legal notions in the social contract, at an abstract philosophical level, and not concerned with concrete and practical matters as to how obedience to the contract is to be ensured. Certainly Foucault's notion of juridico-discursive power depends heavily upon legal models from Hobbes to Austin, but this model of power cannot be his main target, as he believes this model *masks* modern power, the major target, and is totally inadequate for discussing it, as it lacks the concepts. Ultimately then Foucault's target must be Rousseau rather than Hobbes. On this point Walzer is awry for he treats Hobbes and the references to Hobbes as Foucault's main target. But governance and bio-power are Foucault's real targets and Hobbes and juridico-legal theories only a target because they mask bio-power. Hence Rousseau with his highly manipulative form of education designed to bring about the governance of Emile and Sophie is more like his real target. However if Foucault interprets Hobbes as being a mere legal abstract jurist, then he is also mistaken for Hobbes was concerned with general providence and the education of citizens so that obedience to the contract could be assured: "men only become political subjects, ex discipline" (*De Cive*, I,1). In *Leviathan* this is to be achieved through education (see Marshall, 1981).

Foucault believes that what he calls the juridico-discursive conception of power permeates both liberal and marxist approaches to the analysis of power, though he offers no detailed analysis of this notion. Central to this conception is the notion of a Sovereign who owns power and to whom the citizenry are subject. The Sovereign may be monarch, or a conglomerate of individuals or institutions, vested with legislative powers. There is then a postulated superior relationship between sovereign and subjects. Second, this legal notion of prohibition by law permeates the analysis of power relations. In a similar manner to a prohibition by law this model of power "prohibits" by repression. Foucault attacks the adequacy of this concept for the analysis of modern power but scarcely questions its adequacy even as a model for the analysis of legal systems. Nevertheless Foucault believes that questions of the attribution of power and its legitimation - the major concerns of this account - are not adequate for an account of modern power.

In his discussion of power Foucault dismisses the classical questions about the nature and legitimacy of power - the familiar what and why questions - and instead asks a *how* question; How is power exercised? This he refers to as a flat little empirical question, but it is hardly that, and is certainly not treated as such by him. A fundamentally different concept of power as a commodity legitimated by some form of juridic-discursive framework:

> we have in the first place the assertion that power is neither given, nor exchanged, nor recovered but rather exercised and that it only exists in action ..... power is not primarily the maintenance and reproduction of economic relations, but is above all a relation of force. The questions to be posed would be these: if power is exercised what sort of exercise does it involve? In what does it consist? What is its mechanism? (Foucault, 1977a, p. 89)

Foucault is not interested in questions of state power - a serious problem according to some critics (see, Hoy, 1986) - and his concern is not with the dispersion of power to smaller and smaller units of the population. Although his concern is at this micro-level it is not with ownership at this level, but with the *exercise* of power at these extremities or "lowly" levels of the political system. Indeed, Foucault claims, the state can only operate:

> on the basis of other, already existing power relations ... (i.e.) a whole series of power networks that invest the body, sexuality, the family, kinship, knowledge, technology and so forth. (Foucault, 1977c, p. 122)

Foucault, in Nietzschean fashion, runs together the will-to-power and the will-to-knowledge:

> we are forced to produce the truth of power that society demands, of which it has need, in order to function: we *must* speak the truth; we are constrained or condemned to confess or discover the truth. Power never ceases its interrogation, its inquisition, its registration of truth .... it is truth that makes the laws, that produces the true discourse which, at least partially, decides, transmits and itself extends upon the effects of power. In the end, we are destined to a certain mode of living or dying, as a function of the true discourses which are the specific effects of power. (1977a, p. 93)

Knowledge is then for Foucault, as it was for Nietzsche, a function of human interests and power relations. The thesis in Foucault that knowledge "*is*" power, does not identify knowledge and power, but claims that they are closely interrelated so that where there is power there is knowledge, and vice versa; in Foucault's hands this is represented by the concept "power/knowledge", and as is clear from the quotation above power and knowledge are not to be studied separately.

In his earlier writings Foucault treats power as being repressive (Foucault, 1977a, p. 90); "power is essentially that which represses ... nature, the instincts, a class, individuals ..." There is even talk of the hostile engagement of war like forces as he reverse Clauswitz's assertion that war is politics continued by other means to that of politics is war continued by other means. It is almost as if agents, professionals acting in their professional capacity say, *literally* are unaware of this power. For example in questioning an examination candidate I may be concerned only that the candidate should exhibit what knowledge is possessed but, if this is all that I think that I am doing I am mistaken, according to Foucault, as I am also "exercising" modern power, producing normalised or calculable individuals who will lead useful and, perhaps, docile lives. Through the very examination system I am producing or constituting individuals both as objects who are classified in various ways, and as subjects tied to "true" selves. It is through these normalising processes that governance is obtained according to Foucault. The power that is exercised then in some sense *underlies* the day to day practices and discourses. It underlies professional activities and, thereby, poses considerable problems to us as educators.

The kind of knowledge then with which Foucault is concerned with is not then *particular* knowledge of the form, "Children with learning difficulties can be identified in the first year of schooling", but rather with the regimes of discourse/practice (power/knowledge) which permit such statements to emerge and to be legitimated as knowledge. Hacking (1981) sees Foucault as asking Kantian type questions about the conditions which make knowledge possible, though the answers which he gives are that the conditions are to be found in socio-historical contexts, or epistemes (Foucault, 1973a). The episteme does not give truths but permits certain claims to be considered as truth.

So the power/knowledge which is Foucault's concern is the underlying power/knowledge or set of conditions that permit and legitimate certain particular claims to knowledge. For example the notion that to function in modern society, i.e. to be *governable*, one must be literate, might be one of the conditions underlying the statement above on detecting early reading difficulties. Such problem people "need" normalising. Clearly functional literacy permits certain forms of political domination.

Furthermore he is not concerned with knowledge in *general*, with a set of Kantian transcendental Kantian conditions for all knowledge but, rather, the conditions for *particular* knowledges. But these particular knowledges, as we shall see below, are mainly restricted to the human sciences (Gutting,1989: Foucault, e.g., 1984e,f). If in *The Order of Things* his space for the identification of these conditions appears overly linguistic, in *The Archaeology of Knowledge* this space is extended to consider technical, institutional and bureaucratic contexts - what he refers to as discourse/practice.

In the earlier writings (Foucault, 1977a) power is treated as being repressive and war like metaphors such as, power being war, a war continued by other means, are employed. But in his later writings he is to drop this notion of repressions because it "is quite inadequate for capturing what is precisely the productive aspect of power". Power is now seen as productive and as being positive, constituting us as individuals of a certain kind (not all of which is bad).

Power is formally defined in his last discussion of the topic, in relational terms as:

> a mode of action which does not act directly and immediately on others ... (but) ... instead it acts upon their actions ... on existing actions and on those which may arise in the present or in the future. (Foucault, 1983a, p. 220)

It requires that the person upon whom it is exercised:

> be thoroughly recognised and maintained to the very end as a person who acts ... (so) ... that ... a whole field of responses, reactions, results, and possible inventions may open up. (ibid)

It is to be distinguished from a relationship of violence, which has the capacity to force, or to bend, or to break, even though violence may be necessary to bring a power relationship into play. Violence and consent are to be seen as instruments of power and distinguishable from power. Violence merely breaks or destroys, whereas power *makes*: modern power is no longer power over life and death, but the power to *make* life.

At the micro-level, however, power is not owned by any one person, nor, in its "exercise", exerted by agents acting with such intentions. It is brought into existence almost at an unconscious level, even though it requires agents to bring it into existence - for it *only* exists when brought into play. Here he is a strict nominalist.

However this account of power/knowledge raises a set of philosophical problems. For example, is Foucault an epistemologist?; what is the status of his own claims?; what is the status of his "historical" methodology (genealogy)?; and, for now, is he advancing a new type of social theory? (see below, chapter 6, for a discussion of these issues).

The analysis of power which Foucault is trying to bypass, if not transcend, is often attributed by him to Hobbes. It is called by Foucault, "juridico-discursive" power. It is essentially a form of power which is owned, legitimated by the social contract and directed downwards in a repressive manner. If power is essentially owned, it is something which is acquired, seized or shared. This assumes an unegalitarian, repressive and downward direction of power. Furthermore it is seen as *external* to other relations - communication, knowledge, economic, sexual, etc. Now conceived as external to other relations and depending upon how the relationship between power and desire is conceived (in the case of sexuality for example), one is always trapped Foucault argues. How does this entrapment occur?

If power is conceived as external to desire, and we are seen as possessing certain instincts or drives, then one is trapped by laws which define "proper" sexuality in a certain way through rejections, exclusions and prohibitions. An order, legal and illegal, is prescribed for sex by demands within the law, not only of this legality but, also, claims of intelligibility, i.e. true knowledge about ourselves. The hold on sexuality is maintained through law and language; through the discourses that legitimate certain truths about ourselves as proper subjects of sexuality. To seek pleasure in activities outside such definitions is not merely to break the law but, also, to be *delinquent*, by possessing certain instinct and drives and thereby to be a non-normal and ungovernable person. Therefore we are trapped by an external power.

If, on the other hand, power is conceived as not being external to desire, but fundamentally associated with desire so that it can itself constitute desire, then our desires will be formed in various ways such that we become subjects of particular kinds. In this case it is not so much the repression of instincts and desires deemed as givens, but the constitution of such desires through power relations so that we "become" subjects of sexuality (autonomous persons, etc.). Either way as subjects we are trapped and subjugated, tied to our instincts, or to our constituted desires.

At some points in his writings Foucault sounds as though he considered power in the second of these senses, i.e., as power constituting the subject so that (s)he was for ever trapped and subjugated. But he moved in his later writings away from his repressive, deterministic and fatalistic conception, towards an active and positive sense of power (Foucault, 1983a).

If it is granted to Foucault that selves can be constituted - that there is no self *prior* to this social constitution - surely the body, the point of application of bio-power, is beyond relativity, and potential constant modification? Yet both Nietzsche and Foucault seem to be denying this. Foucault's reading of Nietzsche is that not only can the body be used and experienced in many ways, and that desires are related to cultural interpretations, but that, also, every aspect of the body, given the appropriate techniques, is capable of modification. Dreyfus and Rabinow (1983) point out that whether or not Foucault's reading of

Nietzsche is correct, these issues are important in understanding and evaluating Foucault.

This is because the body is the critical focus for Foucault in the exercise of bio-power, it is the point at which the most minute and local social practices are linked with the large scale organisation of modern power (particularly through the notion of sexuality). Yet he is not clear about the extent to which the body is malleable, the extent to which it can be changed. Whilst he rejects the notion that the body has a fixed structure and fixed or given needs, it is unclear in his writing as to the extent to which cultural arrangements can change the body's structure and needs. Does a body have a front and a back? Why can't bodies move backwards more easily than forwards? Are these invariant features of bodies and if so are there others? How specific can we be about these invariant structures?

For those interested in disciplinary techniques these questions must be of great importance. Yet Foucault is silent. His genealogical task had been to show that:

> the body is also directly involved in a political field; power relations have an immediate hold upon it; they invest it, mark it, train it, torture it, force it to carry out tasks, to perform ceremonies, to emit signs. (Foucault, 1979a, p. 25)

Of course Foucault is not the first person to write a "history" of the body. It has been the subject of pathology, as the seat of needs and appetites, and as the locus of physiological and evolutionary processes. But he and Nietzsche gave us a political technology of the body. It is Foucault's conceptualisation of this that is so important.

It would be wrong to think that in 1757 Damiens' body was not involved in political dynamics. The power of the Sovereign was inscribed into his body by the executioner Samson in a controlled and agonizing display of knowledge of the physiology of the body. But genealogy is a to reveal:

> a knowledge of the body that is not exactly the science of its functioning, and a mastery of its forces that is more than the ability to conquer them. (Foucault, 1979a, p. 26)

This knowledge and this mastery are what he calls the political technology of the body. It is the refinement of the techniques that Samson used on Damiens to the techniques used on the soldier, the criminal and the schoolboy, that Foucault explores in *Discipline and Punish.* It is not merely selves or identifies that are constituted by these technologies but also bodies; in so far as bodies can be militarised (see below), so also can they be sexualized. What are constructed or constituted are human bodies which exemplify the characteristics of (modern) sexuality. If we interpret Foucault as saying that sexuality (in his sense) is nothing but a particular socio-historical construct - a unity of anatomical elements, biological functions, sensations, feelings and pleasure - that have been lumped together in some sort of historical accident, then it would seem that he lays a groundwork or basis for feminist critiques of how female bodies are constituted by such things as the media and pseudo-medicine (what a female body really should be). Even though he has scathing criticisms of how women's sexuality was "developed", it seems that he is open to the charge of leaving it just there. He treats women's and men's bodies as one, but by omission.

The disciplinary techniques were well developed by the end of the eighteenth century. By then:

> the soldier has become something that can be made; out of a formless clay, an inapt body, the machine required can be constructed .... one has "got rid of the peasant" and given him "the air of the soldier". (Foucault, 1979a, p. 135)

The soldier is no longer one who bore certain natural signs; on the contrary he can be made out of formless clay. In such passages Foucault seems to be endorsing the theme introduced already of the infinite malleability of the body, because it is a body (loc.cit.) which:

> is manipulated, shaped, trained, which obeys, responds, becomes skilful and increases its forces.

What is new in these techniques is that bodies are no longer treated *in general*: control is not obtained by violent oppression *en masse* of a state, a region, ethnic group, whatever. Rather the body is treated *individually* (Foucault contrasts these treatments with the metaphors of "wholesale" and "retail"). It is the beginning of individuality - no longer is the individual the one who stands out, or above, or in contrast to the crowd, as the crowd has become differentiated and *all* are individuals. These techniques gain control over "movements, gestures, attitudes, rapidity" increasing "the economy, the efficiency of movements, their internal organisation by ensuring an interrupted constant coercion supervising the processes of the activity" (loc.cit) through the ideal Panopticon *gaze*.

Foucault refers to these technologies and the institutions in which they are deployed as disciplines and/or disciplinary blocks. Institutions such as schools, hospitals, and asylums are referred to as disciplinary institutions, but his focus is not upon the institutions per se. *Discipline and Punish* may be subtitled "the birth of the prison", but the prison is not *the* focus of this book. Instead it is the development of the technologies of power. Important as the prison is in the "history" that Foucault is telling, its birth as a prison is the outcome of the search for, and the development of, these technologies.

In the late 18th century, according to Foucault, there existed three mutually co-existing forms of punishment. There was the monarchical, exemplified by Damiens' wretched end; there was the reformed, modified, and restrained version under the aegesis of the legal reformers; and there were the newly emergent prisons. Neither prisons nor the techniques used in them were new, as people had been held in captivity since time immortal. But what was new was the incorporation of imprisonment - the prison - and these techniques as *a form of punishment*. The question which Foucault asks, and answers, is: "how is it that, in the end, it was the third that was adopted?" (Foucault, 1979a, p. 131).

Foucault's central argument is to the effect that the prison is but one amongst several disciplinary institutions, some of them only marginally connected or related to the prison, in which techniques for training and correction were being refined and developed from earlier practices associated with the exercise of power over individuals. Many disciplinary methods had long been in existence - in monasteries, armies and workshops. But in the course of the 17th and 18th centuries the disciplines became general formulas of domination (Foucault, 1979a, p. 137).

Whilst discipline "acts" on bodies, it does not appropriate then as in service or vassalage. It is a policy of coercions, a political anatomy, and a mechanics of power, that define how one may have hold power over other bodies so that they operate as one wishes or desires, but usefully, docilely and efficiently. The powers and forces of the body are turned into trained aptitudes and capacities; resistance is turned or reversed into subjection.

In all of this development there had to be close attention to detail; it is this detail which eventually individualises people. Here Foucault, quoting Marshal de Saxe says (1979a;139):

> Although those who concern themselves with details are regarded as folk of limited intelligence, it seems to me that this part is essential, because it is the foundation, and it is impossible to erect any building or establish any method without understanding its principles. It is not enough to have a liking for architecture. One must also know stone cutting. (1979a, p. 139)

For the disciplined person no detail is to be unimportant. But this is not the outcome of the disciplines, per se, as it comes from Christianity, where in God's sight every detail is important and where education has always revelled in minutiae.

It is not so much the *attention* to detail that is important, but the political awareness of detail for governance that emerges form these earlier times. Whereas in earlier Christian education detail was important, per se, now it becomes transformed so that its importance stems from its political utility in gaining control of bodies, in dominating them and turning then in useful, docile and efficient directions. Detail is important *politically* in the correction and training of bodies, As Foucault says; "discipline is a political anatomy of detail".

According to Foucault bodies are subjected to discipline by four broad techniques:

1. *The Distribution of Bodies*, so that they were enclosed in functional sites where, strictly speaking, bodies occupied spaces according to ranking (i.e. how well the body has been judged to have been normalised or corrected).

2. *The Control of Activities*, so that the aptitudes and characteristics sought can be efficiently and correctly imposed or transmitted. This can be done by specifying how activities are to be carried out and for how long, so that time is intensified.

3. *The Total Programme*, is to be arranged so that there is a progression and development of particular aptitudes and relationships developed between aptitudes. From the incorrect or untrained stage of commencement or initiation, there is a programme that leads to the desired effects.

4. *The Composition of Forces*, whereby all the "new" details, the minutiae of trained and corrected forces, are reformed or recombined into a profitable productive force. What was distributed and trained, has to

be reconstituted into an efficient machine; it has to bind the process together in a new and more productive manner.

These techniques are put into operation by a total observation - surveillance, examination and normalising judgement.

For modern power to be effected it must be induced by other than violent means. The mechanism is observation. What is needed is a means of observation whereby there are "techniques that make it possible to see induced the effects of power" (Foucault, 1979a, p. 170). This phrase is important in understanding what it is that Foucault is saying about power. Consider his description of rooms at the École Militaire:

> The very building of the école was to be an apparatus for observation; the rooms were distributed along a corridor like a series of small cells; at regular intervals, an officer's quarters were situated ..... the pupils were confined to their cells throughout the night ..... (and) a window (was to) be placed on the corridor wall of each room from chest level to within one or two feet of the ceiling. (op.cit., p. 173)

Now the techniques which make it possible for the pupil to be seen are first the confined cell with one window only and through which the pupil is totally visible to an observer. As this is the only window, the pupil is clearly aware not only that he can be seen and that he is totally visible but, also, *when* he can be seen. So by the techniques, i.e. the physical structuring of the spaces and the possibility of always, in principle being visible, the pupil must assume that he is under constant surveillance:

> This infinitely scrupulous concern with surveillance is expressed in the architecture by innumerable petty mechanisms ... (invoked) in the progressive objectification and the ever more subtle partitioning of individual behaviour. (loc. cit)

The perfect disciplinary apparatus "would make it possible for a single gaze to see everything constantly" (loc.cit). Hence Foucault's interest in Bentham's Panopticon.

It is not the gaze per se which the Panopticon offers, but the *techniques* by which the gaze is executed. It is these that are important. The notion of political surveillance by constant observation, culminating in self observation, is to be found in early Chinese thought. But in the panopticon, with its circular structure and its central surveillance post through which prisoners in cells which open towards that central post, prisoners must assume that they are under constant surveillance. The panopticon, idealisation as it is in Foucault's writing, is a "superior" architectural space. It is therefore, the technology involved in the Panopticon that is important, and not merely the notion of continuous surveillance.

The minute techniques identified by Foucault in his micro-analytics of power clearly place the school and its practices into a complex power/knowledge web in which power is exerted over children, whether or not it is in their (best) interests. Clearly not all power relations are "bad" in Foucault's view, but those which involve power/knowledge, and "knowledge" from the human sciences, which can lead to subjection and the imposition of identity, are. But this cuts right across the liberal view of power only acting contrary to the interests of the child.

Liberals tend to believe that the identification of what is in the interests of the child should be located in wide social contexts, so that questions of race, gender, economic and political domination are raised. But this also tends to turn the enquiry outward, so to say, away from particular micro-level exercises of power towards wider issues concerning, ultimately some general political theory. Attention is turned away thereby from the actual mechanisms of power employed at the micro-level in classrooms.

However what remains untouched and not on the educational agenda by such liberal accounts are:

(i) the *mechanisms* of power - how is power exercised?;

(ii) the *normalising* function of power/knowledge brought into play by the legitimated intentional acts of professional people acting in the best interests of the child; and,

(iii) the *professional* activities of educators.

Foucault's approach to power directs our attention towards these matters and away from the macro-level and general theories of state power. For this he is criticised by writers from opposed poles of the political spectrum (e.g. Walzer, 1986: Poulantzas, 1978). In general he was opposed to universal theorising, believing that political action was possible without a general theory of the state, and that the notion of the general intellectual capable of such totalisation (here he refers to Voltaire, but his real target was Sartre and the generation "des Temps Modernes"), is no longer capable of realisation.

But this presents him with serious problems. Refusing any sort of normative or theoretical stance, refusing to take part in theory construction (in spite of Dreyfus and Rabinow's interpretation) he remains a relativist, whose position may be advancing a critique of our present day society; however, he may rest at the level of iconoclast.

Foucault is in no doubt that the school is a disciplinary institution and that such matters as learning to read and write, even if in the best interests of the child, serve normalising functions in the search for governance. He might have conceded further that (under certain conditions) literacy skills were in the best interests of the child. Nevertheless their acquisition involves the exercise of power; under the same optimum conditions it would not for the liberal position. Yet little may differ from a legitimate command in the best interests of the child and an exercise of power, - not in the (best) interests of the child. Foucault in suspending normative frameworks is able therefore to concentrate on the mechanisms, regardless of normative questions about legitimacy and illegitimacy, whereas the liberal framework must first solve normative issues in complex social and theoretical areas as to what are the best interests of the child, before attention can be turned to questions about whether power is exercised.

Power is not always seen by philosophers of eduction as a major topic. For example R.S. Peters, who wrote an excellent book on Hobbes (Peters, 1958), scarcely discussed power in his major education work, *Ethics and Education* (1966), preferring rather to discuss authority, as though that was the legitimate educational concept for the conceptualisation of instances of social control, and the directing, correcting and changing of behaviour. However a philosophical literature has emerged within education on the topic of power, from David Nyberg (1981) to more recently Nicholas Burbules (1986), in the North American literature, and Patricia White (1982), in great Britain. Sociologists of education have addressed power through notions such as ideology, or hegemony, or social reproduction.

Given this limited discussion of power by philosophers of education it might be asked, why power?: why is power so important in education? Why bother with questions about power? Foucault was posed this question by a French newspaper:

> Why is the notion of power raised by so many people today? Is it such an important subject? (1983a, p. 209)

Foucault expressed amazement at the writer's question and the surprise voiced by the questioner that people should raise such questions because, as he was quick to point out, he couldn't believe that such questions had been raised by him, for the first time in the twentieth century. He went on to remind us of the existence of concentration camps and the traditional role of philosophy as critique of the excesses of political rationality. Even so, it might be countered, this need not entail a full blown discussion of power per se; might not the more traditional approach through the concept of authority an the legitimate and illegitimate uses of authority suffice?

Burbules and White (op.cits.), to their credit, do not think so and they have addressed explicitly the analysis of power and the implications of their analyses. These are important correctives within the philosophy of education literature. Yet I would wish to argue that their discussion remains centred in what I will call a liberal view of power, one which, in my view, *masks* certain exercises of power upon people. If the recent philosophical work in education has brought power back onto the philosophical agenda, it remains a circumscribed agenda and one which masks the exercises of power upon the young and the activities of professional educators. Foucault's approach to power identifies a series of power relationships which exist in schools, which are fundamental in the social construction of individuals, and which are not identified by the liberal problematic.

But first we will look at some of these liberal educational approaches to power.

R.S. Peters on Authority and Power

According to Peters authority is inseparably connected with a rule governed form of life. "Authority":

> presupposes some form of normative order that has to be promulgated, maintained, and perpetuated .... it has its natural home in legal systems, armies, and religious communities. (1966, p. 238)

The central point for Peters is that authority is required where decisions need to be made on the correctness or incorrectness of rules.

The distinction between "authority" and "power" which he then draws is:

> "Power" basically denotes ways in which an individual subjects others to his will by means of physical coercion (e.g. infliction of pain, restriction of movement), or by psychological coercion (e.g. withholding food, water shelter, or access to means of attaining such necessities), or by the use of less dire forms of sanction and rewards ... or by personal influences. Authority on the other hand, involves the appeal to an impersonal normative order or value system which regulates behaviour basically because of acceptance of it on the part of those who comply.... Authority, of course, may be and usually is supported by various forms of power. Behind the symbolic gestures of the policemen lies the coercive power which he can summon ... (ibid)

Having drawn this distinction Peters then goes on to talk of being *an* authority - on mathematics say - and being *in* authority for matters of social control - a teacher in a classroom say. But he is quite explicit that "the most crucial concept for discussing social control in the school is that of 'authority'". What is equally clear is that power is off stage - a nuisance which can be resorted to or which *can* be summoned. Power is not *necessary* in the school, or in education.

Power is mentioned by Peters in only four places in *Ethics and Education*. Only two of these have any real educational significance, namely, in the paragraph quoted and in a later footnote, where he notes, somewhat ironically it might be thought, that Stanley Benn had accused him of assimilating authority to power. In general that would be my interpretation also.

What we can note in Peter's account is that power seems to be owned by individual subjects who use "it" on other subjects. It appears to be an ability of a capacity which is owned by a person. Furthermore it seems to bring others under the will of the owner and cannot therefore be in the best interests of those subjected. It is directional, one way from the owner to the subjected, and because it involves physical and psychological coercion, in either dire or less dire forms, it must be repressive. Because individuals become subjected to the will of others, there must be some changes in their behaviours, beliefs, or attitudes. Finally there is a Top-Down notion of power, as if power resides with the Sovereign, and is politically legitimated as a backup for necessary authority. It is almost part of the social contract.

These are the main features of what I call a liberal view of power, and which is endemic in philosophy of education, even in Nicholas Burbules' sophisticated treatment of the topic (Burbules, 1986).

Burbules opens his account by noting that "traditional theories of power" (within the liberal democratic tradition) assume that power is a property of individual persons which is wielded instrumentally to achieve certain intended outcomes. In his view this has provided an inadequate account of the reciprocal nature of power relationship, masked the conservative nature of power "systems" in making resistance difficult, if not impossible, and failed to recognise that power is invested structurally in institutions, independently of agents. He opts therefore for a relational approach to the analysis of power, seeing Steven Lukes' (1974) account as being "much closer to the mark", even though it needs supplementation by a theory for identifying interests. A relational approach makes it clear that power is a relation made more or less necessary by circumstances and wider contexts, including conflicting or competing interests. Also, he claims, there is always a tension between compliance and resistance so that whereas one agent may be "successful" in gaining an advantage this means that a degree of compliance must be obtained and autonomy ceded to the disadvantaged, so that resistance may be possible and, second, that the advantaged's own actions become constrained by the attempt to preserve the power structures.

Power relations are said by Burbules to "suppress, disguise, preserve, or deny conflicts of interests". Where there is no conflict of interests, e.g. concerning the child's safety, there is no power relation, though other social relations may exist. Burbules then argues that the problems inherent in Lukes' account of conflicts of interests may be ameliorated or "solved" through a dialogical or pedagogical (Socratic) approach.

Lukes' (1974) formal definition is that "A exercises power over B when A affects B in a manner contrary to B's interests". Essential to Burbules' account is that "B is influenced against his or her interests" and that "power cannot be exerted to compel an outcome that *is* in B's interests" (op.cit., p. 96). This formal definition is supplemented by the dialogical-pedagogical and therapeutic method of identifying interests, which *must* involve recourse to wider social and economic contexts and, thereby, presumably, hegemony and false consciousness.

With this analysis - explicated and defended in considerable detail - Burbules then turns to consider questions of power in education:

> In order to identify power relations in schools we have to begin with the questions Where are the conflicts of interests? Where

> are the zero-sum games? In principle, education need not involve power relations at all; the learning of one student does not necessarily entail the disadvantaging of another. In principle teachers can function as legitimate authorities, not as authoritarian masters. In principle schools can *educate* and broaden student understandings beyond the facile and hegemonic. At their best moments, schools as institutions, and the educators and students who populate them, minimise power relations and promote the basis for informed, consensual and equalitarian human relations - but these are *moments*. As presently constituted schools are the site of the various conflicts of interests and hence maintain the conditions of power relations even when these are in conflict with the benign and ameliorative purposes educators avow. (op.cit., p. 109)

This paragraph raises some problems inherent in the account of power given by Burbules. Whilst he wishes to eschew the ownership view of power and replace it with a relational approach, the notion of authoritarian masters and the institutionalised conditions for power relations suggest some prevarification by Burbules on the notion of a commodity which can be owned. He is at pains to point out that institutional structures also exercise preventive power (ibid., p. 102); "Such institutionalised forms ... take on a 'life of their own' ... and it matters little whether institutional forms are actively or passively maintained". And, he continues; "it broadens our understanding to view power as a means of prevention as well as a means of direction".

Such remarks as these raise questions about ownership as well as about the status of power relationship. At some points Burbules seems to be saying that deep and underlying conflicts of interests have led to institutions such as schools with vested interests owning a commodity - power - which permeates the social structure of the school in a number of existent power relationships through which power is exercised, either in active or preventive forms, according to conflicts of interests. Burbules is adamant that power must necessarily be defined in terms of conflicts of interests and of advantages and disadvantages. In which case questions of ownership, though replaced by talk of interests and advantaged, are not really abandoned. It is the advantaged - agent or institution - that is on the directed, repressive pole of the power relationship and to this extent a residual ownership thesis persists.

Even with this important relational turn Burbules lies within what I term the liberal view of power (and he sees himself as being within the liberal democratic tradition). This view of power can be characterised as power being independent of knowledge, and as being owned or possessed by someone who exercises it in a Top-Down manner contrary to the interests of the "recipient". In relation to education it is not seen as necessary but as something to be appealed to as a last resort.

As Foucault's account of power differs markedly from this liberal view, it should be helpful at this point to summarise these differences. First, on Foucault's account power is not owned by the sovereign, by the state, or by teachers. It exists as a *relationship* only when brought into play by agents who, often, are unaware of the exercise of this sort of power/knowledge. To the extent that they don't own it, may be unaware that they exercise it, and can't usually be said to impose it intentionally, then individual people may not be held responsible for the spread of modern power [Foucault, 1984b]. Second, Foucault does not see power as necessarily being repressive: on the contrary power can be positive in its effects, as it promotes pleasure for example, and constitutes us as subjects in various ways. Third, power does not act upon beliefs, but upon *actions*, and can always be resisted; also it acts upon bodies, changing abilities and capabilities, and producing docile and calculable bodies to lead useful lives. Fourth, Foucault is not concerned whether power is a legitimate or an illegitimate way of acting on people's actions. Finally this power is not necessarily Top-Down and directed necessarily by State apparatuses: it is capillary, working at the lowest micro level in society. Hence power is to be understood not in terms of a social contract between Sovereign and individual but in terms of the politics of everyday life.

Foucault provides us with an example of how to analyze the exercise of power in *Discipline and Punish* and some general guidelines in his last major discussion of power - "The Subject and Power". But Foucault's warning is that nothing universal *follows* from his analysis of punishment for, say, the exercise of power in eduction, even though he uses educational examples to exemplify the thesis that modern power as developed in the disciplines has come to permeate all of the social fabric. He claims that his works are not to be taken as truths (a problem in itself because it leaves their status unclear), but that at best they might be used as missiles, or bombs.

In general, following Foucault, an analysis of power relations should be conducted under five general heading.

(1) The systems of differentiations established by law, or by traditions, or by economic conditions, etc., which gives some prima facie

position for power relationships to be brought into play. For example the legal, traditional, and pedagogic status of the teacher provides conditions for bringing power into play.

(2) The types of objective pursued intentionally by those who act upon the actions of others when power relations are brought into existence. For example, the teacher may be pursuing pedagogical objectives yet bringing modern power into play through normalisation procedures.

(3) The means of bringing power relations into play, either through force, compliance, consent, surveillance, economic reward, etc.

(4) Forms of institutionalisation; there may be a mixture of legal, tradition, hierarchical structures such as the family, or the military, or the school.

(5) The degree of rationalisation which, depending upon the situation, endows, elaborates and legitimates processes for the exercise of power. In education much of the early talk in philosophy of eduction of a teacher being *in* authority and *an* authority should be conceived int his light.

Genealogy and the analysis of power relations will reveal, according to Foucault, the normalising functions of schools. In the medieval school, according to Ariès (1962), there were no authority structures as we now understand them. Certainly the teacher was not in authority over the students and had little or no authority or power to discipline or punish. Punishments for disorderly or ribald behaviour were imposed by the students themselves and tended to be a fine of some kind. The critical question to be pursued then could be to track out the changing patterns of punishment as the disciplinary block, which we call the school, "emerged". What would be required here is a genealogical investigation of schools which throw up violent contrasts similar to Damiens on the one hand and the quiet, caring way on the other hand. In schools we have the example of the medieval school, the harsh repressive schools of Victorian times, and the modern notions of counselling and pastoral aspects.

CHAPTER 5

ON EDUCATION

As Foucault wrote and said little explicitly on education, it might appear somewhat of a daunting task to write a book on Foucault *and* education. If it is, it is not merely for that reason, but because of the complexity of his thinking, the changes in direction which his work appears to take on several occasions, the problems of understanding where he is coming from and why, and the general lack of knowledge and understanding of continental philosophy and social theory, in Anglo-Saxon educational literature. Arguably it is Pierre Bourdieu's work that is best known to educationalists, and not Henri Lefebvre; or Descartes and Kant to philosophers of education, and not Sartre and Merleau-Ponty; Freud rather than Lacan, to psychologists of education; and so on.

The concern of this book has been to mount a critique of liberal education, in particular the notion inherent in liberal thought of developing personal autonomy. This has been mounted from Foucault's writings on the human sciences (Man), rationality, power and knowledge, and governmentality or reason of state. In this chapter we turn more explicitly to education. Except in *Discipline and Punish* he says little explicitly on education. However, what is said there is to exemplify notions such as power/knowledge, disciplinary blocks and practices, and techniques of domination and is not explicitly directed at education. But if he did not say much about education per se we can, in Foucauldean manner, look at his own *practices* of education. When we look at his pedagogical practices an interesting and contradictory picture emerges - that of a classical academic, concerned about the disciplines, truth, and teaching. In spite of his critiques of disciplinary blocks, some disparaging remarks about his own earlier education, and remarks on the need for reforms in education, his own practices were quite traditional.

In order to understand these contradictions we need to look at his activities whilst at Clermont-Ferand, the events of May-June 1968 and the stormy interlude at Vincennes from 1968-1970. From his practices we can discern a view of education, but in turn these practices need to be sited in a wider educational and social context.

First we need to look at the reforms promoted by the de Gaulle government between 1966 and 1970, and in particular at those reforms of the universities promoted by Christian Fouchet in 1966, and at Edgar Faure's 1968 proposals for the loi d'orientation, which was accompanied by the setting up of the experimental university at Vincennes. Foucault's participation in the reform process and his approach to pedagogy at Vincennes will then be investigated.

French Educational Reforms - 1960's

Educational reforms were introduced by the Fifth Republic mainly by Christian Fouchet in 1967, but also there were the reforms introduced in 1968 by Edgar Faure in response to the events of May-June of that year. In a speech to the National Assembly of France on 19 May 1965, Premier Georges Pompidou had said of French education:

> It stills lives for the most part on postulates bequeathed to it by the Jesuits of the 17th. century and which were only slightly modified at the end of the last century. Of course we have become aware of the increased importance assumed by the sciences and also of the accretion of new knowledge. But we have contented ourselves with adding to the syllabus ... (that which is) ... often increasingly abstract ... children arrive at the end of their secondary studies with a level of knowledge which is becoming more and more worthless. (quoted in Capelle, 1967)

The Fifth republic had marked four major areas for reform on assuming office. Education was one of them and changes were initiated as early as 1959. Within education they aimed initially at "modernising teaching methods, improving methods of selection at the ages of eleven and thirteen, changing the conditions of the baccaleauréat examination and eventually of raising the school leaving age to sixteen" (Pickles,1973;55).

Later there were to be emphases on modernising the universities and taking higher education down the technocratic path deemed necessary by the Fifth Republic for a strong France.

There can be little doubt that at the outset of the Fifth Republic, de Gaulle had a strong commitment to education. Indeed it was said that in the area of educational reforms in the first ten years of the Fifth Republic, France had been "more innovative and dynamic than most other Western European countries" (Safran, 1977). However, de Gaulle's commitment, like that of Napoleon, had been based upon the notion of stability and the grounding of teaching upon "sound principles" (Halls,1976). By the end of his period in office he was generally disillusioned with education; first, with teachers and, second, with the students. Although he desired a form of education that would develop powers of reasoning and reflection as well as a critical attitude, perhaps exemplified by his own earlier reflective and critical behaviour in the Army, he was in turn, and as we have noted already, highly critical of the students' political activities.

Georges Pompidou, who became premier in 1962 and President in 1969, was himself an ex school teacher with a literary and classics background. Yet he never questioned the importance of the need for industrial expansion and growth, and a scientific and technocratic education that would meet such needs. Christian Fouchet became Minister of Education in 1962 and held office for four years and four months, which was the longest tenure by a Minister of Education for a century. He was not a specialist in education but he was certainly a technocrat determined to rationalise educational provision and administration at all levels. However it is with the "reforms" of upper secondary and university education that his name will be associated.

There were considerable rapid changes made in higher education during this decade, but the secondary changes impinged heavily upon higher education also, not only in the demands for places by successful baccaleaurét candidates, but also in the shifts in the curriculum away from essentially a classical, humanistic form of study towards a practical technocratic education through which progress, and the demands of industry, were to be met. This shift reflects Pompidou's notion of worth expressed in his 1965 comments on education to the National Assembly (see above).

A major "reform" which impinged directly upon the universities was the changes to the baccaleauréat examination. At the start of the decade success in the baccaleauréat examination gave unlimited access to all of the Faculties in the Universities. It had been possible for a student whose interests had been in the classics at the lycée to be admitted to a science faculty. Fouchet's reforms were to restructure the course and the examination into a number of sections - five in all - so that access to a university faculty came to be predetermined by the section of the course. The main innovations were the introduction of economics with statistics, to be studied along with Latin or a foreign language (Pompidou even with his leanings towards technology and progress could not foresee abandoning Latin); the opening of modern studies to languages whereas previously it had meant science; and considerable advice for students from the staff council and orientation programmes. Clearly the role of the classics had been diminished, and a major shift from the literary humanistic education that preceded the decade had been initiated, if not put in place and made operational.

In effect selection to the Universities had been introduced. The left, which was almost fanatically attached to a principle of non-selection, held that possession of the baccalauréat was not merely a universally acceptable admission qualification, but also an admission qualification to whatever faculty the student might choose (Pickles,1973). This right of access was regarded as an expression of an irrevocable, bottom line, principle of equality. Principles of selection, for the left, smacked of pre-Revolutionary class privilege. Ironically, in the vast expansion of French higher education, many teachers and administrators, concerned about falling standards, had advocated some form of limitation (Halls,1976, p. 183). Sam White, writing in the *Evening Standard* of 17 May 1968, noted that Raymond Aron was insisting upon this 'solution' to the student unrest (White, 1984). Aron, spokesperson for *Le Figaro*, "saw himself as the lone voice of sanity amidst a general madness" (Poster,1975, p. 356).

Within higher education there were two powerful forces - those of democratisation and those of modernisation. The former, usually expressed as equality of opportunity, represented the increased demand from, in the main, the lower middle classes (and not the working classes) for access to higher education. As late as 1971 OECD reported that the push for access had "not yet started from the urban working class or from the small farmers and agricultural workers" (OECD,1971, p. 68). (It was really middle class students - daddy's little darlings - who revolted in May-June). It was also believed that these demands would be better met by a form of "classless style" and a reduction in the level of correlation between the level of social class and the level of education. To a certain extent these factors required greater access to higher education and greater access to a variety of forms of education. Those pressing for democratisation wanted access then, and open access to all forms of education, whereas those pressing for modernisation wished to control the growth, to control the size of the forms of development, and to control the forms of institution in which such education would be given. These were competing pressures in France and called in question many of the assumptions upon which traditional higher education had been based.

For example, the Universities saw their traditional role widening dangerously and were concerned about a loss of standards in rapid expansions of higher education. For many in the university modernisation involved a distortion, if not an abdication, of the traditional function of the university - its humanising, cultural transmission function. Others, and before the upheavals of 1968, began to look at ways of resolving these conflicts, by looking at curricula, pedagogy and better ways of involving students in the university.

The main tensions identified by OECD up to 1968 were:

(1) *The Pressure of Numbers*. The numbers gaining the baccalauréat and thereby an entry certificate to the Faculties had risen immensely. There were enormous classes and considerable anonymity. However the faculties, which could not select, tried to gain breathing space by failing large numbers at the end of the first year - up to 45% This was bound to cause problems.

(2) *Faculties and les Grandes Écoles*. Les Grandes Écoles were highly selective and access was highly competitive. In Foucault's case this involved two years preparation at Lycée Henri IV and on the first occasion he failed. Whereas the faculties were not overly concerned with their teaching les grandes écoles were very attentive to their teaching. Given their function to prepare the future political and intelligentsia elites this is hardly surprising. But they conducted little research. Whereas their failure rate and drop out rates were low, those of the faculties were high. According to OECD whilst they supported each other they also supported each others' weaknesses.

(3) *Modernisation and the Institutions of Higher Education*. In between these sectors there was a yawning gap with little variety. There was little attempt to meet between faculties and the world of industry and commerce. Whilst industry sought the traditionally liberally educated person from the faculties they were finding that their education was old fashioned and scholarly.

The *OECD* Report was written in 1971. Additional universities had been established throughout the 1960's, and Fouchet addressed these general difficulties in May 1965 with the proposals for implementing the "reform" of the universities from the Implementation Commission. The reforms of the earlier commission (Commission d'Étude de l'Enseignments Supérieure - "les dix-huit" as they were called) proposed to do away with the introductory year (la année propédeutique) tested by the eliminatory exam, and replace the existing structures with three stages of university study. The first stage was to be a two year cycle leading to a diploma in literature or science. In literature, for those preparing to teach, there were six main sections - classics, modern studies, languages, history, geography and philosophy. There were divisions within the sciences but the important feature for science was that students were required to have prerequisites of science or mathematics. In addition to literature and science there were three other sections for psychology, sociology and history of art and archaeology. The second stage was either a further year leading to a licence which was required for secondary teaching or two years which led to a maîtrise or masters degree. Finally there was the competitively won agrégation and a doctorate.

Another major innovation was the creation of University Institutes of Technology for the training of highly specialised technicians with more general education than technicians had possessed in the past. Fraser comments:

> For the universities this did represent the acceptance of a new function: the training of skilled personnel in civil engineering, mechanical construction, dynamics, electronics and automation, chemistry, labour management, applied biology, administration, local government, documentation and statistics. (1971, p. 77)

These changes proposed by Fouchet had major implications for teachers and researchers. First they represented a split between research and teaching and a separation of lycée teaching from university work. Previously professeurs could move reasonably freely between lycée and university - as in the cases of Canguilhelm who had taught Foucault at Lycée Henri IV and taught later at the Universities of Strasbourg and the Sorbonne, and Lyotard, who had taught for several years in lycées and subsequently at Nanterre and Vincennes. But the main problem was that expansion had been so rapid, and the changes so major, that sufficient attention had not been given to the implementation and integration of these major innovations into what had been a very traditional system concerned with the preservation and transmission of culture. Generalist and innovative teachers were required - yet the centralised curriculum and structures militated against such autonomy and innovation.

Within a year of Fouchet's higher education reforms students and workers began a series of revolts and disturbances. The reforms had not been a settlement of student grievances and left and right wing political beliefs and attitudes towards education. The intellectual differences underlying these differences are well summarised by Macrides:

> While Pompidou and his associates never questioned what had become known as the "industrial imperative", that is, the need of

> industrial expansion and growth, many among the intellectuals, some of the left wing parties and some of the trade unions began to subordinate it to social and qualitative requirements: security, leisure, improved conditions of everyday life, education, culture, and above all the elimination of sharp income inequalities. Many people demanded the freedom to control and decide for themselves - in the factory, in the universities, in towns and villages - instead of allowing an impersonal and highly centralised state to make decisions for them. The French men and women began to reject the tutelage of the centralised administrative state and to yearn for what we call "community control". (1975, p. 55)

Fouchet had made a serious mistake in underestimating the students' desire for real participation in the functioning of education (Fraser,1971, p. 140). It was the students themselves who cracked the University system in 1968. This led to the "Loi d'Orientation" in which considerable autonomy was granted to institutions and participation to students. This November 1968 Bill was a response to the revolutionary student challenge of May-June 1968. Fouchet's changes had done little to meet the demands of the left for democratisation, and the demands of the students for participation in 1968 necessitated more serious modification to the system. Given that some people were committed to the system, it "was an object of national pride" (Pickles,1973, p. 153), then it was hardly surprising that opposition to the 1968 Bill came form both left and right.

If it is accepted that the main grievances of the students in May-June were educational and not political (contra *Time*, May-June,1968), then indeed the students had cracked the system. Daniel and Gabriel Cohn Bendit's (1968) account makes the grievances point well, namely that the students were in the main not driven by political but by educational motives (assuming that these can be separated in thought for this discussion).

The main grievances of the students centred on the problems caused by the rapid expansion of the 1960's; shortage of teachers, inadequacies of buildings, irrelevance of courses, remoteness of staff and petty administrative restrictions, particularly in halls of residence; students were concerned about selection and their rights to engage in political activities on university premises (previously restricted to those occasions which arose as part of the normal curriculum). They wanted self management for the universities, a change of teaching methods, and changes to curricula and examinations.

The 1968 Bill did not address selection even though the previous government had announced that selection would be introduced in 1969. It was too difficult politically. In theory political discussions could be held only if they arose as part of an established course, though there was a general toleration of the posting of notices and the holding of meetings. The Bill proposed to allow debates on such political issues providing that the life of the university was not disrupted. On the question of the re-organization and restructuring of the Universities the bill "steered a cautious course between concessions and precautions, with the aim of preventing any irrevocable weakening of the State's fundamental responsibility for education" (Pickles,1973, p. 156). The number of universities was to be increased and universities were defined as possessing financial autonomy, but they were no longer to be composed of the traditional faculties. Instead they were to be composed by smaller units or departments. Universities were to be administratively autonomous and university councils were to be "expressions of the principle of participation, comprising teachers, researchers, students and administration" (ibid.). Yet whilst examinations were to be supplemented by a form of continuous assessment, examinations which conferred the national diplomas remained firmly under the control of the Ministry of Education (as evidenced at Vincennes - see below). Whilst the universities were stated to have financial and accounting autonomy they still depended upon Government grants and their accounts and administration remained firmly under the control of the central administration through auditing and inspection. The demands of the students from June 1968 for total autonomy of the Universities from the state had not been met. Yet in the Parliamentary debates that preceded the bill being passed on 11 November 1968 fears were expressed that "M.Faure had gone too far to meet the students" (Pickles,ibid.).

Nevertheless Faure's successor, Oliver Guichard, continued decentralisation of academic decision making, the establishment of interdisciplinary curricula and the founding of new university centres in the Paris region. The emphasis on a technological business orientated curriculum continued, with further "reforms" of this type introduced by Education Minister René Haby in 1974. For many professors this meant an end of the notion of a cultured person and the cooption of the university for business purposes (Safran, 1977).

Vincennes was part of this response. It was to be experimental, but inter-disciplinary, on the cutting edge of research, and democratic. Hopefully it was to be a magnet to draw the dissidents from the Latin-

Quarter, to isolate them and to confine them. If the Faculty attracted to Vincennes contained idealists, liberals and intolerant ultra-leftists in a potentially interesting intellectual mix, the students were the cream of the militant crop from the street fighting days (Miller,1993, p. 175). Somewhat ironically the site on which this new campus erupted, both physically and politically, was leased from the army which had owned the land for more than one hundred years.

Vincennes was to be a model of the reforms, of the loi d'orientation - it was to be participatory (democratic) and interdisciplinary in the sense of the new structures contained within the reforms. Faure had stressed the need for more participation in a speech to the Assemblée Nationale earlier in July 1968 in a major response to the events of May-June. New relations between teachers and staff, and new structures for the Universities, were said to be of paramount concern. Participation was then the dominant theme of Faure's declaration (1968:7). But how was participation to be understood?

Participation had been a concern of de Gaulle in his immediate post-war government and it almost became a slogan in the later years of the Fifth Republic. As with many Gaullist ideas it was vague and rhetorical but it referred vaguely to notions of shared management and profit sharing schemes.

At Vincennes participation was to be interpreted by students and a number of faculty in a particular way, different from and not at all in the manner envisaged by the Fifth Republic, and this was perhaps the downfall of the philosophy department.

But nor had the teaching of philosophy been addressed adequately by the Fouchet reforms. Philosophy syllabii and teaching methodology were under the control of edicts from the 1920's (see, e.g., M.E.N., 1967) and such methodology compounded the severe overcrowding at the universities. The Fouchet reforms addressed structures but not pedagogy.

Foucault's Pedagogical Practices

In 1960 Foucault was appointed by Jules Vuillemin to the philosophy department at Clermont-Ferrand, where his initial responsibilities were to teach psychology. Later he was appointed professor of Philosophy. Vuillemin was later to "move" to the Collége de France, with Foucault priming Dumezil to promote the candidacy, and in turn being supported by Vuillemin when his own candidacy was at issue. Vuillemin wrote to Foucault at Hamburg, after having read his thesis, but Foucault was but one of many young and subsequently important people for whom Vuillemin had gone "fishing ... in the tank on the Rue d'Ulm" (Eribon,1991, p. 129).

At first sight they would appear to have had little in common, but, according to Eribon, they got on famously in a department "where friendly relations and warm companionship prevailed" (Eribon, loc.cit.). Not only had Vuillemin moved towards philosophy of science and mathematics, and was particularly interested in the work of Bertrand Russell, but he also gradually evolved politically to the right, whereas Foucault, in spite of his Gaullist acquaintances, was essentially on the left despite his lack of sympathy for left political parties and political theories of the left. Both Foucault and Vuillemin demanded rigour and they respected each others' intellectual work. For Vuillemin this respect was to over-ride any other possible judgments that he may have harboured post-1968 and permitted him to support Foucault for the post at the Collége de France (Eribon,1991, p. 132).

However it must be noted that in many of the important formative years of French left politics, leading up to 1968, Foucault was not in France. Nor was he involved in party politics, though he had been a member briefly of le Partie Communiste Francaise in the 1950's. What was clear was that after his experiences in Warsaw he was strongly anti-communist (manifested in a violent series of "attacks" upon Roger Garaudy, formerly a prominent member of the PCF, when he was appointed to Clermont-Ferrand contrary to the wishes of the department for Gilles Deleuze - Eribon, 1991: Macey, 1993). Though he was interested fiercely in politics he remained at a distance from any militant political involvement. Many of his friends from Clermont-Ferrand times were surprised at his later swing to the far left and the radical positions that he was to adopt. His assistant (Foucault's "sister") from 1962 to 1966, Francine Pariente, said of his attitudes and positions in the 1970's (quoted in Eribon, 1991, p. 132): "I never managed to believe it really".

Foucault had several contacts with Gaullist power in the 1960's, often through his friend from Warsaw days, Etienne Burin des Roziers. He said of Foucault that: "when he visited me sometime during 1962 the future of our higher education was his dearest project" (quoted in Eribon, ibid.). He was even considered for an administrative post as assistant director of higher education in the Ministry of Education, but that was to be blocked by those who objected to his homosexuality. An homosexual as a director of higher education was not acceptable to certain people. What is important here, and as Eribon (loc.cit) points out, is that Foucault did not find the idea of such a post repugnant.

Eribon notes:

> this anecdote reveals the sort of man Foucault was in those days - an academic in the most classic sense of the word.

Miller (1993, p. 172), in similar vein, comments that, "during those years, Foucault also seems to have played the academic game with genuine relish and a certain cunning".

In 1965 Foucault took part in elaborating the reforms in education that Christian Fouchet had begun. As we have seen these reforms were an important part of the Gaullist programme, with both de Gaulle and Pompidou committed and involved. Foucault, in a statement in 1966, seems to be very much in accord with the spirit of reform:

> If an honest man, today, has the impression of a barbarous culture this impression is due to a single fact: our system of education dates from the nineteenth century and there still reigns there the most insipid psychology, the most antiquated humanism.....this is the fault of the organisation of education. (1966a:15)

The earlier Commission ("les dix-huits") had produced its report in March 1964, outlining the major principles for the reforms. The Implementation Commission was charged with implementing these reforms. Within the main commission a sub-commission, called the "Commission on the Teaching of Literature and Science", was established in January 1965. Foucault was a member of the Implementation Commission on the suggestion of a former normalien Jean Knapp, who was a technical advisor to the Minister and who was present at all of the meetings of the commission. Foucault was also a member of the sub-commission on the teaching of literature and science. The Implementation Commission met approximately once a month for the next year and Foucault attended assiduously - he is noted as being present in all of the minutes of the meetings. Minutes of the sub-commission are not included with these minutes but reports were received from these and other smaller groups. Traces of Foucault's remarks are to be found in the major Report but he had also prepared other reports, and made verbal reports to the commission (e.g., the meeting of 15 February 1965 when he spoke to a report already circulated). Also, other inputs by Foucault into the discussions are formally noted in the minutes.

There were 22 members of the Implementation Commission and

ten of these were members of les dix-huits. Amongst these were François Chamoux, and Jean Grappin (who later was to have a torrid time as Dean of the Faculté des Lettres at Nanterre). The new Commission included Fernand Braudel, the historian of *Annales* fame, and Robert Flacellière, the Director of the École Normale Supérieur. Julles Vuillemin had been included as a member (his name occurs on the first list but is later omitted) on the request of Foucault to Knapp. Vuillemin held particular views on the disciplines and on quality that Foucault respected (Eribon,1991, pp. 153-169). These qualities would have been important in combating the technocratic thrust of the reforms towards the professions and vocational training. If Vuillemin could not live with that thrust Foucault apparently could and did, though he did attempt to temper those aspects at the meetings.

The Minister, Christian Fouchet, opened the first meeting by thanking those who were attending and stating that the group was charged with examining the problems of higher education. He emphasised that this was a problem, "to which he gave the greatest importance". Whilst he stressed that participants should feel free to speak at all times he, nevertheless, stressed at the conclusion, as he was to repeat at most of the meetings, the importance of confidentiality. Foucault seemed to have ignored this request as he discussed progress of the Commission with students (Eribon, 1991, p. 135).

Fouchet then turned to the terms of reference of the Implementation Commission. Whilst these were listed under five headings it is clear for our concerns that those under the first heading were the most important. Under the first heading of "Mission de L'Enseignment Supérieur" are four categories listed from A-D. It was clear that Fouchet wanted confirmation of the "movement in education" that had underlain already the ideas, proposals and changes in education of the Fifth Republic. For example, under A, was higher education to be concerned with culture or "formation professionelle", or both? And where was research to fit into this complex problem? B was concerned with the preparation of teachers, at all levels, and C with the "formation technique supérieur". D was concerned with how answers to these questions were to be implemented.

The four other major categorizations were concerned with access to higher education, its organisation, its teaching methods, and the conditions of recruitment and service of teachers and other professional staff.

It might be thought, given the work of the earlier commission, that the fundamental issues in 1, and which were listed under A had already been decided. In which case Fouchet must have been seeking confirmation of the technocratic thrust in education that the Fifth Republic sought, and this may have been reflected in the overlapping membership of the two commissions. If this is correct Vuillemin's decision to withdraw makes sense. Moreover there is little doubt that as the "programme" was under considerable attack from many in the Universities, such "solid" confirmation would have been important for the Minister. Certainly the Report of the les dix-huits had been circulated to the members of the Implementation Commission in November 1964.

Foucault's recorded participation concern the following points. At the opening session he urged a unified semester system across the education system. On 15 February he spoke to a report, circulated earlier to members, on higher education in the discipline of philosophy. The concern expressed was that in the proposed changes not enough time would be given to philosophy for prospective teachers of the subject. Foucault proposed technical solutions for agrégation by the amounts of time devoted to philosophy in the broad general changes. At the third meeting on 8 March, and in the closing minutes, he returned again to the subject of the academic year. There was support for his proposals on agrégation by Devril and Braudel on 22 March.

On 5 April concerns on the technocratic thrust were expressed by Foucault. He emphasised the importance of the disciplines in professional training, arguing that any professional training must be *based* upon studies in the traditional disciplines. He returned to this problem at the next meeting of 24 May, questioning the Minister concerning the routes for students from the bachelors degree into the new technical institutes. Would science students have to go into them or could they enter the science faculties? Were the institutes preparing a similar route for arts and law students? The Minister responded that access was not determined in advance but added that professional preparation in the institutes would have different objectives from those of the traditional faculties.

Foucault also made a major contribution on the thesis for the doctorate, arguing that it might be possible to submit a doctorate from a series of published papers. A similar proposal was made by Education Minister Edgar Faure in his address to Senate in November, 1968 (Faure,1968). And it was Faure who was to approve Foucault for the new university campus at Vincennes in 1968.

Foucault's contributions can then be summarised as contributions to technical problems involved in implementing the reforms, major contributions on the teaching of philosophy and the ph.d. thesis, and a number of objections and questions concerning the technological thrust of the implemented reforms. These contributions which included two written reports indicate a person committed to both University education and the traditional approaches to knowledge through a firm foundation in the disciplines, especially for students going down the technical paths in the proposed university institutes of technology.

According to Eribon Chamoux said that Foucault did not at any time dissent from the broad general thrust of the proposed reforms. It is clear however from the minutes that Foucault perceived problems and expressed concerns. The nature of many of these concerns are important. First there is the concern about the teaching of philosophy and the training of future teachers of philosophy. And these are concerns about the *discipline* of philosophy. Philosophy mattered to Foucault. Second there is a concern expressed about ph.d. theses. Foucault believed they took too long and that they were abstracted from the practical professional life of the candidates. The status of the thesis appears to fall under his attacks upon grand abstract and universalising theories. If theory can only be local and specific then it must arise from particular contingencies. Hence Foucault was arguing for the importance of the "intellectual" and professional life of the candidate. The ph.d. must arise from, and be part of, the candidate's lived experience. Faure was to propose much the same as Foucault on the structure of the doctorate in 1968 (and it is now common practice at some English speaking universities).

However the major concern seems to be with the disciplines and the necessity of a sound grounding in knowledge and methodology. Whilst it is clear that he was committed to philosophy from the concerns already noted, it was not so clear in the minutes that he was at those points in time committed more widely. However his questioning of Fouchet on these matters makes that wider commitment clear. But how wide? To all disciplines and to all forms of knowledge? That cannot be discerned from the minutes but if his general antagonism towards the human sciences is now added to the picture, as well as the 1966 statement quoted above, then it is clear that he is talking about the more traditional disciplines within the faculties of science, arts and law, and not about the humanistic social sciences.

Faure must have approved the recommendation of Canguilhelm that Foucault be appointed to the committee at Vincennes for coopting staff. Later he was to become chairman of the philosophy department. But Faure's approval cannot have been accidental. Foucault had proven himself to be committed to the traditional disciplines, he had made major proposals on the subject of philosophy to the Implementation Commission, and he was at the cutting edge of his subject as *Les Mots et Les Choses* had shown.

Vincennes was to be a model of the reforms, of the loi d'orientation - it was to be participatory (democratic) and interdisciplinary in the sense of the new structures contained within the reforms. Faure had stressed the need for more participation in a speech to the Assemblée Nationale earlier in July 1968 in a major response to the events of May-June. New relations between teachers and staff, and new structures for the Universities, were said to be of paramount concern. Participation was then the dominant theme of Faure's declaration (Faure,1968, p. 7). But how was participation to be understood?

Participation had been a concern of de Gaulle in his immediate post-war government and it almost became a slogan in the later years of the Fifth Republic. As with many Gaullist ideas it was vague and rhetorical but it referred vaguely to notions of shared management and profit sharing schemes (Macey, 1993, p. 220).

At Vincennes participation was to be interpreted in a particular way, different from and not at all in the manner envisaged by the Fifth Republic, and this was perhaps the downfall of the philosophy department. Foucault was to depart for Le College de France in 1970. The full details of this tempestuous period, as they impinged upon Foucault, can be found in the biographies of Eribon, Macey and Miller.

But we must note that the Foucault who returned to Paris from Tunisia in late 1968 had been hardened by unrest and violent encounters with the police. Foucault had hoped that the events of May-June 1968 would signal new forms of life and social organisation. But if he was more overtly politicised by his experiences in Tunisia he was also to be attacked for not being there - *in* Paris *in* May-June. This caused difficulties for him at Vincennes for he was seen by some to have been compromised by his absence in Tunisia (Macey,1993, p. 221). But, in addition, his earlier work on madness was taken up the anti-psychiatry movement and by the left in general, so that he began to enjoy a growing reputation as a leftist (Macey,1993, chapt.9).

Jean François Lyotard, who later took up an appointment to Vincennes certainly saw the Faculty (of Arts) as requiring a reconstruction away from the oppression of the normal curriculum towards a praxis that allowed "the critical comprehension of reality in all its forms and the liberation of the power of expression" (Lyotard,1968, p. 44). Yet the forms that this praxis took were problematic at Vincennes. Lyotard who had been prominent at Nanterre in May-June was to say:

> We used to fight a bit. Only once did it lead to anything worthwhile. It was on a day of active strike. What could we do? At the time we were working on the operators in persuasive discourse, making use of Plato's dialogues and Aristotle's Rhetoric and Sophistic refutation. We subjected the statements relative to the strike to the same analysis.... Enter the commando unit armed with clubs, shouting that we were breaking the strike. A fight starts, quickly followed by palavers between the two groups, the besiegers and the beseige. The latter argue as follows: on the one hand our "normal" activity is to study persuasive discourse.... On the other hand, to participate in an active strike is to occupy the workplace and to think together about the discourses that persuade or dissuade us from striking. The difference between these two activities is not distinguishable.... Most of the assailants backed off, admitting that we were as much "out of it" as they were. (1978, p. 70)

The arguments and fights over participation and the continual disruption of teaching, fired by the right wing press, did not make life easy for Foucault. Miller notes that whilst Foucault expressed solidarity with the students, and attempted to modify some of his pedagogic practices yet:

> at the same time, he continued to lecture *ex cathedra*, making no effort (as many radical professors did in those years) to conceal or soften the power and authority of his own intellect. (1993, p. 181)

He quotes Foucault:

> When I lecture dogmatically I tell myself: I am paid to bring to my students a certain form and content of knowledge; I must fashion my lecture or my course a little as one might make a shoe, no more and no less. I design an object. I try to make it as well as possible. I make a lot of trouble for myself (not always, perhaps, but often). I bring the object to the desk. I show it and then I leave it up to the audience to do with it what they want. (loc.cit.)

According to Miller he saw students as apprentices and himself as the master craftsman, even in those difficult times. However he never saw himself as a guru with disciples and offered himself only as an example. His teaching then was compatible with his view of his works, of theory and the general role of intellectuals in society.

The arguments and fights over participation and the continual disruption of teaching, fired by the right wing press, did not make life easy for Foucault. Yet he seems on participation to have aligned himself with the students:

> It seems to me that what students are trying to do ... and what I myself am trying to accomplish in the dust of my books is basically the same thing.... We must free ourselves from cultural conservatism as well as from political conservatism. We must see our rituals for what they are: completely arbitrary things ... it is good ... to transcend them ... show up, transform, and reverse the systems which quietly order us about ... that is what I try to do in my work. (Foucault,1971c)

Yet the phrase "dust on books" cannot be ignored as it represents a certain displacement, a certain lack of praxis, or involvement in the attempt to rethink pedagogical practices. He did not appear to have seen that a fundamental target of May-June 1968 was pedagogy.

Certainly Foucault made a number of very interesting appointments to Vincennes. Gilles Deleuze declined because of his health, but they included: Alain Badiou, Etienne Balibar, François Chatelet, Janette Colombel, Judith Miller (Lacan's daughter), Jacques Ranciere, René Schérer, Michel Serres and Henri Weber. These appointments represented an intriguing variety of political positions, from moderate leftism to the PCF, to an extreme version of Maoism, and to Trotskyism. Eribon suggests that by appointing people from such different positions Foucault sought to moderate the extremisms of some of the appointees. Other possible explanations are that he created a space in which it would be possible for marginalised philosophers to work, and that he sought specialists in power, and specialists in knowledge (Macey,1993, p. 225).

But Foucault did not fully recognise or acknowledge that the first victim of the May-June maelstrom was the teacher, the person professing to knowledge, and the person whose authority was based upon competencies in a field(s) of knowledge (Descombes, 1980: chapter six). Foucault was challenging both political authority and authority in the areas of the human sciences, but in his actions and teaching behaviour did not seem to see that this called in question also his status as a teacher. His emerging interest in power and knowledge was not employed in a self reflective and reflexive manner at Vincennes to critique his own teaching. Lyotard was far more aware of these issues (Marshall,1995c).

Foucault taught courses on Nietzsche and on sexuality and individuality. But the remainder of the programme was much more openly political. (Details of the courses taught are provided by Eribon). The content attracted the ire of the Minister of Education and in January 1970 he announced that because of the specialised content of the courses any degrees awarded would not be recognised nationally. Foucault defended his choice to experiment with freedom at Vincennes in *Le Nouvel Observateur*, on 9 February, 1970:

> We have defined two broad areas of teaching: one that is basically devoted to the political analysis of society and one that is devoted to the analysis of the scientific fact and to the analysis of a certain number of scientific domains. These two regions, politics and science, seemed to all of us, students and teachers alike, to be the most active and the most fruitful.

But if Foucault had selected the right staff and if the curriculum was right his approach to pedagogy did not appear to recognise the critical importance this occupied for any "genuine" reforms of the universities. Participation was interpreted by many of the student factions and faculty as requiring more than agreement on the form of the curriculum. Foucault did not seem to grasp this point. He could not cope with the constant interruptions to lectures, the pickets and demonstrations that became commonplace at Vincennes, and the rambling forums and debates that often replaced formal teaching.

In his inaugural lecture at the Collège de France in December 1970 he addressed projects on the traditional and centuries old subjects of truth, rationality and normality, though emphasising his explicit interest in the subject of power and noting that he was crossing the boundaries of these traditional subjects. Yet he emphasised, particularly in the debts he paid to Hyppolite, that he wished to be "among other things, a scholar among scholars" (Foucault, 1971a). The lecture contained then elements of both scholarship and radical "things to come".

In the ensuing years, and within these parameters, Foucault performed his scholarly duties assiduously.

Yet in 1971 on a visit to North America he was still talking of the particular forms of exclusion that befell university students (Foucault,1971c). First they are "put outside of society, on a campus". There they are "transmitted a knowledge traditional in nature, obsolete, 'academic' and not directly tied to the needs and problems of today". The outcome of this exclusion is the neutralisation of the students. They are "rendered safe, ineffective, socially and politically ineffective". At the end of a specified time they can be reincluded and reabsorbed.

So for Foucault and after Vincennes the university was still problematic as students were cut off from the proletarian change that Foucault saw as still happening. Foucault later saw that the problem for the left had been that they had not been able to articulate an appropriate theory of governance and this would have had to have included an appropriate pedagogy. Though he had planned to work on this and associated problems with Pierre Bourdieu this was not to eventuate.

If Jean Françoise Lyotard had thought the issue of pedagogy through in ways in which Foucault had not appeared to (Marshall,1995c), he had also seen that the student movement would gradually disappear. Writing in 1968 of the events of May-June he said: "whatever we may be able to do here can and will be recuperated by the powers that be, until society as a whole is reconstructed differently" (Lyotard,1968, p. 44).

We are presented then with a series of contradictions in Foucault's approach to education. On the one hand there is the normalising thrust of much of what goes on in universities. Yet he worked in them for the university was a sort of protection.

> I have always been fascinated by living protected in a scholarly environment, in an intellectual milieu. Knowledge is for me that which must function as a protection of individual existence.... (Foucault,1983c, p. 7)

He complained of the inadequacies of the curriculum - being outdated, academic, not meeting needs and interests - yet his contributions to the implementation commission emphasised the importance of the disciplines. Whilst in general he went along with the technocratic thrust of Fouchet's reforms yet he clearly saw the dangers for the left in cutting students off, particularly lower middle class students, from "their real milieu, that is, one which is undergoing a proletarian revolution" (Foucault,1971c, p. 57).

But a major inconsistency must be the incompatibility of his teaching practices, outlined above, with that to which he had objected. Teaching was not erotic, rather it was manipulative and normalising; it transmitted knowledge which was obsolete and academic. Yet Foucault's own teaching seems to have been just that, and almost a banking form of pedagogy, though it was not doctrinally *directive*. He believed that there was knowledge to be transmitted and that he Foucault should serve as an academic model on knowledge and its justification (though he never sought to have disciples). There seemed to be little dialogue with students and he certainly became impatient with the students at Vincennes who desired different forms of pedagogy. Foucault was certainly not into replacing lecturers with students (and nor was Lyotard).

On his own terms it is his practices that he should be judged upon. It is the practices of people in disciplinary blocks that he investigates in detail and similarly it is his own teaching practices that matter and not what he said about the exclusionary nature of the university; for example, that like the insane, students were excluded from normal society on campuses whilst an obsolete academic knowledge, not directed to the problems of the day, was transmitted to them (Foucault, 1971c, p. 65).

Educationalists on Foucault - the Moderns

In this section we will look at some attempts by educationalists to comment upon and use the work of Foucault. I use the term "modern" because I see these authors as working within modern approaches to methodology, as opposed to post-modern (see further in the next chapter for a discussion of the modernity/post modernity debate). It will include those who see genealogy as a viable method for approaching schooling because, as I will argue in the next chapter, I do not see Foucault as falling into the post-modern camp.

Educationalists who are interested in questions of social control and the exercise of power make reference to Foucault. With the exception of a chapter in a book by Madan Sarap (1982), these are generally passing references to his analysis of "power". There are, however, some major exceptions. Valerie Walkerdine in Henriques et.al. (1984), where there is an exploration of the ways in which psychology is involved in constructions of the individual and society, examines the work of Jean Piaget in the section devoted to the effects of psychological practices in the social regulation of practices and the construction of notions of the individual. She adopts a Foucault type approach to argue that the developmental psychology of Piaget, insofar as it has been inserted into a child-centred pedagogy, has not had any hoped for liberating effect. Instead, it has become part of a set of scientifically legitimated practices, the *object* of which is the developing child. She argues that such practices, through surveillance, observation and classification, *normalise* children but that developmental psychology does not seem to acknowledge or even understand the point that the developing child is an "object" produced by those very same practices (see also Walkerdine 1986).

Walkerdine's major interest seems to be the notion of the developing child and the ways in which psychology has produced this "subject" as its object for scientific investigation, rather than some other object and, thereby, prohibited other formulations of the individual/social dualism. Her approach is to concentrate upon Foucault as archaeologist looking for a set of socio-historical conditions which have permitted this "subject" to become an object of scientific investigation. But Foucault is to shift his ground in his later work away from epistemes and archaeology per se, towards bio-power, and how this produces "subjects" of certain kinds. Though he was to concentrate upon modern forms of sexuality his concern was more with how these were produced by modern forms of power. The developing child was not his concern as such, nor were the "truths" of psychology. For Walkerdine the subject of the developing child reveals a *particular* set of parameters along which individuals are normalised. Thus Walkerdine would be compatible with Foucault in that she has "correctly" seen that the notion of the developing child is not necessarily liberating. Yet her project, challenging the reduction of problems to formulations in terms of "the child's acquisition of ...." and "the development of ....", seems to be seen by her as a prerequisite to the reconstruction of a new "liberating" psychological subject. Foucault was not interested in the *truth* of such matters within the human sciences, but with the conditions that permit such "truths" to emerge. Nor would he necessarily have seen any such reconstruction of a psychology subject as liberating.

Jones and Williamson (1979) also adopt an archaeological approach to determine the discursive conditions which made possible the emergence of types of statement on mass popular education and pedagogic practices in the nineteenth century. As they freely admit, they concentrate upon "writings of the nineteenth century" and the relations which occur between these writings. Whilst their conclusion - that schooling cannot be reduced to notions of social control and socialisation but, rather, should be seen in terms of the extension of forms of modern power or the securing of governance - is certainly very compatible with

Foucault. But their approach is, perhaps, rather narrow, concentrating as it does upon discourse as statements (a position which Foucault, if he ever held, was to abandon for discourse in a wider sense to include practices). Foucault insisted also that the site for analysis must be the present. Jones and Williamson's "present" is in the nineteenth century.

Hoskin's interests in relation to Foucault have concentrated on the examination. In Hoskin (1979) examinations are interpreted as essentially normalisation procedures. The examination is an important part of school ritual and for Foucault an essential aspect of the exercise of power. Hoskin concentrates on the written statement, but Foucault's later comments on power relations would direct attention to much wider notions of practices and methodology.

In his (1990) contribution to Ball we are, however, presented with a much more interesting and challenging thesis. There he argues that Foucault is a crypto-educationalist, subtitling his chapter, "the crypto-educationalist unmasked". No doubt this is a pun on Foucault as the masked philosopher in his *Le Monde* interview (Foucault, 1980b). According to Hoskin, what Foucault:

> was doing all the time, was an educational analysis, whether he thought he was talking about power or knowledge. (1990, p. 29)

What Hoskin does is to try to turn Foucault's approach to the familiar, of making it very unfamiliar - eruptions from nowhere as the historian Paul Veyne called it - back upon itself, that is, to take Foucault's unfamiliar *discipline*, and make it more familiar as essentially *education*.

Hoskin argues, in relation to the examination, that Foucault is wrong in claiming that the examination is an invention of modernity, "confusing the invention of formal academic examination with the invention of *modern* formal academic examination" (op.cit.,46: this author's underlining). The point here is that there was an earlier form of oral examination, essentially qualitative and holistic, dating back to the twelfth century, and this was replaced by the modern examination as we know it - written, quantitative and arithmetical (not to forget norm referenced). The changes involve changes in form, content, and technology. Here Hoskin must be correct.

However he goes on to argue that, in relation to power/knowledge, power is not knowledge, and knowledge not power. Therefore, if we are to get behind what might merely be a pun on language (Walzer (1986) raises this possibility), then we have to get some purchase on the hyphen or slash between the two in Foucault's writing (see chapter four). What is needed is a third term to mediate and, Hoskin argues, this must be an educational term. He concludes:

> the operation of power-knowledge demands a third term: it operates perhaps via examination, or inquisitor, or disciplina, or paidea; ... can that third term be other than an educational term? (op.cit., 52)

In a sense Hoskin is correct: but in a major sense he is wrong. For his argument to go through he assumes "the centrality of education in the construction of modernity". This central thesis, "something very simple", was really discovered by Foucault, according to Hoskin. Second, for the thesis to go through, "education" must be interpreted in its widest sense. But in relation to the examination Hoskin correctly points out that Foucault is talking about the modern formal examination: equally he is talking about modern formal education, or compulsory mass schooling.

In relation to the first point it should be noted that Foucault does not see education as being central - the main contributing cause or vehicle for the emergence of modernity - though he does concede that it bears some responsibility (Foucault, 1969, p. 25).

In relation to the second point, Hoskin's thesis holds in relation to modern compulsory mass schooling. Foucault did not have much time for that form of education. For him "real" education could not take place in a disciplinary block where the underlying strategy is the production of normalised and individualised subjects. It would have to be detached from the power/knowledge nexus if genuinely free individuals were to be the outcome. So not any old educational term could go along with power/knowledge and the ones that seem to are those that already have a directional, authoritative, or power loaded connotation. So Hoskin does not convert the unfamiliar to the familiar, but leaves us in Foucault's unfamiliar world of power/knowledge and discipline. But, this implies that instead of liberating, we are dominating; instead of producing free individuals, we are producing *subjected* individualised people. It is important to note that for Foucault this was not necessary; it did not reflect anything other than our existing socio-historical position - the present.

There are further interesting papers in the Ball (1990) collection. These attempt to adopt and use genealogical method on educational issues.

The Post Moderns

In this section we will look at how Foucault has been interpreted in some of the modern/post-modern debates on education. It will be argued in chapter six that Foucault should not be interpreted as a post-modernist, and that therefore he should not be appealed to by those extolling the importance of post-modernist thinking for education.

Beyer and Liston in critiquing the inflated educational claims made on behalf of post-modernism concede that it has:

> helped alert us to the realities and consequences of marginalising voices of "others", to the tendency for a technical, western rationality to become hegemonic and oppressive and the need to become sensitive to the particular and the local. (1992, p. 393)

But, they continue:

> the problems we have identified - especially those regarding the loss of general principles and values that can affect and be affected by the particular and the local, the tendencies towards aestheticism and textualism that embroil us in languages that overlook praxis, the conflation of veracity and power and the denial of community in a reconstructed form - should make us wonder about the efficacy of postmodernism in dealing with the political and moral deliberations and actions that educators must undertake.

It cannot be said that postmodernism has *identified* the issues in the first quotation, for they surface in a variety of critiques of culture and methodology. As examples the voices of others and subjugated knowledges had surfaced in historical methodology and in the "new" social history, Weber had long ago alerted us to the dangers of technocratic rationality, and the need to pay attention to the local and the particular has been evidenced in the use of case studies. If these are the major important issues which postmodernists have helped us to understand then there can be no great claim to originality in identifying the issues.

But the authors' point is that even if this were the case postmodernism has serious defects because it cannot deliver and "provide support for the type of political project that educational transformation must be" (loc.cit.). Foucault has certainly contributed to the areas of which the authors approve and, by implication, they classify him as a postmodernist, but what did he say in relation to these alleged defects attributed to post-modernism?

On the first point it is claimed that for postmodernists there "is no 'grand scheme' of the natural or social world" and "reason cannot deliver universal and valid claims about any alleged reality" (op.cit., p. 374). This is not the case for Foucault in the natural sciences, as he made no such claims for the natural sciences. His approach to the natural sciences was essentially derived from Bachelard and Canguilhelm (see above), and he denied claims that he was attacking the natural sciences by pointing out that he had made no analyses of the natural sciences. On truth he was to say: "all those who say that for me the truth doesn't exist are simple-minded" (Foucault,1984e, p. 295).

In the human sciences, if he sees grand totalitarian theories as useful tools for doing local and particular research, the attempt to think in terms of a totality is said to be a hindrance (Foucault,1977a, p. 80f.). In other words marxism and Freudian psychoanalytic theory can throw up problems and issues but they may be on no help in attempting to resolve the particularity of local issues. Foucault also acknowledged that modern history (e.g., Braudel, the Cambridge School), of which he talked approvingly (Foucault, 1967, p. 13) used analyses from other human sciences.

Foucault certainly talked about the terrorism of grand totalising theory in the hands of philosophers such as Jean Paul Sartre: "philosophy from Hegel to Sartre has essentially been a totalising enterprise" (Foucault,1968, p. 38). Instead it should be seen as "a diagnostic activity" but not one that involves a special meta-language (Foucault,1973b, p. 74).

The authors continue that Foucault like postmodernists is not committed to such things as political revolutions and social transformations because instead he is committed to research into subjugated knowledges that combine erudite knowledge and local memories. He thus seems to be committed to the local level of action. Again if this is true about some postmodernists Foucault does not easily fit the cast. Foucault was un homme de gauche, he was committed to some form of proletarian revolution, he was committed to some form of the welfare state, and he was committed to a form of individualism (though not the neo-liberalism of a Hayek). In the 1960's he was committed to the reform of higher education, and he was committed to knowledge, institutions of learning and the life of scholarship which, itself, provided a defence against oppression and the illusions of progress through the progress of the human sciences. For Foucault local knowledge and subjugated knowledges are important because they show how totalising grand theory pushes aside the complexities and the difficulties inherent in any event. *I Pierre Rivière* (Foucault, 1975a) illustrates this point excellently, as a detailed examination of the discourses revealed shows the very problematic nature of the insertion of psychiatry into the French legal system. How could that important social transformation be discussed even, from a theory post facto of what psychiatry is. But what the book does, with its emphasis on a local incident and subjugated knowledges such as Pierre's own story, is to show how psychiatry itself emerged into the social and established its niche in the medical and legal world. As for psychiatry so for disciplinary punishment in *Discipline and Punish.* If postmodern educators advocate the primacy of the local and draw too sharp a distinction between the local and the more distant that was not what Foucault did in practice. Nor was he merely a scholar as his history of political action makes clear (see details in the biographies of Eribon, Macey and Miller).

It is of course correct that Foucault's political demonstrations were in the main local and particular. But that was consistent with his account of power and resistance. From 1970 he was a very public figure often leading demonstrations physically with his body. But whilst these demonstrations were local and particularised they were against something distant, but *exemplified* in the incidents - racism, the struggles in Palestine and Iran, the plight of prisoners....

If post-modernism in addressing educational reform suffers from these defects it is not clear that Foucault's position suffers from the same defects. It is another matter however as to whether his work can address educational reform.

An example of post-modernist and, it is claimed, Foucauldean critique of education is provided by Kiziltan et. al. (1990). They claim to adopt a Foucauldean perspective to launch an attack upon public education which, conceived as "a discursive formation which functions semi-autonomously to construct its own 'regime of truth' ", has been fractured and dislocated by the challenge of post-modernism (1990, p. 356). For them public education is an ordered ensemblage of educational knowledge, statements and practices crossed by a variety of discourses such as psychology, philosophy. legal, economic and the scientific. Public education is a "space" of intersecting and competing discourses in which regimes of truth are not uncontested. But, according to the authors, post-modernism provides an exceptional undermining of public education because it undercuts the traditional meta-narratives which both justify and contest its regimes of truth. The post-modern condition:

> points to the emergence of a new (dis)order, no longer bound to or legitimated by the systematic set of relations organised by the metanarratives of modernity. (Kiziltan, et al, 1990, p. 359)

The authors note that the postmodern turn is marked with respect "to the grounding of (social) sciences" by an outright rejection of the possibility of validating scientific method and knowledge on independent, a-historical gender-and race-free grounds'. This rests upon Foucault's idea "that all knowledge is traversed by forms of power which cannot be eliminated from the act of knowing" (op.cit., p. 353).

Building upon Lyotard's account of the post-modern condition and Foucault's response to Kant's 'What is Enlightenment?' the authors then proceed to develop an approach to public education based upon the limit attitude which can engender the form, the boundaries, the content and the direction of a new public education. The limit attitude is said to be reflexive and transgressive, stressing dissimilarity, constant decentering, endless deferral, recurring doubt, and the multiplicity of the self, knowledge and the world. It involves the motto: "Dare to transgress".

Lyotard and Foucault should not be run together even though they both objected to grand legitimating meta-narratives (see Marshall, 1995c). But in Foucault's case it is not clear that he rejects all of the grand meta-narratives. Whilst he launched an attack upon reason in general (Foucault,1961) this was later quietly abandoned. Nor does he appear to treat the natural sciences as penetrated by power/knowledge in the same way as the human sciences. Indeed Gutting (1989) makes this point quite strongly. Part of Foucault's critique of the human sciences is that they masquerade as sciences and are not seen as heavily infiltrated by power. They are not like physics or geology because they have Man and, Foucault claims at some length, Man is not a genuine object to talk about. On the other hand it appears that the natural sciences do have something to talk about. Foucault's work then does not provide sufficient grounds to mount a total attack upon public education as, according to the authors, is provided by post-modernism. The motto, "Dare to transgress", would appear therefore to have some limitations in the case of Foucault. Foucault does not provide licence therefore for the destabilisation of all of the metanarratives of modernity which have long sustained public education, as the authors seem to claim. Indeed as we have seen above from his own practices he sustained some of those meta-narratives.

But what Foucault does offer to teachers has been well caught by Pignatelli (1993a,b). This is to do, first, with freedom and teacher agency for Foucault provides opportunities for openings to escape the grasp of categories, objectifications and treatments which affect the teacher/student relationship. Thus it is possible to redefine one's own role as a teacher and provide space and support for one's students, one's colleagues and oneself. And this cannot be done without an understanding of Foucault's critique of the human sciences and an understanding of governmentality.

Second, it provides space for oneself, for freedom becomes a practised attitude towards life, refusing to internalise "fabricated subject categories one learns and is led to rely upon to make sense of one's experiences" (Pignatelli,1993b, p. 385). Rajchman's (1985) reading of Foucault is that essentially he addresses questions of freedom. It is not a question of determining who we really are but of raising questions about whom we might become, not merely in our thinking, but in our lives. But how this can be translated out for human beings in technocratic education systems designed to produce "autonomous choosers" is far from clear.

Unfortunately, on freedom, if Foucault addresses *educationally* the already well educated, it is not so clear that he addresses less fortunate oppressed groups.

In summary then, we can see a number of inconsistencies in Foucault, in both what he said and did, in regards to education. Dissatisfied with his own education and urging reforms, especially in higher education he, at the same time, can be seen as supportive of the traditional disciplines (excluding the human sciences) and of philosophy. Sympathetic to students in 1968 and committed as a man of the left to some form of proletarian revolution he seemed unable to realise that his position as a teacher was itself problematised as he continued as a classical academic.

Educationalists are beginning to look at Foucault's work. However, he cannot be used in general but rather his insights should be used either to problematise certain givens - such as the pursuit of personal autonomy - or in more particular genealogical studies.

CHAPTER 6

PERSONAL AUTONOMY REVISITED

Introduction

In chapter three we looked at the notion of personal autonomy and how from Foucault's perspective the notion of an independent autos "adopting" a nomos was difficult to maintain, or make sense of, because the autos was always contaminated by the nomos. It was argued that technologies of domination and technologies of the self were such as to construct an autos "predisposed" to accept a certain type of nomos, and a type which can lead to subjection and domination.

In chapter four we looked more fully at Foucault's account of power/knowledge and how this posed considerable problems for the liberal account of education in which power is not seen as an integral part of educational processes and activities.

In this chapter, we will look again at Man - the subject and object of knowledge of the human sciences - and at the very notion of personal identity which was left implicit in chapter four. In the rejection of Man we will look at where Foucault stood in the modernity/post-modernity "debate". Finally a post-Foucault critique of neo-liberal education, in so far as it concerns the notions of the individual will be developed. First, we will look in more detail at his attack upon Man.

Foucault's Critique of Man

Foucault wrote an introduction to the 1962 edition by the French publishing firm Colin of Rousseau's, *Rousseau Juge de Jean-Jacques*, in which he comments on Rousseau's creation of the Romantic self, and his subsequent annihilation of that self. According to Foucault, and here I rely upon Gutman (1988), this self is a "pattern that is unified and at the same time unique", but it has to be dissolved because it is a "dissociated subject, superimposed on himself (sic.), a lacuna whom one can only call present by a sort of addition never achieved: as if he appears at a distinct vanishing point which only a certain convergence allows the reader to ascertain" (translation by Huck Gutman, 1988:119).

According to Gutman's (1988) account, Foucault sees Rousseau as writing *in the language* of an early version of the self, not yet invested with modern power relations. What had for so long lain below the threshold of description - ordinary individuality - had surfaced with Rousseau, though later in the disciplines it is to take a sinister turn. In order for there to be subjects, the speaking subject had first to be objectified in language. This is Rousseau's "contribution". If the writing of real lives had until then been essentially associated with important individuals as heroes, Rousseau introduces as objects of description, the real lives of ordinary individuals. Rousseau is hardly an ordinary individual or "bloke", but what he tried to portray in his "own story" was a *real* individual life. He is, perhaps, the first person to insist upon his own unique singularity. This was done initially in *The Confessions of Jean-Jacques Rousseau* (1765) and later he critiqued his views and altered them in *Rousseau Juge de Jean-Jacques* (1771) and *Reveries* (1776-8).

First, Rousseau employs a concept of difference. He sees very clearly that for a subject, a self, or a "me" to emerge, then a boundary must be drawn between the self and all that is not the self; between self and not-self; between me and not-me. It is a harsh employment of this concept of difference, that in splitting the self off from the rest of the world, it produced a self that was a subject of knowledge and examination. Rousseau, though he extolled the importance of reason, also extolled the importance of emotions, as underlying our relations with others. Therefore, in dividing himself off from the "outside" or "exterior" world, he will be able to explore all of his experiences, and the limits or boundaries of his consciousness. And it is these experiences that are to be found in this consciousness, that made him unique. The Romantic self then is one who recounts the "history" of the self, but creates itself in the very writing of the "real" self, and in so doing, affirms that very creation.

But, for Rousseau, the self which he has created in the *Confessions*, becomes an object to be examined in *Rousseau Juge de Jean-Jacques*. Creating the self as a subject has been through the objectification of language in writing, to create an object of knowledge which becomes in turn an object of inquisition. But to realise that it is an object of enquiry is for the self to also recognise that it has its own subjectivity. But this recognition produces for Rousseau a form of paranoia, for the cost of difference for Rousseau has been to realise that the other, what he has divided off in a harsh application of binary "yes/no" logic, is alien and inhospitable. The cost of subjectivity was then for Rousseau high: in fact, personally too high, as the satisfaction of individuality brought with it deprivation, alienation, and isolation. In Rousseau's case it certainly did not bring happiness.

For Rousseau the solution in *The Reveries* (1782: written in 1776-78 and published posthumously) is to abandon the concept of difference. He attempts to undo the boundary which he had drawn between the self and not-self; between me and not-me. This was to be done by abandoning himself to the imaginary; by so doing the self, itself the result of the imagination, is annihilated, and the boundaries between self and not self, me and not-me, and the self and society, are blurred, smudged and, therefore potentially capable of being redrawn. Rousseau aspired to a merged and undifferentiated unity with the other.

Therefore, even if Rousseau made possible the ordinary person as both subject and object, and provided the way in for Man as both subject and object of knowledge, he also provides a way out. This is to show how division, through a relentless application of two dimensional logic and the concept of difference, gives rise to counter forces of difference and repugnance, as the promise of happiness, for Rousseau, is not fulfilled. The creation of a self is, itself, the creation of a counter force that leads to the destruction of the self. This is a very important point for Foucault because it follows for him that the identification of the self with "inner" consciousness which underlies Man is internally incoherent and destructive.

But how did Man replace the Romantic self. The account Foucault gives here is to be found in *The Order of Things* (an excellent exposition of which is to be found in Dreyfus and Rabinow), and to a lesser extent in *The Archaeology of Knowledge*.

According to Foucault at the end of the eighteenth century there was a dramatic epistemic shift away from what he calls language as representation. This heralded the end of the Classical Age and the birth of modernity, according to Foucault. This can be seen as a massive rewriting of the history of philosophy, and a rewriting which, because it implies that there was no philosophy as we now know it prior to the nineteenth century, may not be acceptable to many philosophers. Foucault's claim is that philosophy as we now know it, defined by central problems of epistemology, ontology and meaning, did not exist prior to the nineteenth century. In these earlier times, he claims, philosophy operated at the same level as knowledge of life, labour and language, and could only emerge as we now know it, to ask questions about knowledge, ontology, and meaning, when the "sciences" of life, labour and language, or biology, economics and philology, emerged, or took off. These two major claims need siting in Foucault's work.

Foucault's earlier works, *Madness and Civilisation* and *Birth of the Clinic* are, in one sense, concerned with social institutions. The former opens up the area of the dependence of discursive practices upon social institutions which he is to pursue in later writings, for example, *Discipline and Punish*. The latter emphasises archaeological notions of how epistemes permit the possibility of discursive formations. What is important here is the extension of his interests in the human sciences in *The Order of Things*.

The critical point for Foucault in the emergence of the human sciences is the eclipse of what he calls the Classical episteme. By "episteme" he means:

> the total set of relations that unite, at a given period, the discursive practices that give rise to epistemological figures, sciences, and possibly formalised systems..... The episteme is not a form of knowledge (connaissance) or type of rationality which, crossing the boundaries of the most varied sciences, manifests sovereign unity of a subject, a spirit, or a period; it is the totality of relations that can be discovered, for a given period, between the sciences when one analyses them at the level of discursive regularities. (Foucault, 1972b, p. 191)

The shift in episteme is from what he calls the Classical Age to Modernity, or for Foucault, to the Age of Man. For Foucault, Man is not merely the locus of the human sciences but the very condition of their possibility. According to Foucault, Man, in this special sense of being both total subject of knowledge and object of his own knowledge, did not exist in the Classical Age. It is clear when he invites us to consider that Man is dead, that he sees this "invention" of Man, initially by Descartes but especially by Kant, as a retrograde step in Western thought. Man was meant to have brought freedom and emancipation, but it brings with it certain incoherencies and destructive tendencies which he certainly believed had outcomes that strapped and enslaved us.

What prevented the existence of Man in the Classical Age? Foucault's account now turns to theories of meaning and what he calls the notion of representation. He argues that the Classical Age's episteme can be characterised by a universal method of analysis which was purported to yield perfect certainty by perfectly ordering representations and signs to mirror the order of being, or reality, in the world. The role of the thinker/philosopher in the Classical Age, in his view, was to clarify the order of the world, by clarifying and ordering the signs of discourse so that there was an accurate representation of the order of the God-given order of the world. Discourse then is seen as rather like a chart or map (Cousins and Hussain, 1984).

Charts both signify and analyze a reality: in the representation of reality they both signify the elements of reality and present an analysis of the ordering of reality. Soundings are signified and both soundings and headlands are presented so as to show how the world - land and sea - is ordered. What can we question about the chart? Well we can question its accuracy, as to whether that sounding is correct, and in the correct position, but what we cannot question is charting itself as being a representation of reality. Questions about accuracy of particular soundings and the ordering of soundings presuppose the validity of charting. The general question of the validity of charting is not itself a question that can occur *in the chart*, or *on the chart* (see further, Cousins and Hussain,1984).

Chart talk is of course an analogy of Foucault's very detailed analysis of Velazquez's painting, *Les Meninas*, in *The Order of Things*. This analysis is meant to show us that if various functions of representation can be represented, the very activity of representation cannot, itself, be represented. As with the chart example, where the principles of charting cannot themselves be represented - only the nomenclature and translation of signs - so in *Les Meninas* all that can be done is that the spectator, the person looking at the painting can at best be caught in the obscure mirror in the very "back" of the scene painted in *Les Meninas*. Foucault's interpretation is that Man, the subject and object of the painting could not be in the painting. That was the problematic that represents the move from the Classical Age to modernity.

According to Foucault representation was not a problem until God was dead, and Kant awoke from his slumbers. As God had arranged an order, and arranged language in a corresponding pre-established harmony of correspondence with the order, the questioning of representation was neither necessary, nor perhaps, even possible. Language and reality are ordered and correspond - the problem was to get the orders right.

In the Classical Age human being was simply one more kind of being whose nature could be read off from its proper definition. There was no need for a finite being to make representation possible: the person for whom that representation existed was not part of that representation.

Man is the being who gets the whole picture but also gets into the picture. Man now becomes a subject amongst objects. But Man is not just trying to know about objects but to know about one's self as subject. Man has become both subject and object of his or her own understanding, becoming totally involved with the objects which are wished to be known.

Representation disappears as the sciences of life, labour and language search for the very conditions of possibility of such things as living being, exchange, profit, production, discourse and language (Foucault,1973a, p. 312). This establishes new relationships between words, things and their order, in which representation ceased to play any part. In Velazquez's painting what cannot be shown was the activity of representing and what made it possible. What Velazquez can show is the way that representation works but not what makes it possible. And this is to make representation unstable and eventually to wither away. The appearance of Man as the measure of all things changes the order of the world away from a God given order in which representation could work. Man is no longer just a being amongst others but a subject amongst objects. The field of light of representation clouds over and language becomes opaque and dense. As Man is no longer a pure spectator but a subject of knowledge and the old order has crumbled, questions about the very possibility of knowledge arise. What Man learns is that there are finitudes, that knowledge is exterior to Man, that life is finite, and that history, life, and languages impose limitations.

These limitations are seized upon by Kant and turned to advantage. Foucault expresses this point as follows:

> the limitation is expressed not as a determination imposed upon Man from outside (because he has a nature of a history), but as a fundamental finitude which rests on nothing but its own existence as fact, and opens up the positivity of all concrete limitation. (ibid., p. 315)

Kant takes this notion of finitude positively and makes it the basis of all factual knowledge.

The appearance of Man as the subject of knowledge and an object of knowledge, as the one who is to impose order, makes representation problematic. What has to be shown is under what conditions "representation" is possible and legitimate. Post-Kant, Foucault claims, we find the notion of an *analytic*. This is the attempt to show the possibilities and legitimate extent of representation: "The precritical analysis of what Man is in his essence becomes the analytic of everything that can, in general, be presented to Man's experience" (ibid., p. 341).

The limitations and finitudes are no longer viewed as imposed *upon* Man but imposed *by* Man. This was Kant's insight. This means that Man claims total knowledge not in spite of his limitations but *because* of his limitations. In Foucault's words:

> The modern themes of an individual who lives, speaks, and works in accordance with the laws of an economics, a philology, and a biology, but who also, by a sort of internal torsion and overlapping, has acquired the right, through the very interplay of these very laws, to know them and to subject them to total clarification - all these themes so familiar to us today and linked to the existence of the "human sciences" are excluded by classical thought: it was not possible at that time that there should arise, on the boundary of the world, the strange stature of a being whose nature (that which determines it, contains it, and has traversed it from the beginning of time) is to know nature, and itself, in consequence, as a natural being. (ibid., p. 310)

For Foucault modernity begins with this conception of Man. But in Foucault's eyes it is an enslaved human being. If Man replaces God it is as a "God" bounded by limitations of finitude, trapped in the very conditions that permit its very possibility. This analytic which Foucault attributes to Kant, is called by him the "analytic of finitude". It is an analytic in which, in a series of desperate moves, all that human beings recognise as infinite is made by Man *finite*. Herein lies the crux of Foucault's objections to Man and the human sciences.

The tortured transformations which are made by Man in the human sciences fall into three groupings according to Foucault. They all revolve around the ways in which what he calls the positivities (the limits, or finitudes) are both distinguished from, but equated with, the very conditions that make knowledge possible, or to put it another way, knowledge of Man is contaminated by the conditions that make that knowledge possible, and vice versa. He calls these the doubles of the transcendental/empirical, the cogito/unthought and the retreat/return of the origin. Thus Man appears as a fact among other facts and open to empirical observation and theorising, yet at the same time as the transcendental condition of the possibility of that knowledge, and indeed all knowledge. Second, Man attempts to be rational, to define rationality, intelligence and sanity, yet Man is everywhere surrounded by the unthought, the irrational, and the insane. Finally Man appears as a source of a very long history but it is a history the origin of which can never be attained.

If I understand Foucault correctly he is saying that the human sciences will always involve this messiness, that Man will always have a messy involvement in any such knowledge, that every attempt to posit a version of Man will involve a difference and identity between Man as subject, or condition of knowledge, and Man as object, or the content of knowledge. There is a trick or sleight or hand in the creation of Man. According to Foucault this double has spawned the attempts of Kant to rescue a pure form of knowledge; of giving a firm foundation to the empirical by basing it upon our senses, or other forms of human nature (including Merleau-Ponty's interesting attempt to develop an existential phenomenology of the body); and, finally, the linking of the transcendental to the historical.

Each of these attempts, he believes, involves a belief in a true, neutral discourse but Foucault believes that the status of any such discourse is far from clear. He does not believe that there is any way to overcome this transcendental/empirical double.

The second double is concerned to highlight the puzzlement between Man's being, his existence, and his thought about his existence. Foucault raises the question:

> The question is no longer: How can experience of nature give rise to necessary judgements? But rather: How can Man think what he does not think, inhabit as though by a mute occupation something that eludes him, animate with kind of frozen movement that figure of himself that takes the form of a stubborn exteriority? How can Man *be* that life whose web, pulsations, and buried energy constantly exceed the experience that he is immediately given of them? How can he be that labour whose laws and demands are imposed upon him like some alien system? How can he be the subject of a language that for thousands of years has formed within him, a language whose organisations escaped him, whose meaning sleeps an almost invincible sleep in the words he momentarily activates by means of discourse, and within which he is obliged from the very outset, to lodge his speech and thought, as though they were doing no more than animate, for a brief period, one segment of that web of innumerable possibilities. (1973a, p. 323)

The human sciences in the finitudes posit limits to our thought through a language that Man cannot master, in an organism and desires that he cannot master either. The problem is that Man wants to know itself as object but if so how is the unthought to be made intelligible? Man in his very quest for knowledge has made it impossible to think the unthought.

This is very important for Foucault for he was always attempting to transgress the limits of thought, rationality and experience. This has been seen already in the notions of difference and the other, his attacks upon Descartes, his introduction to Binswanger's work on dreams, his attacks upon exclusionary dividing practices and the suppression of knowledge. He believes then that at the very heart of the human sciences, the concept Man restricts and controls thought at the very time when it is trying to think the unthought. For this reason there is an inherent internal contradiction.

The final double is that of the retreat and return of the origin. The double arises as in the cases of the other two doubles, with the breakdown of the Classical Age's theory of representation. With the breakdown of representation genuine historical questions can be asked about the origins or beginnings of language. But the origins of language, and human beings, retreat into the past, *infinitely*, as these questions are pursued.

The problem as Foucault presents it, is that Man is already in the world. He uses language but cannot get behind it to give an account of its origins and how it works. Language is already a kind of practical knowledge which will interfere with any attempt to find the origins. Language is too "close" to permit historical understanding of its origins: they retreat indefinitely.

It is now time to retrace ourselves to chapter three and the notion of the autonomous person. There it was argued that the autos/nomos distinction was very difficult to maintain. But if one were to maintain that the autonomous person was one of the variants of Man, that being autonomous was to exhibit one's human nature, then these arguments in this chapter begin to bite hard. Suppose we take a position on Man that it is part of human nature to be autonomous and that we now attempt to find out what sort of being this being, *is*. What kinds of answers might we turn up?

One well known answer is that given by Piaget and later in a more advanced and complex form by Kohlberg. Here personal autonomy is associated both with morality and rationality. To be autonomous is to act morally and to act morally is to act rationally. What is claimed is that there are various stages of moral thinking and that children develop from heteronomous to autonomous stages in moral thinking. There is a *development* of the morally autonomous person. This is perhaps not the place to object that both Piaget and Kohlberg have ignored the other aspect in the Enlightenment tradition that morality is linked with the emotions, as in Rousseau and Hume, and is not just reducible to rationality. But it is the place first to develop a critique of how personal autonomy develops.

This can be argued by following Walkerdine's (1984) critique of the notion of the developing child. If a certain version of Man is presupposed as an educational outcome of a set of educational experiences then don't be surprised if the presupposed version of Man is the outcome. Children are exposed in Kohlberg's research to a series of incidents in which their ability to engage in moral reasoning is increasingly explored. Certain stages from heteronomy to autonomy in the moral reasoning of the child are identified and it is claimed that moral reasoning is developmental through six stages. But the autonomous person is not the 'natural' outcome of any unfolding development of human nature. Instead this version of Man was presupposed in the very construction of the research. Carol Gilligan (1982) has objected that girls do not reason in the same way in increasing levels of generality and universality of moral principles. Rather, she claims, they start in more Humean or Rousseauean fashion with the relationships between individuals as governing moral decision making, rather than abstract principles.

But, also, from the preceding discussions of Foucault's Man we can now see that the morally autonomous person, knowledge of whom is to be found in Kohlberg's research on the development of empirical stages, sets a finitude upon morality. For Foucault morality is to do with the exercise of liberty not through the imposition of finite forms of control derived from knowledge about oneself and the laws that one adopts "autonomously", but by *caring* for oneself. To impose a fiction of universal laws upon oneself is to impose a finitude which made one unfree. It made one unfree in that it not only imposed limits upon thought and action but it also imposed limits upon one's identity. Instead one had to transgress these limited and finite situations.

Foucault argued that the discourses of personal autonomy prevented a new form of ethics from emerging. What was unthought had to be thought by thinking differently and not finitely. There were new, unthought things, experiences and pleasures which could not be perceived or conceptualised, that needed to enter the arena of thought concerned with caring for oneself through an appropriate exercise of liberty.

If Man marks the rise of modernity for Foucault, and as he clearly rejected Man, is he also rejecting modernity?: is he a post-modernist? We will now turn to this issue, but first some comments on the notion of Enlightenment.

Enlightenment

In what sense was the Enlightenment meant to be productive of liberating thought and new forms of political and social life? The short answer is that the Enlightenment stood for many things and many different and often opposed thinkers are associated with it. As one historian (Hampson,1968, p. 9) said: "the Enlightenment was what one thinks it was". It was certainly cosmopolitan and not merely French; and it was not merely rationalistic. It is tempting to think of it as being essentially French, and to see Voltaire, Rousseau, Diderot, Condillac and Condorcet - the philosophes - as the precursors of the Enlightenment in action - the French Revolution. But this is surely a very limited perspective or approach.

At the outset *difference* is written historically into the Enlightenment, even though it is perhaps common and in deference to Kant to see its central value as being that of rationality - in some cases scientistic rationality. And while this scientistic or positivist trend is a comparatively easy though very important target, it must not be forgotten that in opposition to this over rationalist emphasis, and in relation to morality, David Hume, Diderot and Rousseau argued for the primacy of the passions. If Kant was woken from his dogmatic slumbers by Hume, this was for him to emphasise eventually the importance of practical reason, as opposed to the passions. Hume and Kant then, two central, and non-French thinkers who are closely associated with the Enlightenment, hold almost diametrically opposed positions on a central value to be associated with it. Indeed one of the Enlightenment's virtues might be seen as its defence of difference.

If reason is seen as a central value, it should then be seen as but one among many values which include autonomy, freedom, equality, curiosity and scepticism. Politically there are the ideas of reform, citizenship and democracy. Giambattista Vico expressed the political dream of the Enlightenment when he said that what human beings have made human beings can understand, and what human beings can understand they can change. But if Cassirer, for example, is correct that the central figures of the Enlightenment are Kant, Goethe and Rousseau then it is clear that the identification of Enlightenment thought with Kant *and* the extension of rationality must be mistaken (Kant did argue for limits to knowledge). If Kant can be represented as urging autonomy, Goethe the limits of knowledge, and Rousseau as attacking the idea of progress, then we have a different view of the Enlightenment to that which is often presented, namely the progress of society and the liberation of human beings through the use of reason.

French warships have on their upper works the words, "liberté", "egalité" and "fraternité". These catchwords of the French Revolution formed in blood and war are also, apparently, to be defended or promoted by war. But the Revolution can be seen also as living out the contradictions of the Enlightenment. If it gave us the language of human rights and the political hopes of putting the Enlightenment into practice it gave us also the violence of the guillotine, pitting citizenship against individual rights, reason against passion, and coercion against autonomy. If the Revolution saw the inauguration of the welfare state through various forms of public assistance it saw also the emergence in practice of the police state, with political coercion and committees protecting individuals from themselves in the name of beneficence but in acts of governance.

The questions which have to be raised are: is the identification of the Enlightenment with rationality, and the identification of "reform" with the dark side, mentioned above, and encapsulated by Adorno and Horkheimer in *The Dialectic of Enlightenment* and in Foucault's notion of governmentality, the only interpretation of the Enlightenment? If the answer is no, and this is possibly Foucault's answer, then we can still work within the message of the Enlightenment for not only are there contradictory messages in the Enlightenment but there may be a way out, offered by the very notion of enlightenment. At least Foucault thought so (Foucault, 1984b), for he sees Kant as being the first philosopher to interrogate the present and that this continual interrogation of the present could provide a way out.

Foucault and Kant

Foucault does not accept the Enlightenment view of the improvement of human beings, particularly through the advancement of reason. For Kant this improvement was to be obtained through the critical use of reason in its universal applications. But, Foucault argues, this thesis has induced in us dogmatic slumbers (Foucault,1984b). What we have lost in Kant's message is an attitude; the attitude of maturity. Kant answers the question, "What is Enlightenment ?", by identifying Enlightenment with the attainment of maturity through the critical use of reason. Foucault agrees with Kant but disagrees upon the nature of reason, rejecting the form(s) that reason has taken. In particular there is no universal form that reason must take according to Foucault. Rather there are multiplicities of reason, and multiplicities of theories in relation to specific local issues. Yet, Foucault believes, Kant was correct in urging that theory must be critical. Where the post-Kantian slumbers were introduced, according to Foucault, was in the failure to address the socio-historical conditions in which Kant produced his own views on the critical use of theory. Slumber was caused by a failure to continually and critically question the application of universal reason to human dilemmas and to respond to changed socio-historical conditions.

Foucault (1984b) interprets Kant as being the first philosopher to interrogate the present. In his article, "What is Enlightenment?" (the title of which Foucault is later to borrow) Kant addresses those actual features of his period of existence which, transgressing history and tradition, designate a form of modernity where self awareness and norms must be created out of themselves. Kant's answer leads him to speculate about a state of freedom, world citizenship and eternal peace, because he interprets revolutionary practices and enthusiasm as a sign of historical progress towards betterment for mankind, especially through the unfolding of reason. Rather than reason unfolding, Foucault the archaeologist would tell us (1971a,1972b), arbitrary formations of discourse, especially those which he designates as the human sciences, have frozen Kant's notion of an unfolding freedom and we have become embroiled in a senseless dynamic of power which continues to dominate and subjugate us as human beings.

It is not the content of Kant's analysis then that Foucault praises but the form or spirit: it is not the search for conditions of truth and revolution that should be our concern but, rather, the need to continually re-evaluate the present, he argues. Kant's question marks for Foucault:

> the discreet entrance into the history of thought of a question that modern philosophy has not been able to answer, but that it has never managed to get rid of either. (1984b, p. 32)

According to Foucault Kant's speculations should not be seen as heralding a return to past traditions and forms of life, or as heralding a point of transition towards some evolving new era. On the contrary

Foucault reads Kant as providing us with a "way out".

The way out for Kant is the process of Enlightenment which by linking will to reason releases us from various forms of authority over us. To accept the authority of others in areas where the use of reason is called for is to be in a state of immaturity. The will to know through reason could lead us from such states of immaturity both individually and collectively, according to Kant.

It should be noted that for Kant this type of reason is not instrumental or technocratic reason, or just any type of reason but, instead, reason for reasoning's sake. If reason can be used instrumentally it can also be used in an unfettered and critical manner to argue freely about, for example, the means towards which instrumental reason is put. The political problem which Kant was trying to reconcile was how individuals could, at one and the same time, meet the demands of bureaucratic reason - to pay their taxes say - and yet exercise reason publicly. Given the times of Frederich II this was indeed an audacious challenge both to individuals and to authorities.

It is these challenges to know and to exercise reason publicly that Foucault sees as the spirit or form of the Enlightenment. Where this has gone wrong, Foucault seems to be saying, is that whereas the heirs of the Enlightenment present the content of Kant's questions they do not present the form or spirit, because they are prisoners of the content of Kant's questions. Because they proceed from the epistemological question concerning the conditions under which the use of reason is legitimate, they become captives of the analysis of truth, ignoring the possibility that their "will to knowledge" is deeply enmeshed in modern power formations. Foucault's analyses trace the unravellings of this will to knowledge, and locate them in modern power formations. They are denounced because they leave us in a state of immaturity - to use Kant's original term. If Foucault denounces the path that the heirs of the Enlightenment have taken, he sees Kant's question and the spirit of the critical impulse underlying the question as being both important and worthy of renewal. In spite of the claim that "the historical event of the Enlightenment did not make us mature adults" he still believes that Kant's critical attitude, conceived as *an attitude towards the present*, as an ethos or philosophical life can, through a form of critical-historical enquiry, establish the limits imposed upon us and, thereby, the possibilities for freedom. Central to this enquiry, he believed, was a critical ontology of ourselves.

Critical Theory

In commenting on these Enlightenment beliefs, hopes and aspirations Richard Bernstein has this to say:

> many of these beliefs that led to such high hopes and expectations in Enlightenment thinkers have turned sour. There seems to be a natural progression from early Enlightenment ideals to contemporary positivist and empiricist modes of thought. What were once great liberating ideas have turned into suffocating strait jackets. There is a hidden nihilism in the dialectic of this development which Anglo-Saxon thinkers have not often honestly confronted. The history of intellectual life during the past two hundred years has imposed ever more severe restrictions on what counts as genuine knowledge and on limits of rational argument. (1976, p. xxiii)

One way, after Habermas, of distinguishing modernity is as an achievement in human culture, as reaching processes of rationality which are essentially institutionalised in a society. It is this institutionalisation which makes possible the preservation and transmission of culture. Habermas believes that Weber's view of modernity as an iron cage was not merely pessimistic but mistaken. It was mistaken according to Habermas because Weber's concept of rationality was too narrow and encompassing. Whereas Weber was correct that rationality conceived as bureaucratic or technocratic rationality leads to the conclusion that the normative and affective areas of thought are "imperfect", by the standards of rationality so conceived, there is no need to be so restrictive or constrained.

Thinkers of the Enlightenment could not have foreseen the narrow identification of rationality with scientific reasoning and its subsequent usurpation by a narrow positivistic and technological "scientific" approach. It is this technological means/end form of rationality that has come to be taken for rationality in practice - indeed it is this notion of rationality which has come to be identified with Western capitalism.

It can be argued that technocratic rationality has come to permeate all forms of social and cultural life: it is just not in the control of the physical environment but in economic structure, in the law, in business management, increasingly in government structures and welfare agencies, and in education. The educational reform literature and practices of the Western capitalist world are structured by, and articulated within, forms of technocratic rationality. Weber's mistake was to see technocratic rationality as encompassing of all forms of rationality. Not surprisingly it is in conflict with normative and affective areas of social life.

If modernity is to be conceived in terms of rationality it is a mistake, Habermas argues, to construe rationality in such a narrow way. Modernity can be construed in terms of rationality but in wider forms to capture the normative and non-cognitive areas of social life. To be modern on his view is to have reached a certain state of maturity measured by the institutionalisation and development of three different forms of reason. These forms are derived from three different but complementary ways of relating to and experiencing the world. Life for Weber was experienced as a unity, but a unity which was defective because parts were inaccessible to reason and, thereby, marginalised.

Bernstein says that at the heart of Habermas's intellectual project are certain questions:

> A "theory of rationalization" requires not only the elaboration of categories and concepts for a systematic examination of the character and different modes of rationality, but an explanation of how they are concretely embodied in social and cultural life.... To speak of "the pathology of modernity" and "the deformed realization of reason in history" presupposes a normative standard for judging what is pathological and deformed. Can we still, in our time, provide a rational justification for universal normative standards? Or are we faced with relativism, decisionism, or emotivism which hold that ultimate norms are arbitrary and beyond rational warrantability? ... the very possibility, of a critical theory of society depends on giving an affirmative answer to the first question and a negative answer to the second. (1985, p. 2)

Habermas may deservedly be seen as the leading exponent of critical social theory; at one point (Habermas,1981, p. 13) he identifies himself as the defender of modernity (at least against certain, mainly French, critics), but in that source against Lyotard (1984) in particular. His concern is that without criteria of rationality the distinctions between the true and the false, the naked and the masked, and indeed theory and ideology break down, and "the" Enlightenment vision of the ongoing rational criticism of social institutions becomes empty. Without criteria of rationality there can be no such criticism. There can still be criticism but this will be of an ad hoc indeterminate nature, lacking an epistemological, ethical or political stance or position. In Habermas' view this is to abandon not only the spirit of the Enlightenment but, also, the very important reforms which have marked the history of Western democracies for two centuries or so. This is to open up the possibility of the resurgence of conservative political and social forces and to betray liberal political thought and practice in a resurgence of traditionalism and conservativism. Thus Habermas refers to these French critics as the "young conservatives" (ibid.). Caught by this net are Lyotard, Foucault, Derrida and Deleuze at the least.

Post-Modernity

Foucault does not address the modernity-post modernity distinction directly, though he would have been required to in a planned debate with Habermas. Unfortunately this did not happen. Whilst we have considered Foucault's interpretation of Kant, it does not answer the question as to whether Foucault is still enough of a modernist, and still too committed to the voice of reason, to have become a post-modernist. At this point we will turn to consider more fully the notion of the post-modern.

Defining the Post-Modern

The term surfaces in the 1930's and 1940's mainly in relation to the arts, including history, and architecture. However to talk of modernism and post-modernism as periods or epochs, may be itself to adopt a modernist stance, namely that it is possible to delineate the characteristics of a period and, thereby, to be beyond that period. It may be better to see it as a complex map of late 20th. century thought and practice rather than any clear cut philosophic, political and/or aesthetic movement.

Is the distinction between the modern and the post modern a polemical or a philosophical distinction? Either way philosophers will have to take cognisance (Hoy,1988): otherwise, especially if it is the latter and a "Kuhnian" style paradigm shift is occurring in philosophy, then some philosophers may be "left behind". The paradigm shift question has been formulated explicitly, and debated, by Lyotard and Habermas among others. Whereas Lyotard rejoices in the shift away from post-Enlightenment thought, totalising thought, and the philosophical "certainty" of meta-narratives, Habermas wishes to preserve what was important in the Enlightenment's view of reason.

Fredric Jameson begins his forward to Lyotard (1984) with this observation:

> [post-modernism] involves a radical break, both with dominant culture and aesthetic, and with a rather different moment of socioeconomic organization against which its structural novelties and innovations are measured: a new social or economic moment (or even system).

Lyotard's (1984) well known definition is that "post-modern" is an "incredulity towards meta-narratives". His major working hypothesis is that the status of knowledge is altered as societies enter what is known as the post-industrial age and cultures enter what is known as the post-modern age. Lyotard uses the term "post modern" to describe the condition of knowledge in the most developed societies. He follows sociologists and critics who have used the term to designate the state of Western culture "following the transformations which, since the end of the nineteenth century, have altered the game rules for science, literature and the arts" (1984, p. 3). Lyotard places these transformations within the context of the crisis of narratives, especially those Enlightenment meta-narratives concerning meaning and emancipation which have been used to legitimate both the rules of knowledge of the sciences and the foundations of our institutions.

By "transformations" Lyotard is referring principally to the effects of the new technologies since the 1950's and their combined impact on the two functions of knowledge - research and the transmission of acquired learning. Significantly, the leading sciences and technologies have all been based on language related developments - theories of linguistics, cybernetics, informatics, computer languages, telematics, theories of algebra - their miniaturization and commercialization. In this changed context the status of knowledge is permanently altered: its only preservable form as an international commodity becomes the basis for national competitive advantage and security in terms of commercial and politico-military strategies. Already knowledge has become the principle force of production, changing the composition of the workforce in developed countries. The mercantilization of knowledge will further widen the gap between nation states and the information rich multinationals, raising new legal, ethical, political and educational problems.

As knowledge becomes a question of government, the problem of legitimation necessarily arises: who decides what is "true" ("scientific") or "just"? The post-modern condition reveals that knowledge and power are simply two sides of the same question. The problem of legitimation is highlighted with a recognition of the crises of narratives and specifically the inability of the sciences to legitimate themselves by reference to the grand narrative of philosophy. In contrast to the modern era Lyotard defines "post-modern" as an incredulity towards meta-narratives, a distrust of stories which purport to justify certain practices or institutions by grounding them upon a set of transcendental, a historical, or universal principles. The post-modern condition of knowledge begins with scepticism about the rule of consensus: that the truth value of a statement between the sender and addressee is acceptable if it is cast in terms of a possible unanimity between rational minds. The crisis of narratives is symbolised in the post-modern dispersal of language elements. There is no principle of unitotality or universal meta-language, as there are many languages: a multiplicity of language games each with specific pragmatic valencies. Lyotard's reading of Wittgenstein emphasises the pluralistic and incommensurable nature of language games, each with its irreducible body of rules defining its properties and uses (also Lyotard,1988). There is an *agonistics* of language in which utterances are understood not as the transmission of information or message but rather as an unstable exchange between communicational adversaries. The rules do not have a bedrock justification; they are the object of a contract between players. If there are no rules, there is no game. Every utterance is a "move" in the game where to speak is to fight (in the sense of playing). Progress in knowledge is conceived of in two ways: the first is construed as a *new move* within the established rules; the second is construed as the invention of *new rules*, that is, the development of a new game.

This basic conflict model of language, then, challenges the rules of consensus not only as it underlies the Enlightenment narrative of the hero of knowledge working towards good ethico-political ends but also contemporary accounts of the fully transparent communicational society as advanced by Habermas, on the basis of the ideal speech community, where validity claims are said to be discursively redeemable at the level of discourse. The model is ultimately used for understanding the nature of the social bond - each of us lives at the intersection of many games - and science itself.

The interpretation of language games as heteronomous (untranslatable) and paralogous (undermining rules) shatters the grand legitimating meta-narrative of science as the supreme voice of reason. Science is not only incapable of legitimating other language games but is incapable of legitimating itself, and metaphysical philosophy is forced to relinquish its legitimation duties in face of the proliferation and splintering of language games. The idea of modernity, of science as the exemplification of rationality, is revealed as one narrative among others: the grand narrative, but one which has broken apart and splintered into many different forms.

Yet in the post-modern age, decision makers still proceed on the assumption that there is commensurability and that the whole is determinable. But in the post-modern age the legitimation of knowledge is formulated in terms of performitivity. Increasingly science has fallen under the sway of another game, technology, whose goal is not truth but optimal performance, and whose criteria are minimising input and maximising output, rather than truth or justice. Research and progress in knowledge are relegitimated in terms of the performative or efficiency criterion.

Foucault as Post-Modernist

In his first major book, as we have seen, Foucault (1961) launches an attack upon Western reason, and Descartes in particular, arguing that by excluding madness in the *Meditations* Descartes had attempted to confine reason, thereby limiting the potential of the imagination (see also, Foucault,1986), and limiting creativity and freedom. There is a sense then in which Foucault may be close to Lyotard but only in a superficial way, for if Foucault had entertained a complete rewriting of reason this was abandoned after Derrida's (1963) critique. He was not opposed to reason and was certainly not opposed to the natural sciences. He was not opposed to knowledge and his works should not be interpreted thus. However, in typical Canguilhelm fashion he does argue that truth is not so obvious, or as straightforward, or as simplistic, as positivistic accounts would have it to be.

Nevertheless Foucault maintained that there was no universal form that reason must take. Rather there are multiplicities of reason, and multiplicities of theories in relation to specific local issues. If there are no meta-narratives in this sense then the role of intellectuals must be local and specific (see 1972a). Yet, Foucault believes, Kant was correct in urging that theory must be critical. Slumber was caused by a failure to continually respond to socio-historical conditions, and failure to question the development of responses to human dilemmas through the critical questioning of the application of universal reason. Rather than reason unfolding, Foucault the archaeologist would tell us (1972b), arbitrary formations of discourse, especially those which he designates as the human sciences, have frozen Kant's notion of an unfolding freedom and we have become embroiled in a senseless dynamic of power, modern power or bio-power, which continues to dominate and subjugate us as human beings (1979b). These arbitrary discourses are the result of the break down of the notion of language as representation (1973a) and its dispersion and fragmentation. To be modern is to attempt to control this dispersion and fragmentation. Foucault appears to take no general stand (1973a, p. 307) on this issue.

Indeed whereas Lyotard's concerns are with the natural sciences Foucault's are with the social sciences. Foucault both refused to side with Lyotard, because he did not wish to be seen as an enemy of reason and enlightenment, and to accept the label of "post-modernist", even if he did wish to point up the dangers of attempts to put Enlightenment ideas into practice, particularly in the applications and practices of the human sciences.

However there is a sense in which Foucault may still be considered as a post-modernist. This sense is developed by Hoy (1988) and concerns how to think the *unthought*. Both modernists and post-modernists attempt to think the unthought but *how* they approach it is different. According to Hoy there are four major differences between modernists and post-modernists on this issue.

First modernists lament the inability to think the unthought. The Enlightenment thesis involves the extension of rational thought so as to leave nothing as unknown. Rather than lamenting the inevitable inability to extend rational thought according to the Enlightenment programme, the post-modernist accepts the inevitability of being unable to carry out the programme.

The second feature has to do with *how* post-modernists attempt to think the unthought. What post-modernists would reject is the attempt to bring the unthought from out of the darkness, so to say into the light, with some traditional form of thought - clear and distinct ideas or transcendental deductions of the unthought conditions of experience. According to Heidegger the unthought will appear, forced to the surface so to say, when problems or anomalies force to the forefront the background assumptions and/or practices that had been unseen, or had functioned imperceptibly.

For Foucault *power* is forced to the forefront in his examinations of the human sciences. It is the great unthought that conditions those kinds of knowledge. In the Enlightenment tradition knowledge is seen as logically independent of power. At best the tradition answers questions concerning the relationship between knowledge and power as being either, that knowledge confers power, or , that those with power can define or determine knowledge. In both cases the relationship is essentially contingent and interest-free knowledge is the norm. What Foucault shows is that interest free knowledge in the social sciences, is far from being the norm. The unthought of power is forced to the forefront by the investigation of social practices, of how that knowledge was obtained and how people were treated in the social institutions in which the human sciences were developed. In Foucault's case this involved the investigation of suppressed knowledge, the unthought of schedules, daily routines, strategies and techniques of discipline, etc. But for Foucault power cannot be thought in the modern way by being encapsulated in a theory. He advanced no theory of power because power is no one thing or object to be explained by a theory.

The third feature of the post-modern is that there is no one, privileged way to think the unthought, or indeed to think there is one unthought or that the unthought is even a single "thing". This involved shifts for Foucault from the autonomy of language to making social practices explicit, to the notion of discursive practices, to how subjectivity is "constructed" by the unthought - by unthought social practices and discourses, or by poorly articulated and partially conscious ethical self-fashionings.

The final characteristic identified by Hoy is that post-modernism has moved beyond the rhetorics of progress and nostalgia. Essentially this involves not taking one self seriously or too seriously, or of making Man the centre of philosophical investigation. Whether or not we are progressing tends not to worry post-modernists because complexity and the lack of meta-narratives makes criteria for progress most unclear. The Enlightenment programme of improvement then is a story, and a simple story from a post-modern perspective. Nor is there any need for regret or nostalgia. A complementary thesis in *Discipline and Punish* is that what appears as irrational in the Ancien regime, - torture - was according to beliefs about guilt and the espousal of truth quite rational. Thus Foucault argues our modern day notions of rationality are not necessarily better but different. Thus we should be more tolerant of what appears not merely as irrational but inhumane. He could be said to be "refining our sensitivities to differences" (Hoy,1988;30). Foucault probably takes himself too seriously in *The Archaeology of Knowledge* where he seems to be making strong claims about his notion of archaeology, giving it a privileged position as a serious discourse concerned to give the historical a priori conditions of knowledge (Hacking,1981).

Hoy concludes however that Foucault is neither a modern nor an anti-modern (see further chapter five below). But he is, according to Hoy, a post-modern in that he has no nostalgia, there is no looking back over the shoulder, nor is there a desire to control and predict the future. Foucault refused to accept the label of post-modernist. If he was a post-modernist he was surely correct in refusing any such label. Nor was he ever, like Lyotard, an advocate or persuader to join post-modernism. For him (and Deleuze) that would have involved the vast indignity of presuming to speak for others.

The Critique of Neo-Liberal Education

Foucault had begun to address the neo-liberalism that was about to sweep Europe and other areas of the Western world. He was well aware that the left was ill-prepared for neo-liberalism. He had, for example, critiqued Hayek and had planned a book with Pierre Bourdieu, but that was not to happen. Just as the left was ill-prepared for neo-liberal attacks upon the welfare state in general so also were teachers ill-prepared for the "reforms" in education that were to be launched. Underlying the reforms in education are certain views of the individual which need to be submitted to a Foucauldean critique. This will now be developed.

Fundamental to the reform literatures have been notions of freedom and choice. Students (parents, guardians, etc.) are presumed to be persons not merely capable of deliberating upon alternatives, and choosing between alternative educational programmes according to individual needs and interests, and the qualities of programmes, but it seems to be the case that it is part of the very nature of being human to both make, and want to make, *continuous* consumer style choices. But the notions of autonomy needed to make choices, and the notions of needs and interests, presuppose that such choices are the student's (or chooser's) *own*, that they are *independent*, and that needs and interests have not been manipulated or imposed in some way upon the chooser. Therein lie problems for the notion of the autonomous chooser.

It is said that people should be free to choose the school that provides the best quality education in accordance with their needs and interests. For example in the major document in the New Zealand reform literature, concerned with secondary education reform, it is said:

> Consumers need to be able to directly influence their learning institution by having a say in the running of it or by being able to turn to acceptable alternatives. Only if people are free to choose, can a true co-operative partnership develop between the community and learning institutions ... choice will involve providing a wider range of options both for consumers and learning institutions. (Department of Education, 1988, p. xii)

> And:

> If institutions and consumers are to be able to co-operate in any meaningful way at the local level ... they must have some degree of choice. (ibid., p. 29)

In these comments, very representative and central to the New Zealand literature, the notion of the autonomous chooser is paramount.

There is also the major claim that the quality of educational choices made by the consumer *as* consumer is superior to that offered to a consumer by the choices of providers. Consumers know better than providers about education. Thereby the professional knowledge of educators is relegated to second position, at best! There is the notion also that the quality of the community, and the relations between learning institutions, are enhanced by the consumer driven activities of autonomous choosers.

From a Foucauldean position these are merely *changes* in the forms that *governmentality* takes (Foucault,1979b). Governmentality carries with it notions of leadership and husbandry, and policy from successive governments in New Zealand has carried strong overtones of both. Governments have overridden traditional methods for setting agendas - educators were excluded from the educational agenda setting forums - providing leadership through what can be called a *busnocratic* form of rationality (Marshall,1995, a&b). At the same time they have claimed to be providing a better form of security for those in need of health care and those for whom access to educational services has been difficult. They have not abandoned security but reassessed it in terms of individualism and the autonomous chooser in particular. In so doing they have exercised a form of power, which can be called busno-power, which impinges both on individuals as individual living human beings, and also on them as subjects of a population. In producing and reproducing a form of human nature - autonomous choosers - this busno-power also impinges upon the population as a whole, as individual consumer activity "improves" both society and the economy. By busno-power I mean a form of power directed at individuals to turn them into autonomous choosers and consumers (Marshall,1995a). In busnocratic rationality and the exercise of busno-power there can be seen a merging of the economic, the social and the activity of government.

Foucault saw the emergence of liberal doctrines as an attack upon policing. In a similar manner these neo-liberal doctrines can be seen as an attack upon welfarism and the welfare state. Critiques of the welfare state in general, and education in particular, are of course well known in Western liberal democracies (see e.g., Marshall and Peters, 1990;1991: Peters and Marshall,1990). The theoretical neo-liberal remedies are: a return to the principles of a so-called free-market economy; a revival of the classical articles of faith of economic liberalism; and a re-privatization of the public sphere aimed at capital accumulation. Foucault had attacked social security but argued that this needed to be rethought in line with increasing demands for autonomy, and not that social security was unnecessary.

There is little doubt that in the twentieth century we have a more humane approach to schooling, and that we have changed our attitudes towards children, away from the Dickensian type schools of Creakle and Squeers. Liberal views on the importance of the individual, psychological theories of development or growth, demands to respect the needs and interests of children, and more enlightened social and political views have, to a certain extent, penetrated the modern school. Personal autonomy and not social control is now seen as a fundamental aim, if not the *aim*, of modern education.

Against a utilitarian, authoritarian and teacher directed pedagogy in the traditional school, progressives urged that education should start from the child, from the child's needs and interests and from the child's nature and growth patterns (but see Dewey's (1938b) critique of progressivism). Dearden (1968) is a good example of a liberal philosopher of education who saw something important in the child centred movement's notions of needs, interests and growth. He argues that properly construed these notions are important for the development of personal autonomy based upon reason. By this he means (Dearden,op.cit., p. 46): first, independence from authorities; second, that of testing the truth of things for oneself, whether by experience or by a critical estimate of the testimony of others; and that of deliberating, forming intentions and choosing in accordance with a scale of values which is self formulated. Both understanding and choice, or thought and action, are therefore to be independent of authority and based instead upon reason. From this broad philosophical position personal autonomy is construed as an ideal, to be aimed at by educators, and to which children are to be enabled to grow. This general approach *respects* the child as an individual person, as having a distinctive point of view, and distinctive purposes to pursue. This, Dearden himself concludes, is the only moral way for pedagogy to proceed. The autonomous chooser of neo-liberal theory might seem to be a logical outcome of Dearden's position. But this is not so. Traditional liberal philosophy of education is well aware that talk of such things as needs and interests is ambiguous between what the child sees as its needs and interests, and what adults and educators see as the "real" needs and interests of the child to be. Needs and interests, after such fundamental notions as food and warmth, can be seen to reflect value positions, and whilst there is a sense in which we cannot avoid introducing our children to value positions in just living our everyday lives (see e.g., Smeyers, 1992), these value positions are not unproblematic. But the busnocratic notion of the autonomous chooser collapses such a distinction and what the chooser chooses is the "real".

But the needs and interests of autonomous choosers are being shaped also through ideologies and multi-media forms of presentation which emphasise the need for skills, the continual need during a working lifetime to be reskilled, and the economic motives for both getting educated and purchasing quality education. Underlying these reforms is a certain form of human nature encapsulated in the notion of the autonomous chooser. It is not the homo economicus of traditional liberal economic theory but "an individual" that does not merely act as an autonomous chooser, but acts *because* of its very nature. Busnocratic rationality actively encourages, and busno-power promotes, this kind of individual (Marshall, 1995f).

There seems then to be then a major shift in the objects or individuals of the new theory(ies) from classical economic theory. There is almost a postulation of a fundamental human *faculty* of choice, which is both part of human nature and which humans need to exercise to be "proper" human beings. This is different from an autonomy which in traditional liberal theory could or could-not be exercised. Now, it seems, choice can't be resisted. It is not just that human beings are autonomous, or that their autonomy can be developed, or that it is a duty to exercise autonomy, but instead there is said to be a faculty of choice which is necessarily continuously exercised on commodities, and which sweeps aside or over-rides the traditional categories and frameworks on human nature of the human sciences.

These new economic theories with the further twist of behaviourist doctrines, see an autonomous chooser as perpetually responsive to the environment. In which case the autonomous chooser is capable of infinite manipulation by the structuring of the environment. If so, then the environment can structure the choices of the individual. Hence economic intervention in the social can manipulate the individual, thereby transgressing the fundamental rights of non-violation of the individual, and the individual's self formulated purposes and projects, of earlier liberal thought, encapsulated in the liberal view of personal autonomy as an aim of education.

The logical implication is that one's life becomes an enterprise - the enterprise of the autonomous chooser. But it is not the self of classical liberal theory, where the right to formulate one's own purposes and projects was seen as inviolate. It is not just that the insertion of the economic into the social *structures* the choices of the individual but that, also, in behaviouristic fashion it manipulates the individual by penetrating the very notion of the self, structuring the individual's choices, and thereby, insofar as one's life is just the individual economic enterprise, the lives of individuals.

Needs, interests and growth then become contaminated as both needs and interests become constituted by the insertion of the economic into the social. The very autos is penetrated by these economic, individualistic needs and interests, setting growth patterns towards, e.g., freedom *from* and choice. If the older liberal version of autonomy had some historical justifications, it is clear that these "new" autonomous choosers have different needs and interests and that their autonomy is problematic.

If the liberal model was aware of the problems associated with the possibility that needs and interests themselves are socially constructed, nevertheless it believed that personal autonomy provided one with some independence. The autonomous chooser is quite a different construction, and one which can be continually restructured. By emphasising skills and downplaying knowledge and understanding, and by emphasising information and information retrieval as characteristics of the educated person, neo-liberal education can be seen to be heavily embroiled in the security of state and international capitalism, as there is both a particular kind of person sought under the form of an autonomous chooser and a clear intention by state institutions to foster and reproduce such individuals.

Security for the state and the economic enterprise can be monitored in a variety of ways but in education the production and reproduction of choosers goes hand in hand with autonomous chooser modularisation - break whole programmes down into small units and monitor skill outputs from each module. Surveillance becomes almost total. But, thereby, the whole person is ignored and will founder. Where is the holistic skill of balance, and wise judgement (Oakshott,1971) in knowing when to exercise these "little" skills?

These general points on autonomy were grasped by Jean François Lyotard (Lyotard,1993), but in a slightly earlier and different context. Writing in the heady times of the 1960's, in the times of de Gaulle's technocratic reforms of education, and as a member and supporter of the movement of 22 May in the 1968 student (and workers) revolution in France, Lyotard saw the autonomy offered by the Fouchet educational reforms as a sham. What this autonomy offered was a false independence. This was merely an independence from the other, and one which permitted the individual to be picked off and allotted to a slot in the technocratic structures of the capitalist state. By structuring interests and choices, allotting to slots was masked in the educational reforms as autonomous choice of career. But Lyotard went further on this notion of autonomy. The autonomous chooser gained independence but at a tremendous price for the community. He argued that independence in this sense was gained at the expense of discarding social obligation for the other members of the community. The faculty of choice, deeply imbedded in human nature in the theory of the autonomous chooser, has no theoretical need for the other, for the needs of self and the other, and social justice, are "met" by the individual choices of the autonomous chooser. Hence there is no need for obligation to the others of the community. If there is no need to consider the other, to converse and to consult, and to enter into dialogue, then the independent autonomous chooser is further cut off from a shared community form of life and more liable to be "picked off" by the information systems, consumer products and media, through which individual choices increasingly come to be policed.

This notion of personal autonomy, which was meant to lead to emancipation, was a bitter fraud according to Lyotard:

> This "emancipation" is the story of a Faust who didn't need to sell his soul because one had not been denoted to him, so he was

under no obligation to return it to the donor, nor did he have the power to steal it from its donor. (1993, p. 151)

Conclusion

Individualism has become a necessary feature of many Western states and, as in the case of Eastern Europe, a condition almost for their very security. However the form of individualism offered by the autonomous chooser is not the free person offered by Enlightenment thought and liberal education. The autonomous chooser will be a product of both busnocratic rationality and busno-power. Needs, interests and choices can themselves be manipulated because the autonomous chooser is highly manipulable and easy to pick off.

Liberals and the liberal left have had no real response to these educational changes, either intellectually or in practice, except to provide critique and/or to repeat the principles and policies of the past. If Foucault is correct, what is needed in response to neo-liberalism is an increased vigilance, and an increased imagination and inventiveness, for there is a complex problem space brought into play by such neo-liberal reforms (Gordon, 1991). What is required is a neo-social democratic approach to these crises of education (and the welfare state) and the increasing demands for autonomy. This is not explicit in the extant works of Foucault.

CHAPTER 7

DOING PHILOSOPHY OF EDUCATION

In philosophy of education we seem to have arrived at an impasse. From a position where analytic philosophy of education was seen to be at a cross-roads, to where it was seen to have been surpassed by marxism, we seem not to have settled upon any one methodology as a "paradigm". Perhaps that is healthy. However it will be argued in this chapter that Foucault may have something to offer philosophy of education, not merely in some post-structuralist or "after- philosophy" sense, but in the way that he looks genealogically at historical data and concepts, in what he called the history of thought (in contrast to history of ideas).

In order to do this we will contrast Foucault's "philosophical" approach to issues and problems with a more traditional philosophical approach. This will be done by looking at a particular issue - the punishment of children - first, from a traditional analytical approach, and second from the approach of Foucault.

Punishment involves important educational and philosophical questions. But these differing philosophical approaches generate different and possibly conflicting answers to philosophical questions, and thereby pose several puzzles for educators trying to talk about the punishment of children. It will be argued that the insights offered by Foucault in the second approach have similarities to Wittgenstein's approach to doing philosophy. A conclusion which might be drawn is that insofar as Foucault and Wittgenstein have some affinities, Foucault might not be so divorced from Western Anglo-Saxon philosophy as some of his detractors would wish to argue, though some within that group might wish to exclude Wittgenstein anyway, for heralding the end of philosophy.

Punishment has been a recurring topic in both philosophy and philosophy of education. There is both an educational literature and a philosophical literature, and identifiable recent debates in journals such as *Philosophy of Education* (1984) and *The Journal of Moral Education* (1984-6-9). The analytic approach dominated philosophy of education in the Anglo-Saxon "world" for nearly two decades. It will be *illustrated* by reference to the account of punishment by R.S. Peters in *Ethics and Education* (1966). Peters' work is used only to illustrate a general analytic position on punishment, which is readily available, and which has set the grounds for debate on the meaning of "punishment" and its legitimation in philosophy of education. Foucault's approach to punishment is to be found in *Discipline and Punishment* (1979a). Philosophical puzzles for talk of the punishment of children vis-a-vis the punishment of adults are raised by different answers given by these two accounts.

It will be argued that a "solution" to these puzzles is to use the insights of Wittgenstein. In particular his views on concepts, following a rule, and how concepts are learned. The "solution" will be closer to the position of Foucault than to Peters and analytic philosophy which, from a Wittgensteinian point of view, was mired in a mistaken search for necessary and sufficient conditions for the concept "punishment", and a mistaken interpretation of Wittgenstein's notion of a rule. Such an approach would be incompatible with the later Wittgenstein. Foucault may then have something to offer to doing philosophy.

In Part I of the chapter we look at the traditional legalistic model of punishment, exemplified in Richard Peters' *Ethics and Education* and normally known as the Hart-Flew-Benn model. In Peters' work there are references to the authority of Wittgenstein to claim justification for this approach to punishment. This approach generates philosophical puzzles about talk of the punishment of children (Marshall, 1975, 1984a & b). Part II looks at Foucault's approach to the concept of punishment in *Discipline and Punish.* But Foucault's account also generates puzzles for talk of punishment. In Part III it is argued that Foucault may be closer to Wittgenstein, at least on this issue, than at first sight may have seemed possible. The conclusion suggests following Foucault in approaching the discussion of punishment in education, rather than seeking "insight" from analytic philosophy of education.

Analytic Philosophy of Education

Traditional philosophical approaches to punishment have tended to concentrate upon two major questions. These are questions concerned with *meaning* and *justification*. The questions, What is the meaning of "punishment"?, and, How is punishment to be justified?, have almost come to dominate philosophical literature (see the selection of papers edited by H.B. Acton,1963). This philosophical literature concerns itself with a particular model of punishment, one which is essentially a legal model. H.L.A. Hart, drawing upon earlier work of Antony Flew and

Stanley Benn, presents this model in *Punishment and Responsibility* (1968), as an answer to philosophical questions on punishment. The model is sometimes referred to as the Flew-Benn-Hart model of punishment. This model was to be adopted by R.S. Peters in his enormously influential writings on philosophy of education (e.g., *Ethics and Education*, 1966). In general this model has set the framework for subsequent discussions in education of the tricky notion of punishment. It will become obvious in this chapter that this model, in relation to the punishment of children, is seriously flawed.

The Flew-Benn-Hart Model

Hart says that he is merely drawing upon "recent admirable work scattered through ... philosophical journals". Hart added the qualifier "English" to his list of journals but this does not represent a certain insularity or philosophical myopia, for Hart was probably correct at that time that there was little need to go beyond this literature in English speaking philosophy (see Acton, 1963). It should be noted however that he is also writing from within an established legal tradition and with more than merely an analytic methodology as he relates his approach to that of Locke's discussion of property. This latter aspect is ignored by Peters (1966).

Along with Flew (1954) and Benn (1958), Hart defines the standard case of the concept of punishment as containing five elements. According to Hart (1968, p. 4f) punishment must:

(i) involve pain or other consequences normally considered unpleasant;
(ii) be for an offence against legal rules;
(iii) be of an actual or supposed offender for the offence;
(iv) be intentionally administered by human beings other than the offender;
(v) be imposed and administered by an authority constituted by a legal system against which the offence is committed.

Hart immediately regulated the following to the position of *sub-standard or secondary cases*: pain or consequences for breaching other than legal rules - here he gives as specific examples, the family and the school; by other than authoritative officials; and unpleasantness or pain imposed deliberately by authorities but upon non-offenders.

Philosophical puzzles are posed for educators by this position. How can educators talk meaningfully about the punishment of children, if at all, in more than a sub-standard sense of the term "punishment"? This will rest as a puzzle for now.

This is the account which is to be found, essentially, in Peters (1966). First, Peters adopts Hart's fourfold division of meaningful questions about punishment. These are said to be (Hart, 1968;4) questions of *definition*, *justification* and *distribution*, with the latter divided into questions of *who* should be punished, i.e., *entitlement*, and the *form* including severity. Peters, however, sees the first two questions only as being philosophical questions, with the remaining two being the province of jurists and administrators. He presents us then with a philosophical division of labour, with the efforts of philosophers directed at the first two questions about punishment, and the relegation of the last two questions to the status of administrative, juridical or, in Peters' case, educational questions. We will return to these questions below.

Peters' account of punishment in education did not meet with universal approval (see, e.g. P.S. Wilson, 1971; John Wilson,1977). Yet, nevertheless, the model was to set the form of the debates that ensued in philosophy of education. For example, and even in protest, on analytic grounds the author argued that something was awry with this model in talk of the punishment of children (Marshall, 1975). But I adopted the *form* of the debate and, in general, the protest fell upon deaf ears (see however Kleinig,1982, chapter 18).

Punishment and discipline are two central concepts for understanding social control in schools. In general philosophers of education have adopted their concepts in these areas from traditional liberal political philosophy. Thus according to Peters; "the most crucial concept for discussing social control in the school is that of authority" (Peters, 1966, p. 237). Peters discusses several closely related concepts, namely "discipline", "authority" and "punishment". In his own case he is drawing upon traditional political philosophy (e.g., Benn and Peters, 1965), but in this account of authority in *Ethics and Education* he is also clearly drawing upon a reading of Wittgenstein, conceding to Winch (Peters, 1966,p. 246) that authority is necessarily linked with rule governed behaviour in Wittgenstein's sense, which is stronger than his earlier announcement (op.cit., p. 238) that "the concept of authority is inseparably connected with a rule governed form of life". It:

> presupposes some sort of normative order that has to be promulgated, maintained and perpetuated ... (by) ... procedural

> rules which give such people the right to decide, promulgate, judge, order and pronounce ... (it) would be unintelligible unless we first had the concept of following rules with the built in notion that there are incorrect and correct ways of doing things. (loc.cit.)

It is not at all clear that Peters has interpreted Wittgenstein correctly on rules as, for example, there is too much of the command sense of a rule here - see Marshall (1984b) for an account of Wittgenstein and rule following behaviour.

In the school then authorities pronounce upon the rules, which are themselves related by Peters to Wittgenstein's notion of rule following behaviour, and are the authorities which in turn administer discipline and punishment (though for Peters punishment is a necessary evil - in contrast to John Wilson who holds that it is in some sense logically necessary - for a critique of Wilson see Marshall, 1984b).

But if Peters has misunderstood Wittgenstein he has also smudged the notion of a rule, from its legal sense in the Flew-Hart-Benn model. It is no longer a legal rule, but a school rule, or family rule or any old rule. But Hart, as we have seen, rejected these school and family rules as being part of the paradigm examples of punishment. Punishment in the Peters' account is then for the breaking of a rule, but the philosophical puzzles remain and have, perhaps, deepened.

Both Peters and Hart assume that analysis and considerations of an adult legal situation will set the conceptual and justificatory framework for the discussion of the punishment of children, as if, apriori, history and sociology, for example, have no contribution to make to these framework questions. By "settling" framework questions in this manner, the alleged punishment of children in family and school is relegated by Hart (1968, p. 5) to the position of sub-standard or secondary cases of the use of the concept "punishment". Peters extends this notion of punishment to children by smudging the notion of a rule. But in both writers it is almost by definition that the history of the punishment of children has nothing important to offer to the meaning of the concept "punishment". A consequence is that debates on punishment in education are complex and perplexing, especially when one considers the morality of taking retribution against children.

Might it not be argued that punishment itself is a natural reaction, an emotional expression in relation to some perceived wrongdoing, by an individual who has been the recipient of that wrongdoing? In which case the punishment of children and punishment between individuals, without the legal sanction of laws, might assume "the" logical priority? Thus punishment would be detached from laws and rules and rationality and would become an aspect of the emotions, as in a Humean or Rousseauean approach to moral notions.

Rather than taking that philosophical path here it will be argued instead that historical and sociological issues arising from a consideration of the second two questions - entitlement and amount (form and severity) - are germane to answering questions about the meaning and justification of punishment in general, and the punishment of children in particular. The thinker who has turned these questions on their head, so to say, is Michel Foucault. Foucault (1979a) starts with questions of entitlement and amount and ends, albeit perhaps implicitly, with questions about meaning and justification. Also, whilst sensitive to language, he turns to *practices* and accounts of what was done to people in the name of punishment.

Foucault on Punishment

Whereas Foucault bypasses the traditional questions asked by philosophers on this topic, they are not excluded. What he says on the methods and techniques of punishment impinges explicitly and implicitly upon traditional philosophical concerns with questions of the meaning and the justification of punishment. It is because these traditional concerns have impinged upon education and philosophy of education that Foucault has something to say to philosophers of education. If his approach is different its worth must be assessed ultimately by its fruitfulness. It will be argued that, on this topic at least, Foucault brings to us as philosophers of education important *philosophical* insights. We will see below how he confronts the Hart-Flew-Benn model of punishment, the extent to which Wittgenstein can be seen as a support for his position, and what he means by disciplinary punishment.

Foucault's starting point is in historical data about the prison. According to him (1979a) the modern prison dates from the end of the 18th century. Whilst the prison had existed before then, imprisonment as a major form of punishment, had not, as the prison had been a place for holding prisoners awaiting "proper" punishments such as death, or torture, or banishment. Punishment was not listed in France as a serious penalty except, for example, as a substitute for those women, children and infants who could not serve in the galleys (Foucault, 1979a, p. 118).

Foucault's central thesis is that, from the outset, the modern prison was concerned with techniques of transformation based upon individualisation and normalisation. These techniques were then directed at the criminal and not at the act. As a form of punishment then imprisonment marked a change in the *target* of punishment, according to Foucault.

The key events for Foucault's account of the modern prison were the reorganisation of the Maison De Force at Ghent in Belgium in 1775, the building of the Gloucester Penitentiary in 1779, and the reorganisation of Philadelphia's Walnut Street Prison in 1790. Exhibited in each of these new prisons were disciplinary techniques associated with individualisation and normalisation: the work ethic with strict timetabling; solitary confinement (though not total); surveillance (Ghent was built on Bentham's panopticon as model); and individualisation. Knowledge of the individual was a prerequisite for transforming the individual. Hence the question "Who are you?" became important. The answer was to be obtained through surveillance and careful documentation. Such knowledge was seen as necessary for the transformation of inmates and not merely for their control within the prison. This new knowledge was not directed towards the acts which the prisoners had performed, but towards "the potentially of danger that lies hidden in an individual and which is observed in his observed everyday conduct" (Foucault, 1979a,p. 126).

Foucault claims that this transformation in the form of punishment is not to be treated as a mere rearrangement of penalties. If the new form was also future directed "not to efface a crime, but to prevent its repetition" (Foucault, 1979a,p. 126), the major difference is to be found in the new techniques:

> in the procedure of access to the individual, the way in which the punishing power gets control over him, the instruments that it uses in order to achieve this transformation. (ibid.,p. 127)

These new techniques are applied to the body, time, everyday gestures and activities to produce the obedient subject who, by subjection to rules, orders, imposed habits and authority continually exercised around him and upon him, "must allow (these) to function automatically in him" (ibid., p. 129). This represents a move from reacting to an offence in terms of a judicial subject willingly breaking a social pact, to that of shaping an obedient subject through a form of power based upon knowledge of that subject. It is not just a question of coercion, for that applies in both cases but, rather, that the new forms bring with them different consequences, namely individuals "corrected" by the power matrix that in enveloping individuals comes to function automatically within them.

Foucault provides considerable gruesome detail in discussing the changes that took place in the forms and techniques of punishment. But the opening and harrowing pages of *Discipline and Punish* are not there to shock or titillate but, rather, to draw a sharp contrast a few pages later with the timetable of activities drawn up for offenders in the house of young offenders in Paris. This timetable was devised by the criminologist Faucher in 1838, some 80 years after the earlier example of the harrowing execution of the regicide Damiens.

First, it can be noted that punishment is no longer a spectacle. The ceremony, theatre and public participation that accompanied Damiens' execution are to be eliminated. Far from the public spectacle of the scaffold, punishment is instead to be private, secluded behind walls, and "behind" legal and human science knowledge. The public spectacle was needed so that people could see the Sovereign reassert his power on the body of the condemned. As Foucault says:

> It brought to a solemn end a war, the outcome of which was decided in advance, between the criminal and the sovereign... A body effaced, reduced to dust and thrown to the winds, a body destroyed piece by piece by the infinite power of the sovereign constituted not only the ideal, but the real limit of punishment. (ibid.,p. 5)

If this physical confrontation was revolting and cruel it was also dangerous, because it threw down a further challenge to the people. If reformers such as Beccaria (1764) influenced change, nevertheless Foucault argues, there was a legal and bureaucratic thrust towards the control of populations in a more regular and efficient manner. Power was to be exerted more efficiently by separating the right to punish from the personal power of the sovereign and by setting up a new "economy" of power. The reform of criminal law can be seen as a strategy for reorganising the power to punish so as to make it more effective and at less economic and political cost. In this strategy of "reform" the spectacle of the scaffold had no place. As the new established form of punishment, imprisonment makes the punishment private.

There is also a shift in the target of punishment, away from the body per se. The account of Damiens' execution identifies the target of punishment as being the physical body - unbearable pains are inflicted upon the body for the purpose only of pain. By contrast, later, the guillotine is to administer a quick and sudden death to the body but not attack those parts of the body where "exquisite" and unbearable pain could be produced.

In the new form of punishment there is a new relation between the body of the condemned and punishment as the target shifts to the "soul" of the offender. Punishment is directed at the "soul" but "through" the body, not so that power produces unbearable pain, but so that power envelopes individuals to the extent that they function automatically within certain norms. The "soul" then is sited within a wider target area that includes the body, but it is a body so timetabled that everyday gestures and all activities are minutely observed and controlled. It is this matrix that is the new target of power.

For Foucault punishment must be analysed so as to be part of a general network of power relations that extends beyond the penal regime, for the techniques that he discusses are to be found also in the hospital, the workplace, the military, the asylum and, of course, the school. In many of these areas, where power of the same form is exerted, the law has little or no application. Furthermore in widening the scope of the application of such techniques to both the law breaker and the law abider, Foucault is able to show that punishment serves certain ritual functions associated with sovereignty and the functions of correction and reform. Punishment as an exercise of power is not merely repressive then, and is not merely directed at the breaking of law, but it can have positive effects, normalising people to take an effective (if docile) place in society, in forming the "self", and in promoting pleasure.

In *Discipline and Punish* Foucault identifies a penal theory of punishment as exemplified in and developed from the writings of Thomas Hobbes (*Leviathan*, 1664). This he calls "juridico-legal punishment" and is to be sharply distinguished from those modern forms of punishment which he calls "disciplinary punishment". It is to be distinguished by such notions as the target of punishment and the forms that the punishment takes. In his view modern penal theories essentially exemplify the juridico-legal and thereby obscure the exercise of modern power (see Foucault, 1979b). To this extent they are mystifying he believes because, whilst they talk of acts against the law and of the repressive nature of punishments which uphold the law (and thereby property in a wide Lockean sense), in fact, modern disciplinary punishment is concerned with the individual, the character of the individual, and the normalising of behaviour so that the individual can take a "responsible" place in society. In disciplinary punishment power is exerted not in a repressive but in a positive way (Foucault, 1979a). Foucault's account, which analyses punishment independently of criminal illegalities, is possibly the first major attempt to do so since Rusche and Kirchheimer in *Punishment and Structure* (1939).

From Foucault's position and in reference to Hart's model and his five necessary and sufficient conditions (section I), we can now say this:

(i) punishment need not involve unpleasant consequences;
(ii) punishment is not for an offence but for the good (the "soul") of the individual;
(iii) it is of an offender, not for an offence but for the offender's sake;
(iv) given that the ultimate aim is self-surveillance and self-domination punishment can be administered by the self;
(v) as power can be exercised by anyone, and a punishment is an exercise of power, there need not be an authority for punishment to occur.

There is disagreement with the Flew-Benn-Hart model on all five conditions.

In Foucault's account of disciplinary punishment the punishment of children is not a non standard case. Indeed disciplinary punishment is heavily situated in the school so that the school becomes a primary site for the application of this concept of punishment. Punishment is now justified because it has positive normalising and productive effects.

But now we have a new set of puzzles. How are we to adjudicate between the two concepts? Is legal punishment or disciplinary punishment the appropriate "model" for determining standard or non-standard uses of the concept of punishment? Is Foucault arguing that the concept of punishment has changed its meaning? How exactly are we to justify the use of disciplinary punishment?

Foucault and Wittgenstein

Peters' account of punishment seems to be firmly within the juridico-legal model of punishment. As we have seen we are left with some puzzles. To summarise them more succinctly, which account of punishment are we to adopt? Here, it will be argued, recourse to Wittgenstein is of some assistance.

One of the issues is over how concepts can change their meaning.

As we have seen above in this chapter, Foucault offers us an account of the shift in meaning of the concept of punishment from juridico-legal to disciplinary. Foucault achieves this through a version of historical explanation called genealogy (see above). But Wittgenstein also offers explanations as to how and why concepts change their meaning. In order to see this in Wittgenstein's case something needs to be said about his notion of the use of a sign. Wittgenstein says (1953,I, # 87): "the sign is in order - if, under normal circumstances, it fulfils its purposes". The qualifying clause here is important because it points to the purposes, aims and practices of human beings. According to Wittgenstein much of what human beings do and say is habitual, though this *need* not be to say that it is *merely* habitual or that there is no intelligence associated with these actions - see also Dewey's (1938a) sense of 'habitual'. In these cases actions are mainly predictable as no other alternative is needed or even occurs to human beings. However, as Dewey points out, the regularities in our experience are the results of our orderings of experience and our habitual actions are intelligent responses to our perceived regularities. Similarly for Wittgenstein because, where regularity is perceived, the rule is already "laid down"; if the present situation is sufficiently like previous situations, then there is warrant for following the rule. Nevertheless, even in the dullest and most repetitious action which accords to a rule, there is a creative "act" so that the rule is both made and remade by this creative practice. In more complex situations vigilance and flexibility will be required so that the rules, if followed, will not be followed in a merely habitual manner with little or no associated consciousness. In such situations rules may need to be adapted or refined.

Normally then a rule is followed because the "reason" for following a rule is that regularities are perceived in the world. However this is not to offer either a reason or an explanation of following a rule *in terms* of the perception of regularities in the world. Following a rule and perceiving regularities are essentially the same thing (Bolton, 1979, p. 142). Indeed no reason can be given for following a rule in the sense of providing a reason as support for following the rule. Although reasons can be given for following a rule in such-and-such a way, e.g. from past experience, teaching, past practice, etc., these can be given only on the condition that this way is the way to follow the rule. But whether it is *the* way will be judged from practice. As Bolton (1979,p. 143) says: "reason is not a 'super-cause' responsible for our following the rule". Wittgenstein says:

How can he *know* how he is to continue a pattern by himself -

> whatever instruction you give him? - Well, how do I know - if that means 'Have I reasons?' the answer is: my reasons will soon give out. And then I shall act, without reasons. (1953 I, # 211)

Wittgenstein provides a sceptical argument in the *Philosophical Investigations* (# 143-242). The force of this argument is that the use of such things as sign posts and tables as expressions of rules, is meant to establish that the expression of the rule cannot carry with it an interpretation *which is not potentially equivocal.* It is *practice* which provides the interpretation of the expression of the rule. We follow the direction of the finger in the sign post example, as we have been taught this practice by people who also followed the direction of the finger, and who, after letting us try it on our own, offered us guidance until the practice was "grasped". A limited (i.e. finite) number of examples are offered of the use of the sign post; what the learner must acquire is the ability to make a potentially unlimited number of judgements. But the future path to be followed is left unsaid; it cannot be grasped in this sense. Whilst we can grasp it *now*, this does not guarantee how the sign post is to be interpreted in the future. Furthermore the rule is grasped in conjunction with other rules in an interlocking web of human practices.

The rule then is made in practice through time and this practice is not merely habitual but, rather, is *creative*, because there is a potentially equivocal situation. There are some similarities here to Foucault's notion of the other and his notion of transcendence. Built into the notion of the other is the fundamental notion of *difference* which, as we have seen above in chapter one, arises in turn in logic and the interpretation of the copula "is". When the copula is interpreted *not* as the "is" of identity, but instead as involving a certain non-being, then a notion of difference is always included in the application of a concept, as opposed to being excluded. Every application of a concept then for Foucault involves a potentially equivocal situation in which the other may surface or predominate.

Where or when the applications of concepts do not fulfil their purposes then either the rules must change or different concepts be adopted. For Foucault this has important implications in relation to the self. Freedom is to be obtained for Foucault by transcending the rule, by attempting to change agreements, by attempting to change rules for the application of concepts. Because of the notion of difference built into every concept each application of a concept involves an equivocal situation for Foucault - as in the Wittgensteinian paradox developed in Kripke's (1982) reading of Wittgenstein, where it appears that any new practice at all can be in accord with the rule. In the equivocal situation when there are no longer rational criteria which compel me to follow the rule, whereas the "conservative" Wittgenstein says that if I am to follow the rule I must feel *moved* to follow the rule, Foucault says that we just "know" when to reject the rule. At best Wittgenstein is a conservative transgressor of rules: Foucault is a positive transgressor, for it is through transgression that freedom lies. Instead of being moved to follow the rule I must be moved to transgress the rule.

Freedom is associated with concepts and descriptions of the self for Foucault. He is interested in the use of concepts to describe oneself, and how classifications such as being a homosexual can describe, objectify and subjectify the self, making the self unfree. However, for Foucault, the applications of concepts is not an all or nothing affair, as included in the concept "X" are notions of "not-x". So the very use of "X" to describe carries within it notions of otherness. The political problem is to resist these classifications which constitute the self as a subjected being, by turning them back into the other, and through an ethics of the self, constituting the self differently. But how is one to know when to resist or when to reject such classifications? Foucault is criticised for failing to provide criteria either for resistance to following rules (to accepting the description of oneself as an X say), or for accepting and following rules, principles or practices. For Foucault then, if the sign is not in order, it is unclear how this is known. He does not provide us with an ethics or a political stance which could provide a basis for resistance. It is not enough just to say that people know when they are oppressed and that oppression, and of course the possibility of resistance, are all around.

Much of Foucault's insight into psychology and psycho-analytic theory was gained from his early study of Freud. Foucault talks a lot about the clinical examination underlying psychoanalytic theory and the ways in which, said to the "right" professionals, one's identity could be constituted in certain ways that left one subjected (Foucault, 1980a). Wittgenstein has a similar insight:

> Analysis is likely to do harm. Because although one may discover in the course of it various things about oneself, one must have a very strong and keen and persistent criticism in order to recognise and see through the mythology that is offered or imposed on one. There is an inducement to say, "Yes, of course, it must be like that". A powerful mythology. (1966, p. 52)

Wittgenstein has a prolonged attack upon psychological theory. His major point was that causal *explanations* did not provide understanding of human "behaviour"/action. Instead of turning to psychological theory then we must come to *understand* puzzling behaviour by seeing what is distinctively human about that behaviour. We must find connecting links between that puzzling behaviour and other non-puzzling behaviour. So we must lay out the facts, "placing things side by side", only placing together what one knows, and see the *connections*. In commenting on Fraser's *Golden Bough* he says:

> I think one reason why the attempt to find an explanation is wrong, is that we have only to put together in the right way what we know, without adding anything, and the satisfaction we are trying to get from the explanation comes of itself ... and the explanation isn't what satisfies us here anyway. (1979,p. 2e)

And:

> We can only *describe* and say, human life is like that. (ibid.,p. 3e)

In *The Order of Things* Foucault mounts sustained attacks upon the human sciences. Elsewhere he tracked the "history" of psychology (Foucault, 1987). It is clear that he has philosophical doubts about the very basis of the human sciences. He sees them as internally incoherent and their explanations as being potentially politically dangerous, because their descriptions and explanations of human beings involve classifications and objectifications which, in turn, lead to treatments. In his early work on psychology (Foucault, 1987) he seeks answers to the questions, "Why did we start to treat madness as *mental illness*?", and, "Why do we assume a unitary pathology in the psychological and pathological domains?" He argues that mental "pathology" requires methods of analysis different from physical pathology. Here there are close parallels to Wittgenstein's approach to psychology.

But Foucault stands with Wittgenstein (e.g., 1980) not only in the rejection of a psychology based upon the natural sciences but also on the notion of the laying out of facts. On this latter point we need only turn to *Discipline and Punish* to see his clear rejection of former marxist approaches to punishment (e.g. Rushke & Kirchheimer, 1939), of legal/criminology theory (dismissed in his attacks upon the juridico-legal model of punishment) and in his rejection of the humanistic interpretation of changes in the forms of punishment. Instead we have a long protracted attempt to lay out the detail of what we know about the practices of punishment and the detailed daily lives of people suffering punishment. But he lays out the facts also of practices and daily lives in asylums, hospitals, military barracks and schools. He places things side by side and, thereby, we see connections. Punishment is not concerned with laws and offences as the legal model would have us believe but with the offender and his soul - it is *disciplinary*. Especially in *I Pierre Rivière*, Foucault lays out the facts (Foucault, 1975a). He provides a cacophony of sound where several competing descriptions of the murders by Pierre Rivière of his mother, his sister and his brother, and of his own life history, occur side by side. His motives in laying out the facts are to question the early psychiatric descriptions and explanations, and to question their truth and ascendency over the other descriptions and stories.

The creative aspect of rule following in Wittgenstein is derived from my reading of Kripke (1982). If this reading of Wittgenstein is correct then there are marked similarities between Foucault and Wittgenstein. If not, but if the creative position on rule following is sustainable independently, then it would have these similarities also to Foucault's thought on the application of concepts.

Resolving the Puzzles

Wittgenstein emphasises the close connections between the meaning of a concept and how it is learned. Louise and David McCarty (1995) emphasise this connection, arguing that there is a form of conceptual connection between the two. Whilst they claim that the scheme, "In order to grasp the concept X, one has already to have undergone a process of teaching/learning via p" (where "X" and "p" are stand ins for *specific* descriptions) is not a logical truth, nevertheless, there are connections, stronger than mere historical contingency. The connections which they identify might be called therefore "conceptual". If this general point is now applied to punishment we can discern marked similarities between the account of Foucault, and Wittgenstein's general position. Foucault asks how questions, inviting us to look at practices of punishment and thereby arrives at a concept of disciplinary punishment. Whilst he does not emphasise learning per se, many of the disciplinary blocks which he writes about, are learning institutions - as well as the school, there is the army, the reformatory and the asylum. He shows how people are not only shaped up in disciplinary blocks but also how concepts fundamental to disciplinary blocks - concepts like "soldier", "madness", and "punishment" - are themselves developed upon learning paths as human beings are shaped up by increasingly sophisticated and refined techniques to function along various parameters according to certain norms. That is the modern concepts of "madness", "soldier", ... cannot be understood independently of the learning paths about madness, etc., that have been established and refined in the disciplinary blocks.

If we follow the later Wittgenstein on the notion of understanding and how this is to be achieved by recourse to a laying out of the facts and that there are conceptual connections between the meaning of "punishment" and how it is learned, then we would tend to follow Foucault's account of punishment as being disciplinary, and that the punishment of children is directed in a disciplinary fashion at their "souls".

Foucault, by asking *how* questions about the practices of punishment, by contrasting Damiens' punishment with those of the young offenders in Faucher's reformatory, shows us the concept of punishment has possibly changed - it has different *empirical* content. Certainly there are two concepts of punishment: the juridico-discursive concept and the disciplinary concept. In Wittgensteinian fashion the child must learn the meaning of "punishment" in child rearing practices, in family and later at school, and these are contexts where clearly the punishment of the child has logical and temporal priority (though Wittgenstein would see this as a logicist distinction). Necessarily the learning of the abstract legal model of punishment must come later as a theoretical abstraction.

Wittgenstein would probably reject approaching the understanding of the punishment of human beings from a form of legal theory, because of his opposition to theory in the understanding of human behaviour. In the understanding of human behaviour he was opposed to theory and, at best, theory must be translated back to forms of life and language-and-the-world. The Hart-Flew-Benn model of punishment, in which the punishment of children is seen as a secondary or peripheral use, would run counter to Wittgenstein's notion of translation back into forms of life and the contexts in which concepts are learned. If the punishment of children is secondary and peripheral then there can be no translation back to a form of life in which punishment in the legal sense is learned. No, the order of learning must be different. From this perspective it would be the legal model concept of punishment, with its derived and abstract character, which is secondary and peripheral, or which needed to be translated back.

What is the resolution of the puzzles? How, as educationalists, are we to talk meaningfully about the punishment of children. Wittgenstein says (1953 I, # 87) that the sign is in order if it fulfils our purposes. Does "punishment" fulfil our educational purposes in either of its above senses? If not can we be creative about the rules? I believe that both Foucault and Wittgenstein show us that the punishment of children must have priority over the legal model and that punishment, if we follow Foucault's "creative act", is more like disciplinary punishment than legal juridico punishment.

A conclusion which can be drawn then is that the way to approach philosophical problems is through the facts, by a laying out of the facts. The original puzzles were generated by contrasting analytic approaches to a philosophical issue, with the archaeological/genealogical/historical approach of Foucault. What Foucault shows is that historically a concept of disciplinary punishment has come to displace the legal model. What the first approach shows us is that analysis of "punishment", whilst (arguably) arriving at a coherent concept, has lost touch with the practices of punishment. The second approach asserts the necessity of starting with the practices. But if Wittgenstein asserts the importance of laying out the facts he does not provide "analytic" tools for such a practice, whereas Foucault does - see e.g., Foucault (1991).

Finally, what recourse to Foucault and also Wittgenstein shows us, but with different approaches, is that indeed language went on holiday in the case of the educational discussion of the punishment of children by philosophers of education. This has important implications for the practices of those of us who might claim to be philosophers of education. By accepting the juridico-legal (Hart-Flew-Benn) model the concept "punishment" had ceased "to come to where it was meant to be working". Where our concepts are working *now*, must be our concern and not where they were working, if indeed they were at all, in the past.

CONCLUSION

The aim of this book has been twofold: first to provide an introduction to Foucault for educators and students of education and to draw out the educational implications of some of his writings: and, second, to provide a critique, derived from Foucault, of the notion of personal autonomy in so far as this is conceived in liberal writings as an important aim, if not *the* aim, of education. It has not attempted to engage with critical theory and writings on education in that area on education - that must wait. Nor has it attempted to prescribe from his writings what should be done in education. On Foucault's own grounds that would have been improper. The book, properly in my view, rests at the level of a *critique*, and in this case a critique of the notion of personal autonomy, especially because this notion of personal autonomy has been re-interpreted in neo-liberal views and recent "reforms" of education in western capitalist democracies. Instead of personal autonomy however we have what I call the notion of the autonomous chooser. This is not the notion of an independent and free chooser but someone whose choices have been structured through the manipulation of needs and interests by what I call busno-power. I have launched several Foucauldean based critiques upon this neo-liberal version of autonomy (Marshall, 1995a&b).

In the Introduction we looked at Michel Foucault, the person, and at Foucault the genealogist. The very brief introduction to his personal life cannot substitute for the much more detailed comment available in the three biographies - Eribon (1991), Macey (1993) and Miller (1993). These biographical details are very important, I believe, for understanding the tracks that his work was to take, and to a certain extent he began to acknowledge these influences in later life. Eribon, who interviewed Foucault on several occasions for *Le Nouvel Observateur* is always the journalist. At times, e.g., the encounters with, and funeral of, Jean-Paul Sartre, his book is quite racey. It does not have the stronger blend of academic work with daily life that is to be found in Macey, which is the best of the three biographies I believe. Macey has a good feel for the philosophical aspects and what was at stake philosophically and personally for Foucault. Miller is also strong on these aspects but his book is marred, I believe, by its sensationalism - for example the unnecessarily detailed exposition of sado-masochistic practices and the association by guilt of Foucault, it seems, with all of these practices. Miller, to his credit, is explicit about aids, whereas Eribon is more coy.

In the second half of the introduction the notion of genealogy as practised by Foucault, is introduced. After outlining general aspects of genealogy vis-a-vis more traditional approaches to history I look at the structure of *Discipline and Punish*, as an example of genealogy.

Chapter One looks at the influences upon Foucault. In many ways Foucault defined himself *against* other philosophers, especially Sartre. But he was also influenced at key times by Heidegger, Nietzsche, and the philosophy of science of Bachelard and Canguilhelm. In retrospect more time should have been found for Heidegger. The chapter looks at those philosophers who were central in his time as a student - what I called the philosophers of the Enlightenment - and then those who influenced him, to the extent that he adopted but adapted some of their ideas. This section I called the voices of the others. By the use of the term "other" I do not mean exclusion but inclusion in the sense that the other is always logically included (for Foucault). From his early attack upon rationality, which was quietly abandoned, through his "liaisons" with Bataille, Blanchot, Nietzsche and Bachelard/Canguilhelm, he remains quietly Kantian - a treatise on Kant was part of his Ph.D. But Kant is addressed again, quite late, in his very important paper "What is Enlightenment?" (Foucault, 1984b). In his view Kant asked the right question for his times, but the question and answer had both ossified. What was important in Kant's question, Foucault believed, was the attitude of Enlightenment. In Chapter Two I outline an account of liberal education, in which I identify three strands. First I look at liberalism as a political doctrine, concluding that there is no one central set of principles which cris-cross and sometimes in their emphases, contradict one another. Thus the principle of equality seems to have been over-ridden in recent neo-liberal doctrines by the principle of freedom which, in turn, is conceived only in the negative sense of freedom, as freedom *from*. Then I outline three approaches to education which can be called liberal. First within the socio-democratic view of politics and the role of education I looked at the ideas of Richard Peters and John Dewey. In both of these thinkers personal autonomy is paramount though, as I suggested, in Dewey there are aspects of social control, by the group or scientific community, which may subsume autonomy under wider notions of social or group authority. Strike's emphasis on freedom in education is also within the liberal sphere, but it does provide some basis for the notion of the autonomous chooser which is found in the recent educational reform literature. Certainly the notion of personal autonomy is central in his writings.

Personal autonomy is developed in chapter three. First some of the accounts of autonomy are identified and a number of issues and questions raised. Then the chapter moves towards answering these questions from a Foucauldean position, looking at power/knowledge and technologies of domination and the self. Finally a more recent account of personal autonomy is outlined.

Chapter four develops the notions of power/knowledge and associated technologies, introduced in chapter three. It does this by looking at Foucault's notion of governmentality.
With this developed notion of power relations it then revisits education and the concepts of authority and power in liberal educational writing. The conclusion drawn is that liberal education, in its pursuit of personal autonomy, masks the power relations operating, and hence the thrust for governmentality, by its talk of authority and the development of mind.

The critique has been developed from Foucault's writings, as it is mainly implicit. Chapter five turns then to look at what Foucault said and did explicitly in relation to education and schooling. He says little explicitly but when in Foucauldean fashion one turns to his educational practices an interesting picture emerges. It is certainly different from the transgressor and political activists. From his work with government, and his explicit teaching practices, e.g., at Vincennes, we must draw the conclusion that he was a traditional university academic, concerned with hard work and getting things "right".

The sixth chapter turns again to personal autonomy, further deepening the argument to consider the liberal humanist notion of Man, which underlies personal autonomy, and why Foucault rejects liberal humanism. Finally, in this chapter, the extent to which Foucault is a post-modernist is considered. It is argued following (Hoy,1988) that there is a sense in which he is - that of no regret - but that this is a rather trivial sense.

In the final chapter we look at what Foucault has to offer to doing philosophy. I take a central issue for both philosophy and education, that of punishment, and look at how an analytic philosopher of education such as R.S.Peters approaches it, and then contrast this with the genealogical approach of Foucault. I argue that Foucault's concept of disciplinary punishment and his approach is more appropriate for understanding the meaning and justification of punishment in education. In this chapter I also draw some parallels between Wittgenstein and Foucault and suggest that Foucault may be closer to Wittgenstein, and thereby to Anglo-Saxon philosophy, than might be apparent from from reading some of his critics.

The book has been mainly expository of Foucault and has attempted to use his ideas to critique personal autonomy as an aim of education. It has not provided a detailed critique of his work, except for his educational practices in chapter five. There is ample general philosophical critique and the reader could start with Hoy (1986). Instead I have taken what I see as a sustainable set of his ideas to critique the notion of personal autonomy as an aim of education.

A general conclusion which might be drawn is that Foucault has little to offer to practising educators in terms of a way forward or a way out. What he does provide is a devastating critique of the subtle and complex power relations that pervade educational institutions, which shape our identity, and which make us governable by masking the reality that our identities are being constituted. What he does not provide is an alternative approach to social institutions and their accompanying practices which are themselves informed by the social sciences. Hence some educators have become ambivalent about the value of Foucault's work for education (see e.g., the discussion between Covaleskie and McDonough, 1993).

At the level of critique, however, Foucault's analysis of power/knowledge has disturbing implications for educators as *professionals*, in addition to the critique of personal autonomy.

(i) Foucault suspends the normative notions of legitimacy and illegitimacy. He directs our attention with his concept of power/knowledge to a host of shaping up processes -learning to speak, read and write, for example - which the liberal framework would not normally identify as being contrary to the interests of the child, and therefore not as instances of *power* relations. Instead the liberal framework uses the concept of authority, particularly rational-legal authority which, because it is rational, carries with it implications of legitimacy.

(ii) Foucault directs our attention here because, in pursuing these educational objectives, we are bringing into play modern power which is directed towards governmentality and a form of political domination. Even in classical liberal theory there is a fragile element, for in the case of Hobbes, as Pasquino (1986) reminds us, there is a need for discipline to ensure obedience to the contract. In *De Clive*, I, 1, Hobbes says: "men can only become political subjects *ex discipline*". And in *Leviathan* there is considerable discussion of how this is to be achieved through education (Marshall, 1981). Much of the talk of liberal education ignores what Hobbes, and Rousseau, were very well aware of, namely, discipline. This modern power has become further contaminated by busnocratic rationality and has become what I call busno-power. It is particularly unfortunate that the concept of authority and the notion of choice permeate recent educational discourse masking these forms of power.

(iii) Whilst modern power permeates all of modern society, according to Foucault, it was developed and refined essentially in the disciplines and still has important homes and sources of legitimation in the disciplines and "associated" human sciences. Busnocratic rationality and busno-power have penetrated further into the disciplines - modern theories of human capital theory and management - and into public schooling. The schools then, as disciplinary blocks, become the first site of 'choice' in the development of autonomous choosers.

(iv) In the disciplines there are found certain views of Man as a moral agent, sexual being, learner, and now autonomous chooser. In the normalising procedures of examination and "confession" people are classified as objects and the truth, about themselves "revealed" to themselves. In constituting the subject in these ways busno-power produces autonomous choosers who are highly governable individuals (cf. Ivan Illich's (1973) comments on schooling as the first site of manipulation and alienation into the schooling mentality).

Foucault seemed extremely pessimistic at times about the possibilities of resistance and deinstitutionalising knowledge and information, as we seem so enmeshed in power processes which we are hardly conscious of and, therefore, may not understand. It is not therefore a question of the redistribution of education, its reorganisation, or its cleansing of ideological content, which are familiar enough demands from the left and those concerned about equality and Education. Education, because of modern power, must take on a new form in which the promise of freedom is not the traditional freedom which is meant to be achieved under the guise of personal autonomy, nor indeed in its modern variant, the autonomous chooser. But Foucault neither articulated nor practised such a form of education.

Clearly Foucault is arguing for a form of freedom but it is not one that he was ever to fully articulate (Rajchman, 1985).

(v) As professionals we must take note of Foucault's violent landscapes. He claims that he is not trying to ridicule, supplant or falsify other approaches to power but, rather, that he is trying to offer us another aspect, or another mask, that reality "wears". In his view we don't have to have a total world view to resist and oppose forms of political subjection and domination; we can do it at any point of time, as the various resistance groups in the western world are showing us. But the problem is to recognise when modern power is being exercised and whether resistance is the appropriate response.

This book has, in general, been sympathetic to Foucault, but there are, of course, a number of traditional philosophical objections which can be brought against his work. As has been said these are well identified in the critical reader by Hoy (1986). They need not be repeated here.

Both Foucault and Wittgenstein see and live the philosophical task as being that of human self understanding. In Wittgenstein's case Janik and Toulmin say:

> So that same humane and cultivated Viennese who had begun, in his youth, by mastering the mechanics of Hertz and the thermodynamics of Boltzmann; whom had gone on, in his thirties, to play a leading part in the development of symbolic logic; who had abandoned philosophy, at the age of thirty, in favour of other, humanly more valuable occupations - that same philosopher found himself, at fifty, urging his hearers to reflect more carefully on the ways in which children do in fact learn (or might alternatively learn) the standard patterns of behaviour within which our language has a practical function, and on the metaphysical confusions that can flow from any failure to keep these practical functions in mind. Yet, for all its seeming changes, his intellectual Odyssey had been directed along a single, constant compass bearing. A man (sic) could obey the Socratic injunction, *Know Thyself*, only if he came to understand the scope and limits of his own understanding: and this meant, first and foremost, recognising the precise scope and limits of language, which is the prime instrument of human understanding. (1973,p. 224)

Janik and Toulmin use the "know thyself" metaphor but with some adjustment of the quotation towards "care for thyself", and abandonment of the section on symbolic logic, much of this applies also to Foucault.

Towards the end of his life and perhaps in some difficulty, though with increasing confidence, Foucault attempted to outline the peculiarly personal aspect of his intellectual, scholarly, and public life and work. There is little doubt that his work had been for him a particular kind of test or "essay" (to use Miller's (1993) term to describe Foucault's notion of a trial or experiment or *assay*) in which the philosopher changes or transcends the self in the pursuit of "truth" or understanding. The philosopher must be able to understand oneself and thereby to change oneself in the process of philosophy. Transgression was not merely an exercise in thought for Foucault but, also, a transgression in reality, and a transgression which reconstituted the self. It was not therefore a mere rejection of ideas or customs. Transgression had to be a reflective *reconstitution*. In the insight and understanding of the self brought about by the injunction *Care for Thyself* the self was to be transformed by the central notion of care, and secondarily by the notion of knowledge. Foucault argued and claimed that the Delphic maxim had been transformed to *Know Thyself* whereas it should be understood as *Care for Thyself*, though not in any narcissistic sense.

For Foucault then the purpose of reading and doing philosophy is essentially a matter concerned with the exploration and knowledge of the self.

On that note I will end.

REFERENCES

Aaron, Richard I. 1955. *John Locke*, (2nd.edition). Oxford: Oxford University Press.
Acton H.B. (ed.). 1963. *The Philosophy of Punishment*. London: MacMillan.
Althusser, Louis 1976. *Essays in Self-Criticism*. London: New Left Books.
Anderson, Perry 1976. *Considerations on Western Marxism*. London: NLB.
Arac, Jonathan (ed.) 1988. *After Foucault: Humanistic Knowledge and Post-modern challenges*. New Brunswick and London: Rutgers University Press.
Ariès, Phillipe 1962. *Centuries of Childhood*. New York: Vintage Books.
Bachelard, Gaston 1953. *Le Matérialisme Rationnel*. Paris: P.U.F.
Bachelard, Gaston 1969. *The Philosophy of No* (transl. G.C.Waterson). New York: Orion Press.Original French version, P.U.F.,1940.
Bachelard, Gaston 1984. *The New Scientific Spirit*. Boston: Beacon Press. Original French Version, 1934, Alcan.
Baier, Kurt 1973. 'Moral Autonomy as an Aim of Moral Education.' In Glenn Langford & D.J. O'Connor eds. 1973: 96-114.
Ball, Stephen (ed.) 1990. *Foucault and Education: Disciplines and Knowledge*. London: Routledge.
Barnes, Hazel E. 1968. 'Introduction.' In Jean-Paul Sartre, *Search for a Method*. New York: Vintage Books: vii-xxxi.
Barrow, Robin 1975. *The Philosophy of Education*. London: Methuen.
Beauvoir, Simone de. 1985. *Adieum*. Penguin: Harmondsworth.
Beccaria, C.B. 1764. *An Essay on Crimes and Punishment*.
Benn, S.I. 1958. 'An Approach to the Problems of Punishment.' *Philosophy* 33: 325-341.
Benn, S.I. and Peters, R.S. 1965. *The Principles of Political Thought*. London: The Free Press.
Bernauer, James and Keenan, Thomas 1988. 'The Works of Michel Foucault 1954-1984.' In James Bernauer and David Rasmussen, eds. 1988: 119-158.
Bernauer, James, and Rasmussen, David 1988. *The Final Foucault*. Cambridge, Mass.: M.I.T. Press.
Bernstein, Richard 1976. *The Restructuring of Social and Political Theory*. New York: Harcourt Brace Jovanovich.

Bernstein, Richard (ed.) 1985. *Habermas and Modernity*. Cambridge: Polity Press in assoc. with Basil Blackwell.

Beyer, Landen E. and Liston, Daniel P. 1992. 'Discourse or Moral Action? A Critique Of Postmodernism.' *Educational Theory* 42(4): 371-393.

Binswanger, Ludwig 1986. In Keith Hoeller, ed. *Dream and Existence*. Seattle: Review of Existential Psychology and Psychiatry: 79-105. Originally published 1954. *L'Réve et L'Existence*, transl. Jacqueline Verdeaux. Paris: Desclée de Brouwer.

Bolton, Derek 1979. *An Approach to Wittgenstein's Philosophy*. Atlantic Highlands: Humanities Press.

Bouchard, David F. (ed.) 1977. *Language, Counter-Memory, Practice*. Ithaca, N.Y.: Cornell University Press.

Bowles, Samuel and Gintis, Herbert 1976. *Schooling in Capitalist America*. New York: Basic Books.

Boyne, Roy 1990. *Foucault and Derrida: the Other Side of Reason*. London: Unwin Hyman.

Brown, S. C. (ed.) 1975. *Philosophers Discuss Education*, London: Macmillan.

Burbules, Nicholas C. 1986. 'A Theory of Power in Education.' *Educational Theory* 36(2): 95-114.

Burchell, Graham, Gordon, Colin and Miller, Peter (eds.). 1991. *The Foucault Effect: Studies in Governmentality*. Chicago: The University of Chicago Press.

Canguilhelm, Georges 1977. *Ideologie et Rationalité*. Paris: Vrin.

Capelle, Jean 1967. *Tomorrow's Education: the French Experience*, transl. W.D. Halls. London: Pergammon Press.

Cohn-Bendit, Daniel and Cohn-Bendit, Gabriel 1968. *Obsolete Communism: the Left-wing Alternative*, transl. A. Pomerans. London: Deutsch.

Condorcet, Marquis de. 1795. *Sketch for a Historical Picture of the Progress of the Human Mind*. Quoted in J.S. Schapiro, 1958: 104.

Condorcet, Marquis de. 1792. *Report on the General Organisation of Knowledge*. Quoted in J.S. Schapiro, 1958: 110.

Cooper, David E. (ed.) 1986. *Education, Values and Mind: Essays for R.S. Peters*. London: Routledge and Kegan Paul.

Cousins, M. and Hussain, A. 1984. *Michel Foucault*. London: Macmillan.

Covaleskie, John 1993. 'Power Goes to School: Teachers Students and Discipline'. *Philosophy of Education*. Proceedings of the

Philosophy of Education Society.
Cuypers, Stefaan 1992. 'Is Personal Autonomy the First Principle of Education?' *Journal of Philosophy of Education* 26(1): 5-18.
Cuypers, Stefaan 1995. 'What Wittgenstein Would Have Said About Personal Autonomy'. In Paul Smeyers and James Marshall, eds. 1995:127-142.
Dearden, R.F. 1968. *The Philosophy of Primary Education*. London: Routledge and Kegan Paul.
Dearden, R.F. 1972. 'Autonomy and Education.' In R.F. Dearden, P.H. Hirst and R.S. Peters, eds. 1976: 448-465.
Dearden, R.F. 1975. 'Autonomy as an Educational Ideal.' In S.C. Brown, ed. 1975: 3-18.
Dearden, R.F., Hirst, P.H. and Peters, R.S. (eds) 1976. *Education and the Development of Reason*. London: Routledge and Kegan Paul.
Deleuze, Gilles 1968. *Différence et Répétition*. Paris: Paris University Press.
Department of Education. 1988. *Administering for Excellence*. Wellington: Government Printer (known as the Picot Report).
Derrida, Jacques 1963. 'Cogito and the History of Madness'. In Derrida,1978, *Writing and Difference*. London: Routledge and Kegan Paul.
Descombes, Vincent 1980. *Modern French Philosophy*. Cambridge: Cambridge University Press.
Dewey, John 1916. *Democracy and Education*. New York: The Free Press.
Dewey, John 1938a. *Logic: the Theory of Inquiry*. New York: Holt, Rinehart, Winston.
Dewey, John 1938b. *Experience and Education*. New York: Macmillan.
Dewey, John 1946. *The Problems of Men*. New York: Philosophical Library.
Dewey, John 1962. *Individualism Old and New*. New York: Capricorn Books (first published 1929).
Donnelly, M. 1982. 'Foucault's Genealogy of the Human Sciences.' *Economy and Society* 11(4): 363-379.
Donzelot, Jacques 1980. *The Policing of Families: Welfare Versus the State*. London: Hutchinson.
Dreyfus, Hubert and Rabinow, Paul 1983. *Michel Foucault: Beyond Structuralism and Hermeneutics*. Chicago: Chicago University Press.

Dunn, John 1979. *Western Political Theory in the Face of The Future*. Cambridge: Cambridge University Press.

Dworkin, G. 1981. 'The Concept of Autonomy.' In J. Christman, ed. 1989, *The Inner Citadel: Essays on Individual Autonomy*. Oxford: Oxford University Press.

Eribon, Didier 1989. *Michel Foucault (1926-1984)*. Paris: Flammarion.

Eribon, Didier 1991. *Michel Foucault*, transl. Betsy Wing. Cambridge, Mass.: Harvard University Press.

Faure, Edgar. 1968. *Déclaration de M.Edgar Faure, Ministre de l'Éducation Nationale Devant le Parlement*, National Assemblée, le 8 Octobre, et Senat, le 24 Octobre. Paris: Ministère de l'Éducation Nationale.

Flew, Anthony. 1954. 'The Justification of Punishment'. *Philosophy* 29: 291-307.

Foucault, Michel 1954a. 'Introduction' to Binswanger's *Dream and Existence*. In Keith Hoeller, ed. 1986.

Foucault, Michel 1954b. *Maladie Mentale et Personalité*, revised as *Maladie Mentale et Psychologie* in 1964. This version published University of California Press in 1987 as *Mental Illness and Psychology*.

Foucault, Michel 1961. *Folie et Déraison: la Histoire de la Folie à l'Age Classique*. Paris: Plon.

Foucault, Michel 1966a. 'Entretien.' *La Quinzaine Littéraire* 5 May 16: 14-15.

Foucault, Michel 1966b. 'L'Homme est-il Mort?' *Arts et Loisirs*. June 15: 8-9.

Foucault, Michel 1967. 'Deuxieme Entretien avec Michel Foucault: 'Sur le Facon d'Ecrire l'Histoire'. *Les Lettres Françaises*. June 15: 8-9. (Reprinted as 'The Discourse of History,' in *Foucault Live*, 11-34).

Foucault, Michel 1968. 'Foucault Répond à Sartre.' *La Quinzaine Littéraire* 46, 1-15 Mars: 20-22. (Reprinted in part in *Foucault Live*: 35-43).

Foucault, Michel 1969. 'Michel Foucault Explique Son Dernier Livre.' *La Magazine Littéraire* 28, April-May: 23-25.

Foucault, Michel 1970. 'Le Piège de Vincennes.' *Le Nouvel Observateur*, 9 February. Quoted in Macey, 1993.

Foucault, Michel 1971a. 'The Discourse on Language.' In Foucault 1972b.

Foucault, Michel 1971b. 'Correspondence de Michel Foucault.' *La Pensée* 159. Sept-Oct: 141-144.

Foucault, Michel 1971c. 'Rituals of Exclusion.' In part in, *Foucault Live*: 63-72. The quote is from the original paper, 'A Conversation with Michel Foucault.' *Partisan Review* 38 (2):201, and was not in the version reprinted as 'Rituals of Exclusion.' I take the quote from Miller 1993: 180.

Foucault, Michel 1971d 'Nietzsche, Genealogy, History.' In D. Bouchard ed. 1977: 139-164.

Foucault, Michel 1972a 'Intellectuals and Power.' In D.Bouchard ed. 1977: 205-217.

Foucault, Michel 1972b. *The Archaeology of Knowledge*. London: Tavistock.

Foucault, Michel 1972c. 'On Popular Justice: a Discussion With Maoists.' In: C.Gordon ed. 1980, *Power/Knowledge*. New York: Pantheon: 1-36.

Foucault, Michel 1972c. 'Table Ronde.' *Esprit*, 413 Avril-Mai: 678-703. Foucault, Michel 1973a. *The Order of Things*. New York: Vintage.

Foucault, Michel 1973b. 'L'Intellectual Sert A Ressembler Les Idees, Mais...."Son Savoir Est Partial Par Rapport Au Savoir Ouvrier".' *Libèration* 16, 26 Mai: 2-3.

Foucault, Michel 1973d. *Madness and Civilization*. New York: Vintage.

Foucault, Michel 1974. 'Michel Foucault: an interview.' *Impulse*: 50-55.

Foucault, Michel 1975a. *I, Pierre Rivière, Having Slaughtered My Mother, My Sister, and My Brother...* New York: Random House.

Foucault, Michel 1975b. 'Prison Talk.' In C.Gordon, ed. 1980: 37-54.

Foucault, Michel 1976. 'Questions on Geography.' In C.Gordon, ed. 1980: 63-77.

Foucault, Michel 1977a. 'Two Lectures.' In C. Gordon, ed. 1980: 78-108.

Foucault, Michel 1977b. 'Power and Sex.' In L.Kritzman, ed. 1988: 110-124.

Foucault, Michel 1977c. 'Truth and Power.' In C.Gordon, ed. 1980: 109-133.

Foucault, Michel 1977d. 'The Eye of Power.' In: C. Gordon 1980: 146-165.

Foucault, Michel 1977e. 'Nietzsche, Genealogy, History.' In D.Bouchard, ed. 1977: 139-164.

Foucault, Michel 1978a 'The Dangerous Individual.' In L.Kritzman, ed. 1988, 125-151.

Foucault, Michel 1978b. 'A Quoi Revent Les Iraniens.' *Le Nouvel Observateur* 726, 8 Oct: 48-49.

Foucault, Michel 1979a. *Discipline and Punish: the Birth of the Prison.* New York: Vintage.

Foucault, Michel 1979b. 'Governmentality.' *Ideology and Consciousness* 7: 5-26.

Foucault, Michel 1980a. *The History of Sexuality*, Vol.1. New York: Vintage.

Foucault, Michel 1980b. 'Le Philosophe Masque.' *Le Monde Dimanche* 10945, 6 Avril: I and XVII. Republished in L.Kritzman, ed. 1988: 323-330.

Foucault, Michel 1981a. 'Les Reponses De Pierre Vidal-Naquet Et De Michel Foucault.' *Libération* 185: 12.

Foucault, Michel 1981b. 'Notes Sur Qu'on Lit Et Entend.' *Le Nouvel Observateur* 893: 21.

Foucault, Michel 1981c. 'Politics and Reason.' In L. Kritzman, ed. 1988, 57-85.

Foucault, Michel 1982a. 'Truth, Power, Self: an Interview.' In H. Martin et al., eds. 1988: 9-15.

Foucault, Michel 1982b. 'Technologies of the Self.' In H. Martin, et al., eds. 1988: 16-49.

Foucault, Michel 1982c. 'The Political Technology of Individuals.' In H. Martin et.al., eds. 1988: 145-162.

Foucault, Michel 1983a. 'Afterword: The Subject and Power.' In H.Dreyfus and P.Rabinow, 1983: 208-226.

Foucault, Michel 1983b. 'On the Genealogy of Ethics.' In H. Dreyfus and P. Rabinow, 1983: 229-252.

Foucault, Michel 1983c. 'The Minimalist Self.' In L. Kritzman, ed. 1988: 3-18.

Foucault, Michel 1983d. 'Critical Theory/Intellectual History.' In L. Kritzman, ed. 1988: 17-46.

Foucault, Michel 1983e. 'Social Security.' In L. Kritzman, ed. 1988, 159-177.

Foucault, Michel 1984a. 'Polemics, Politics and Problematisation.' In P. Rabinow, ed. 1984: 381-393.

Foucault, Michel 1984b. 'What is Enlightenment?' In P. Rabinow, ed. 1984: 32-50.

Foucault, Michel 1984c. 'The Ethic of Care for the Self as a Practice of Freedom.' In J.Bernauer, et al., eds. 1988: 1-20.

Foucault, Michel 1984d. 'Entretien: L'Intellectual et les Pouvoirs.' *La Revue Nouvelle* 80 (10), October: 338-345. Recorded 14 May 1981.

Foucault, Michel 1984e. 'The Concern for Truth.' Reprinted in *Foucault*

Live, 293-208. An interview conducted by François Ewald which appeared in *Le Magazine Littéraire*, May.

Foucault, Michel 1984f. 'Michel Foucault, 1926-...' Reprinted in Gary Gutting, ed. 1994: 314-319. This was originally signed 'Maurice Florence' but this seems to be Foucault.

Foucault, Michel 1985a. *The Use of Pleasure: the History of Sexuality, Vol II*. New York: Vintage.

Foucault, Michel 1985b. 'The Return of Morality.' In L.Kritzman, ed. 1988: 242-254.

Foucault, Michel 1986. 'Dream and Existence.' Foreword to Binswanger 1986: 29-78.

Foucault, Michel 1987. *Mental Illness and Psychology*. Berkeley: University of California Press.

Foucault, Michel 1988a. (Laurence J. Kritzman, ed.) *Politics, Philosophy, Culture: Interviews and Other Writings, 1977-1984*. London and New York: Routledge.

Foucault, Michel 1988b. 'The Political Technology of Individuals.' In H. Martin et al, eds. 1988: 145-162.

Foucault, Michel. 1989. *Foucault Live: Interviews 1966-1984*. New York: Semiotexte.

Foucault Michel 1990. *The Care of the Self: the History of Sexuality*, Vol III. Harmondsworth: Penguin.

Foucault, Michel 1991. 'Questions of Method.' In D.Burchell et.al., eds. 1991: 73-86.

Frankfurt, Harry. 1988. *The Importance of What We Care About: Philosophical Essays*. Cambridge: Cambridge University Press.

Fraser, W. R. 1971. *Reforms and Restraints in Modern French Education*. London: Routledge and Kegan Paul.

Fraser, Nancy 1985. 'Michel Foucault: a Young Conservative.' *Ethics* 96: 165-184.

Gilligan, Carol. 1982. *In a Different Voice: Psychological Theory and Women's Development*. Cambridge, Mass.: Harvard University Press.

Goldstein, Jan 1984. 'Foucault Among the Sociologists: the Disciplines and the History of the Professions.' *History and Theory* 23(2): 170-192.

Gordon, Colin (ed.) 1980. *Power/Knowledge: Selected Interviews and Other Writings*. New York: Pantheon.

Gordon, Colin. 1991. 'Governmental Rationality: An Introduction.' In D.Burchell et al., eds. 1991, 1-52.

Green, T.H. 1889. 'Liberal Legislation and Freedom of Contract.' In R.L.

Nettleship, ed. 1948. *Works of T.H. Green*. London: Longmans Green.

Gutman, Huck 1988. 'Rousseau's Confessions: a Technology of the Self.' In H. Martin et al., 1988: 99-120.

Gutting, Gary 1989. *Michael Foucault's Archaeology of Scientific Reason*. Cambridge: Cambridge University Press.

Gutting, Gary (ed.) 1994. *The Cambridge Companion to Foucault*. Cambridge: Cambridge University Press.

Habermas, Jurgen 1981. 'Modernity versus Postmodernity.' *New German Critique*, 22 (Winter): 3-14.

Hacking, Ian 1981. 'The Archaeology of Michel Foucault.' *New York Review of Books*, 14 May, 32-37.

Hall, Stuart. 1986. 'Variants of Liberalism.' In J. Donald and S. Hall, eds. 1986. *Politics and Ideology*. Milton Keynes: Open University Press.

Halls, W.D. 1976. *Education, Culture and Politics in Modern France*. Oxford: Pergammon Press.

Hampson, Norman. 1968. *The Enlightenment*. Harmondsworth: Pelican.

Hare, R.M. 1975. 'Chairman's Remarks on the Symposium "Autonomy as an educational ideal".' In S.C.Brown, ed. 1975: 36-42.

Harris, C.K. 1977. 'Peters on Schooling.' *Educational Philosophy and Theory* 9 (1): 33-48.

Hart, H.L.A. 1968. *Punishment and Responsibility*. Oxford: Clarendon Press.

Hayek, F.A. 1947. *Collectivist Economic Planning: Critical Studies on the Possibilities of Socialism*. London: Routledge.

Hayek, F.A. 1960. *The Constitution of Liberty*. Chicago: Chicago University Press.

Heidegger, Martin. 1982. *The Basic Problems of Phenomenology*. Bloomington: Indiana University Press.

Henriques, J. et.al. 1984. *Changing the Subject*. London: Methuen.

Hirsh, Arthur 1981. *The French New Left: an Intellectual History from Sartre to Gorz*. Boston: South End.

Hirst, P.H. 1965. 'Liberal education and the Nature of Knowledge.' In R.D. Archambault, ed. 1965. *Philosophical Analyses in Education*. London: Routledge and Kegan Paul: 113-138.

Hobbes, Thomas. 1664. *Leviathan*.

Hobhouse, L.T. 1911. *Liberalism*. London: Williams and Norgate.

Hoeller, Keith. (ed.) 1986. *Dream and Existence*, Seattle: *Review of Existential Psychology and Psychiatry*. Originally published as L'Réve et L'Existence, transl. Jacqueline Verdeaux. Paris:

Desclée de Brouwer 1954.

Hoskin, Keith. 1979. 'The Examination, Disciplinary Power and Rational Schooling.' *History of Education* 8 (2): 135-146.

Hoskin, Keith. 1990. 'The Crypto-educationalist Unmasked.' In S. Ball, ed. 1990: 29-53.

Hoy, David Couzens. 1981. 'Power, Repression, Progress: Foucault, Lukes and the Frankfurt School.' *Triquarterly* 52: 43-63.

Hoy, David Couzens (ed.) 1986. *Foucault: a Critical Reader*. Oxford: Basil Blackwell.

Hoy, David Couzens. 1988. 'Foucault: Modern or Postmodern?' In J. Arac, ed. 1988: 12-41.

Jameson, F. 1984. 'Forward.' In Jean François Lyotard, 1984. *The Postmodern Condition: a Report on Knowledge*. Minnesota: University of Minnesota Press, vii-xxi.

Janik, Allan, and Toulmin, Stephen 1973. *Wittgenstein's Vienna*. New York: Simon and Schuster.

Jay, Martin. 1984. *Marxism and Totality: the Adventures of a Concept from Lucacs to Habermas*. Berkeley: University of California Press.

Jones, K, and Williamson, K. 1979. 'The Birth of the Schoolroom.' *Ideology and Consciousness* 5-6: 58-110.

Kiziltan, M., Bain, W.J., and Anita Canizares M. 1990. 'Postmodern Conditions: Rethinking Public Education'. *Educational Theory* 40 (3): 351-369.

Kleinig, John. 1982. *Philosophical Issues in Education*. London: Croom Helm.

Kohlberg, Lawrence. 1981. *The Philosophy of Moral Development: Moral Stages and the Idea of Justice*. San Francisco: Harper and Row.

Kojéve, Alexandre. 1947. *Introduction to the Reading of Hegel*, (1969 ed. transl., James H. Nicholls Jnr). New York: Basic Books.

Körner, Stephan. 1966. *Experience and Theory: an Essay in the Philosophy of Science*. London: Routledge and Kegan Paul.

Kripke, Saul A. 1982. *Wittgenstein on Rules and Private Language*. Oxford: Basil Blackwell.

Kritzman, Lawrence. 1988. *Michel Foucault: Politics Philosophy Culture: Interviews and Other Writings 1977-1984*. London: Routledge.

Langford, Glenn, and O'Connor, D.J. 1973. *New Essays in the Philosophy of Education*. London: Routledge and Kegan Paul.

Lankshear, Colin J. 1982. *Freedom and Education: Toward a Non-*

Rational Philosophy of Education. Auckland: Milton Brookes.

Lasch, Christopher. 1979. *Haven in a Heartless World: the Family Besieged*. New York: Basic Books.

Lecourt, Dominique. 1975. *Marxism and Epistemology: Bachelard, Canguilhem and Foucault*. London: NLB.

Lemert, C.C. and Gillen, G. 1982. *Michael Foucault: Social Theory as Transgression*. New York: Columbia University Press.

Libération 1984. 'Le Canard et le Renard ou la Vie d'un Philosophie.' 1 July, 16-19. Obituary for Foucault.

Locke, John. 1690. *Two Treatises of Government* (1924 ed.). London: Everyman's Library.

Lukes, Steven. 1972. *Individualism*. Oxford: Blackwell.

Lukes, Steven. 1974. *Power: a Radical View*. London: Macmillan.

Lyotard, Jean-François. 1968. 'Preamble to a Charter', reprinted in 1993 *Political Writings*, trans. Bill Readings. London: UCL Press: 41-45.

Lyotard, Jean-François. 1978. 'Endurance and the Profession.' In J.F. Lyotard, 1993: 70-76.

Lyotard, Jean-François. 1984. *The Post-Modern Condition*, Manchester: Manchester University Press.

Lyotard, Jean-François. 1988. *The Differend*. Manchester: Manchester University Press.

Lyotard, Jean-François. 1993. *Political Writings*, transl. Bill Readings and Kevin Geiman. London:U.C.L. Press.

Macrides, Roy C. 1975. *French Politics in Transition: Three years After de Gaulle*. Cambridge, Mass.: Winthrop.

Macey, David. 1993. *The Lives of Michel Foucault*. London: Hutchinson.

Marshall, James D. 1972. 'On Why We Don't Punish Children.' *Educational Philosophy and Theory* 4(2): 57-68.

Marshall, James D. 1973. 'The Problem of Identity.' Unpublished Ph.D. Thesis: The University of Bristol.

Marshall, James D. 1975. 'Punishment and Education.' *Educational Theory* 24(2): 148-157.

Marshall, James D. 1981. 'Thomas Hobbes: Education and Obligation in the Commonwealth.' *Journal of Philosophy of Education* 14(2): 322-331.

Marshall, James D. 1984a. 'Punishment and Moral Education.' *Journal of Moral Education* 13(2): 79-85.

Marshall, James D. 1984b. 'John Wilson on the Necessity of Punishment.' *Journal of Philosophy of Education* 18(1): 97-104.

Marshall, James D. 1985 'Wittgenstein on Rules: Implications for

Authority and Discipline in Education.' *Journal of Philosophy of Education* 19(1): 3-11.

Marshall, James D. 1989. 'Foucault and Education'. *Australian Journal of Education* 33(2): 97-111.

Marshall, James D. 1990. 'Foucault and Educational Research'. In S. Ball, ed., *Foucault and Education: Discipline and Knowledge*. London and New York: Routledge, 11-28.

Marshall, James D. 1990. 'Asking Philosophical Questions about Education: Foucault on punishment.' *Educational Philosophy and Theory* 22(2): 81-92.

Marshall, James D. 1995a. 'Foucault and Neo-Liberalism: Biopower and Busnopower'. In Alven Neiman (ed.) *Philosophy of Education 1995, Proceedings of the Philosophy of Education Society*. Illinois: Philosophy of Education Society.

Marshall, James D. 1995b. 'Skills, Information and Quality for the Autonomous Chooser'. In Mark Olssen and Kay Morris Matthews, eds. 1995. *Education, Democracy and Reforms*. Auckland: New Zealand Association for Research in Education.

Marshall, James D. 1995c. 'Pedagogy and Apedagogy: Lyotard and Foucault at Vincennes.' In Michael Peters, ed. *Education and the Postmodern Condition*. New York: Bergin and Garvey, 167-192.

Marshall, James D. 1995d. 'On What We May Hope: Rorty on Dewey and Foucault'. In James Garrison, ed. 1995. *The New Scholarship on Dewey*. Dordrecht: Kluwer.

Marshall, James D. 1995e. 'Wittgenstein and Foucault: Resolving Philosophical Puzzles.' In Paul Smeyers and James Marshall, eds. 1995. *Wittgenstein and Education: accepting the challenge*. Dordrecht: Kluwer: 205-220.

Marshall, James D. 1995f. 'Needs, Interests, Growth and Personal Autonomy: Foucault on Power'. In Wendi Kohli ed. *Critical Conversations in Philosopy of Education: from Theory to Practice and Back*. New York: Routledge, Chapman Hall: 364-378.

Marshall, James D. and Peters, Michael. 1990. 'The Insertion of New Right Thinking into Education: an example from New Zealand', *Journal of Education Policy* 5(2): 143-156.

Marshall, James D. and Peters, Michael. 1991 'Educational "Reforms" and New Right Thinking: an Example From New Zealand.' *Educational Philosophy and Theory* 23(2): 46-57.

Martin, L.H., Gutman, H., and Hutton, P.H. 1988. *Technologies of the Self*. Amherst: University of Massachusetts Press.

Maxcy, S.J. 1977. 'A Structuralist View of American Education.' *Paedagogica Historica* 17(2): 333-346.

McCarty, Louise and David 1995. 'Wittgenstein On The Unreasonableness of Education.' In Paul Smeyers and James Marshall, eds. 1995: 63-76.

McDonough, Kevin. 1993. 'Overcoming Ambivalence About Foucault's Relevance for Education.' *Philosophy of Education*, Proceedings of the Philosophy of Education Society: 86-89.

Megill, Alan. 1979. 'Foucault, Structuralism and the Ends of History.' *Journal of Modern History* 51: 451-503.

Ministère de l'Éducation Nationale. 1967. *Horaires, Programmes, Instructions - Philosophie*. Paris: M.E.N.

Merleau-Ponty, Maurice 1973. *Adventures Of The Dialectic*. Evanston, Ill: Northwestern University Press.

Mill, John Stuart. 1859. *On Liberty*.

Miller, James 1993. *The Passion of Michel Foucault*. New York: Simon and Schuster.

Norman, Richard 1982. 'Does Equality Destroy Liberty?' In Keith Graham, ed. 1982. *Contemporary Political Philosophy: Radical Studies*. Cambridge: Cambridge University Press.

Nozick, Robert 1974. *Anarchy, State, Utopia*. Cambridge, Mass: Harvard University Press.

Nyberg, David 1981. *Power over Power*. Ithaca, N.Y.: Cornell University Press.

Oakeshott, Michael 1971. 'Education: the Engagement and Frustration.' *Journal of Philosophy of Education* 5(1): 43-76.

O.E.C.D. 1971. *Reviews of National Policies for Education*. Paris: O.E.C.D.

O'Hear, Anthony. 1986. 'Education and Rationality.' In D. Cooper, ed. 1986: 89-110.

Pasquino, Pablo. 1986. 'Michel Foucault (1926-1984): the Will to Knowledge.' *Economy and Society* 15(1): 97-109.

Peters, Michael A. and Marshall, James D. 1960. 'Children of Rogernomics: The New Right, Individualism and the Culture of Narcissism.' *Sites* 21: 174-191.

Peters, R.S. 1958. *Hobbes*. London: Pelican.

Peters, R.S. 1966. *Ethics and Education*. London: George Allen & Unwin.

Phenix, P.H. 1964. *Realms of Meaning*. New York: McGraw-Hill.

Pickles, Dorothy. 1973. *The Government and Politics of France* (Vol. 2), London: Methuen.

Piel, Jean. 1986. 'Foucault à Uppsala.' *Critique*, August-September, 471-472.

Pignatelli, Frank. 1993a. 'What Can I Do?: Foucault On Freedom and the Question of Teacher Agency.' *Educational Theory* 43 (4): 411-432.

Pignatelli, Frank. 1993b. 'Dangers, Possibilities: Ethico- Political choices in the Work of Michel Foucault.' *Philosophy of Education*, Proceedings of the 49th Conference of the Philosophy of Education Society: 378-387.

Poster, Mark. 1975. *Existential Marxism in post-war France: From Sartre to Althusser*. Princeton, N.J.: Princeton University Press.

Poster, Mark. 1984. *Foucault, Marxism and History: Mode of Production Versus Mode of Information*. Cambridge: Polity Press.

Poulantzas, Nicos. 1978. *State, Power, Socialism*. London: New Left Books.

Rajchman, John. 1985. *Michel Foucault: the Freedom of Philosophy*. New York: Columbia University Press.

Rorty, R. 1982. *Consequences of Pragmatism: Essays, 1972-1980*. Minneapolis: University of Minnesota Press.

Rusche, G. and Kirchheimer, O. 1939. *Punishment and Structure*. New York: Columbia University Press.

Safran, William. 1977. *The French Polity*. New York: McKay.

Said, Edward. 1988. 'Michel Foucault 1926-1984.' In J. Arac, ed. 1988: 1-11.

Sarap, Madan. 1982. *Education, State and Crisis: a Marxist Perspective*. London: Routledge and Kegan Paul.

Sartre, Jean-Paul. 1956. *Being and Nothingness: an Essay on Phenomenological Ontology,* transl. Hazel E. Barnes. New York: Philosophical Library.

Sartre, Jean-Paul. 1962. *Nausea*, transl. Lloyd Alexander. London: Hamilton.

Sartre, Jean-Paul. 1968. *Search For A Method*. New York: Vintage.

Sartre, Jean-Paul. 1973. *Critique of Dialectical Reason: Theory of Practical Ensembles*. London: New Left Books.

Schapiro, L.J. 1958. *Liberalism: its Meaning and History*. New York: Van Nostrand Reinhold.

Seigel, Jerrold. 1990. 'Avoiding the Subject: a Foucaultian Itinerary.' *Journal of the History of Ideas* 51(2), 273-299.

Sheridan, Alan. 1984. 'Diary', *London Review of Books*, 19 July-1 August. An obituary for Foucault.

Smart, Barry. 1983. *Foucault, Marxism and Critique*. London: Routledge.

Smart, Barry. 1986. *Michel Foucault.* London: Routledge.

Smeyers, Paul. 1992. 'The Necessity for Particularity in Education and Child-Rearing: the Moral Issue.' *Journal of Philosophy of Education* 26(1): 63-73.

Smeyers, Paul, and Marshall, James. (eds.) 1995. *Philosophy and Education: Accepting Wittgenstein's Challenge.* Dordrecht: Kluwer.

Spencer, Herbert. 1851. *Social Statistics*, Quoted in Schapiro, 1958.

Strike, Kenneth. 1982. *Educational Policy and the Just Society.* Urbana,Ill.: Illinois University Press.

Taylor, Charles 1986. 'Foucault on Freedom and Truth.' In D.C.Hoy, ed. 1986: 69-102.

Taylor, Charles 1989. *Sources of the Self: the Making of Modern Identity.* Cambridge, Mass.: Harvard University Press.

Trombadori, Ducio 1981. *Colloqui con Foucault.* Salerno: Cooperative Editrice.

Tuck, Bryan 1983. 'Education and Tests of Scholastic Ability: Is There a Baby in the Bath Water.' *New Zealand Journal of Educational Studies* 18(2): 165-171.

Veyne, Paul 1984. Quoted in Goldstein (1984).

Voltaire, F.M.A. de. 1673. *Treatise on Tolerance*, Quoted in Schapiro 1958.

Walkerdine, Valerie 1984. 'Developmental Psychology and the Child Centred Pedagogy.' In J.Henriques et al., 1984: 157-174.

Walkerdine, Valerie 1986. 'Post structural Theory and Everyday Social Practices: the family and the School.' In S. Willkinson, ed. 1986. *Feminist Social Psychology: developing theory and practice.* Milton Keynes: Open University Press: 51-68.

Walzer, Michael 1986. 'The Politics of Michel Foucault.' In D.C. Hoy, ed., 1986: 51-68.

White, Pat 1983. *Beyond Domination.* London: Routledge and Kegan Paul.

White, Sam 1984. *Sam White's Paris.* Seven Oaks: New English Library.

Wilson, John 1977. *Philosophy and Practical Education.* Henley: Routledge and Kegan Paul.

Wilson P.S. 1971. *Interest and Discipline in Education.* Henley: Routledge and Kegan Paul.

Wittgenstein, Ludwig 1953. *Philosophical Investigations.* Oxford: Blackwell.

Wittgenstein, Ludwig 1966. 'Lectures and Conversations on Aesthetics.' In C. Barrett, ed. 1966. *Psychology and Religious Belief.* Oxford:

Blackwell.

Wittgenstein, Ludwig 1979. 'Remarks On Fraser's Golden Bough.' In C. Luckhardt, ed. 1979. *Wittgenstein: Sources and Perspectives.* Hassocks, Sussex: Harvester Press: 61-81.

Wittgenstein, Ludwig 1980. *Remarks On The Philosophy of Psychology* Vol 2. In G.H. von Wright and H. Nyman, eds., transl. C.G. Luckhardt and M. Aue. 1980. Chicago: The University of Chicago Press.

INDEX OF NAMES

INDEX OF SUBJECTS

Philosophy and Education

1. C.J.B. Macmillan and J.W. Garrison: *A Logical Theory of Teaching*. Erotetics and Intentionality. 1988 ISBN 90-277-2813-5
2. J. Watt: *Individualism and Educational Theory*. 1989 ISBN 0-7923-0446-2
3. W. Brezinka: *Philosophy of Educational Knowledge*. An Introduction to the Foundations of Science of Education, Philosophy of Education and Practical Pedagogics. 1992 ISBN 0-7923-1522-7
4. J.H. Chambers: *Empiricist Research on Teaching*. A Philosophical and Practical Critique of its Scientific Pretensions. 1992 ISBN 0-7923-1848-X
5. I. Scheffler: *Teachers of My Youth*. An American Jewish Experience. 1995 ISBN 0-7923-3232-6; (Pb) 0-7923-3236-9
6. P. Smeyers and J.D. Marshall (eds.): *Philosophy and Education: Accepting Wittgenstein's Challenge*. 1995 ISBN 0-7923-3715-8
7. J.D. Marshall: *Michel Foucault: Personal Autonomy and Education*. 1996 ISBN 0-7923-4016-7

KLUWER ACADEMIC PUBLISHERS – DORDRECHT / BOSTON / LONDON